EPIC SALADS

EPIC SALADS

Jessica Prescott

For every mood, craving
and occasion

Hardie Grant
BOOKS

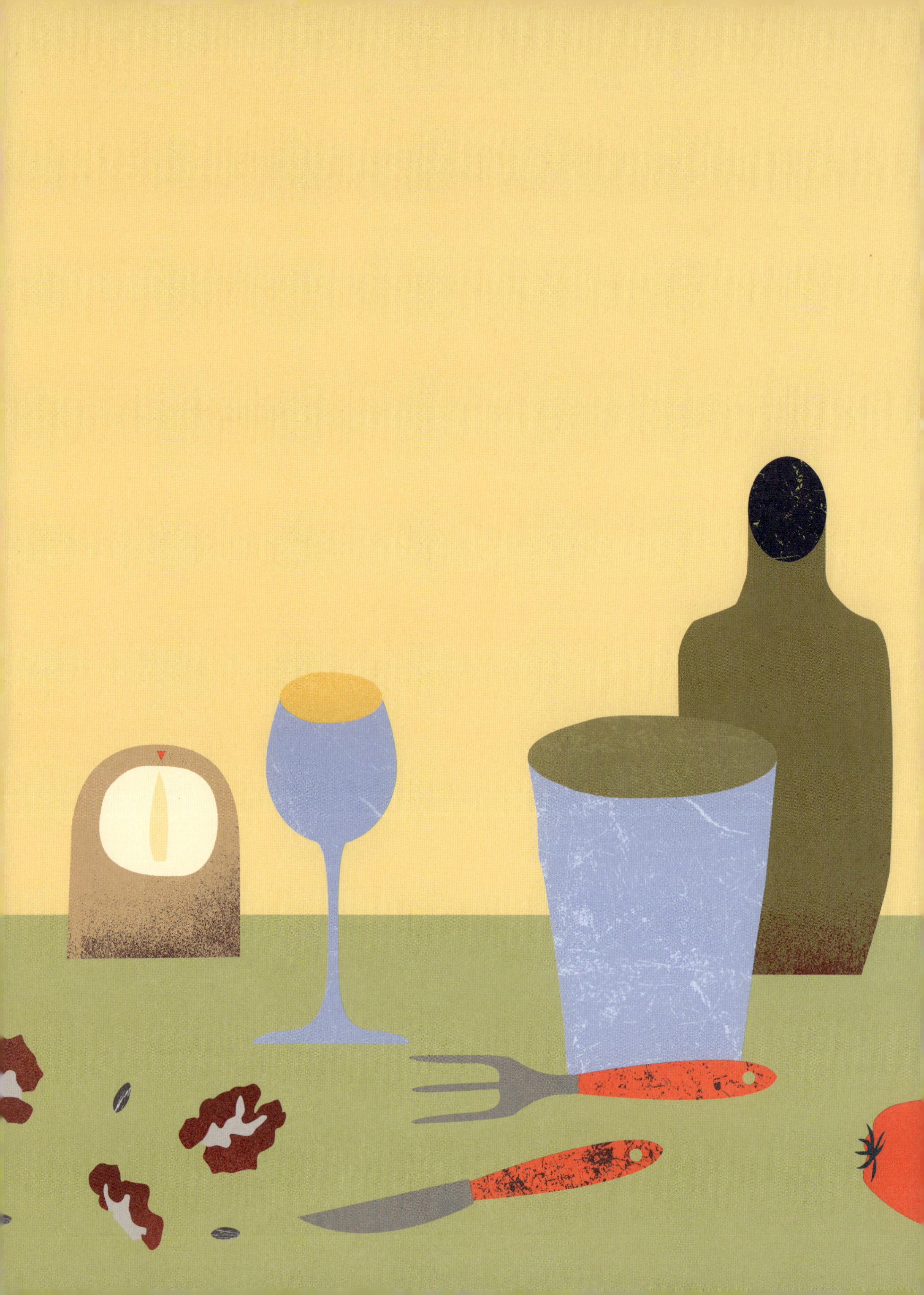

To Andy,

None of my books could have happened without your love, support or willingness to tackle the endless mountains of dishes. Thank you for giving me the space to be the harebrained creative that I am, and for riding the waves of my book-writing journeys with me. I love you.

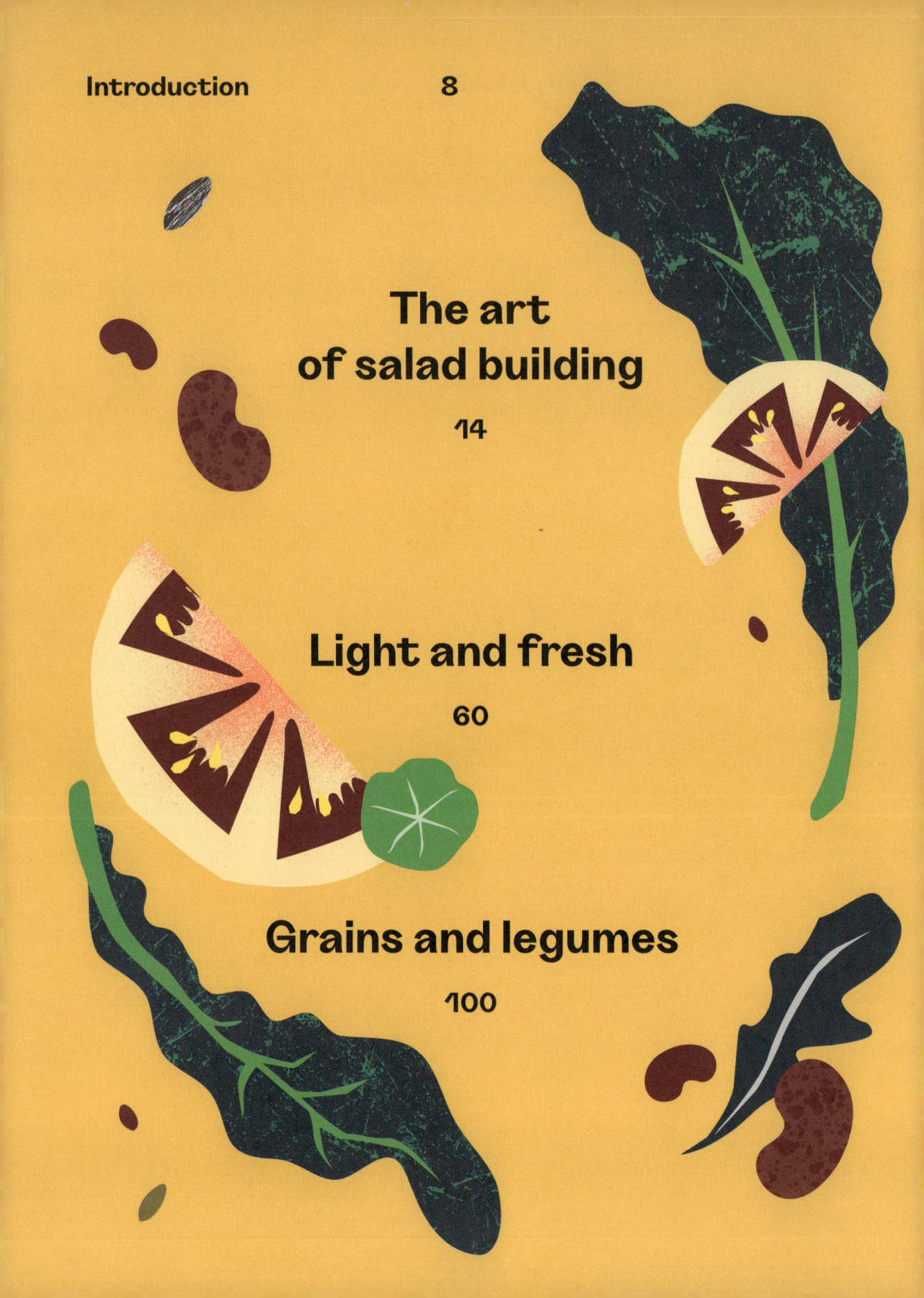

Introduction 8

The art of salad building
14

Light and fresh
60

Grains and legumes
100

Pasta and noodles
136

Showstopping sides
166

Make it a party
192

Index 218
Acknowledgements 222

Introduction

I love salad. I love eating it, thinking about it, talking about it, cooking it. I love that sometimes it requires no cooking at all. To me, salad is synonymous with flavour, crunch, health, versatility and feeling good.

While this book is about salad (duh) and I do harp on about the importance of healthy ingredients, I want to be clear about the way I eat. I most certainly do not eat salad every day. I try to have leafy greens every day, but I don't always manage that either. I love hot chips and ice cream as much as the next person, and I'm entirely capable of devouring half a loaf of sourdough in one sitting. Sometimes I have cheese and crackers for lunch, and often I eat an egg on toast for dinner (yum). The point here is not to promote a salad-centric diet, but to highlight the ways we can incorporate salads into our meal rotations. I firmly believe that the quality of our food directly influences how we feel, and maintaining a varied, well-balanced diet has long been touted – both anecdotally and scientifically – as being the key to overall wellbeing.

I also cannot understate the impact that world travel and city living has had on the way I cook, especially the five years I spent living in a Turkish neighbourhood in Berlin. While my cooking has been influenced by the immense privilege of seeing the way food is celebrated in other parts of the world, I have made a concerted effort to not misrepresent or oversimplify the rich cultural traditions that have inspired my recipes. My intention is to celebrate the culturally diverse world we live in and to pay homage to the flavour combinations that stop me in my tracks.

I hope that within these pages you discover recipes that you love and will return to time and time again – dishes that become your own signature creations. In this book, you will find recipes that invite you to put plants at the centre of your plate, for the sake of both your health and our planet. You will find recipes that transcend the conventional boundaries of salad, remind you of all the wonderful things you can do with plants, and show you how to turn a few humble ingredients into a delicious salad – the kind that leaves you fully satisfied and not foraging for snacks an hour later. In other words, an Epic Salad.

Simply salad

These recipes all consider accessibility, practicality, usability and convenience. While you may discover a few new ingredients (mostly condiments) in my shopping lists, most of these recipes call for ingredients you're probably already cooking with, or can easily find at your local supermarket. No monk's tears or special flowers that only bloom once a year under a full moon here!

I've kept those who love to cook in mind, as well as those who are completely and utterly burnt out by or have lost their joy for cooking. I flip-flop between these two states, and when I find myself in the latter category, I gravitate towards versatility and ease.

While these recipes are all vegetarian, they can be easily tweaked to suit all kinds of diets, and I encourage you to adapt whenever and wherever you want and need. They all fit seamlessly into a weekly meal prep routine, and can also be used as inspiration when throwing something together on a whim. They can be eaten for quick dinners or work lunches alike. Leftovers usually store well for a couple of days, and if you're not onto salad parties yet, turn straight to the 'Make it a party' chapter on page 192 and let me introduce you to my favourite way to share food with friends.

Meal planning and prepping

Many of these recipes will easily fit into your meal planning and prepping routine, with dressings able to be made in bulk, grains and legumes cooked in advance, and veggies prepared ahead of time. Some of them can also be made ahead and stored strategically, mixing right before eating so the ingredients stay fresh – à la the 'salad jars' you may have seen on the internet over the past few years. You can do this in any container you have at home. If you build it with the dressing on the bottom and the leaves on top, it will last for days. When you're ready to eat, simply dump it into a bowl and give it a stir.

Cook's notes

Each recipe assumes you are working with washed and dried leafy greens, and that you are working with a 'medium-sized' vegetable.

Oven temperature
The oven temperatures I share are for fan-forced ovens. If your oven is not fan-forced, increase the temperature by 20°C (35°F).

Measurements
All recipes in this book are made using Australian measurements. That means a tablespoon is 20 ml (¾ fl oz), not 15 ml (½ fl oz) as it is in the rest of the world, and a cup is 250 ml (8½ fl oz). If you live outside Australia, don't fret, just be extra generous when pouring those tablespoons and remember, you can adjust and adapt to your own liking.

I know the term 'handful' can be obscure. Some people only cook in handfuls, while others like to work with grams. While I have included both, it is worth noting that my handfuls of anything usually weigh around 30-or-so grams (1 oz). Learning what a 30 g (1 oz) handful feels like can be helpful when following my recipes, which are, for the most part, very forgiving, and don't require you to weigh or measure your ingredients to get a delicious result.

Garnish
I always reserve a few whole herb leaves for a garnish, even if the recipe calls for them to be chopped.

Improvise
The recipe notes suggest some swaps and substitutions, but feel free to improvise and use up what you've got to hand. Red onions, shallots and French shallots can all be used interchangeably, as can most leafy herbs, lettuces, root vegetables, nuts, etc.

Climate consideration

It would be remiss of me not to take a moment to share why I eat a vegetarian diet. It's no secret that animal agriculture is a leading contributor to climate change.

While I strongly believe that far too much responsibility has been put on the consumer when the leading polluters and destroyers of our planet are allowed to keep on doing what they're doing with no repercussions, I also believe that we, as consumers, wield significant influence.

Our role in shaping the world's trajectory is undeniable, and adjusting our dietary choices is one of the most powerful decisions we can make for protecting our planet.

I used to think veganism was the answer and I gave it a red-hot go for a good number of years, but I have now realised that I don't have to take a black-and-white, all-or-nothing approach to food. I have settled on a happy medium that still prioritises plants but also uses egg and dairy now and again. I'm not here to try and convince you to adhere to any kind of diet – you'll figure out what works best for you in your own time, and that's likely to be fluid and ever-changing – but I am here to remind you that we as consumers can choose to be part of an important shift to help slow climate change.

Our impact should not be underestimated; every time we spend money we are casting a vote for the type of world we want to live in. When we shop small and prioritise ethical brands, eco-friendly practices and, above all, a diet that emphasises plants over meat and dairy, we are voting for a cleaner, greener world. Our future is quite literally in our hands.

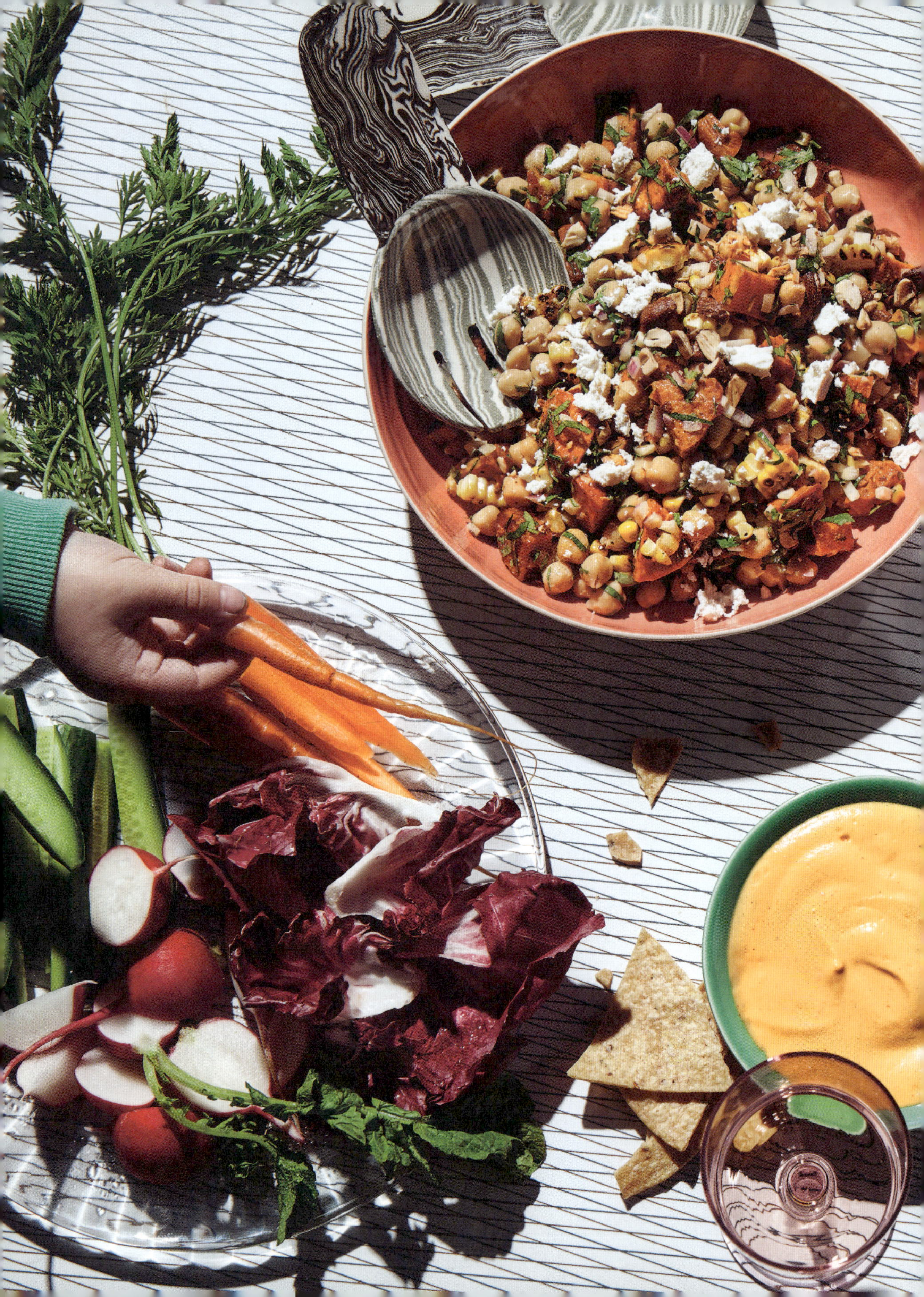

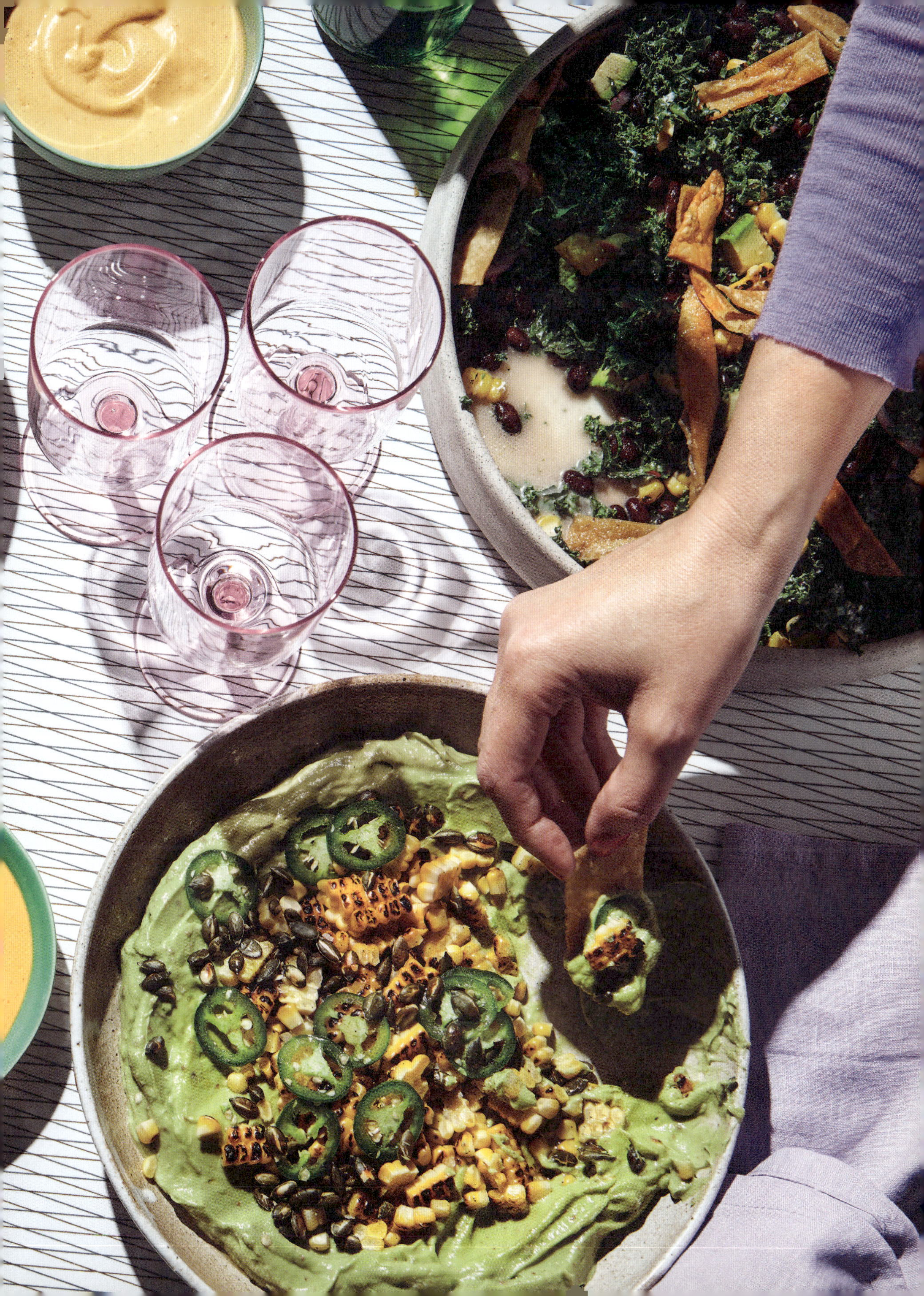

THE ART OF

SALAD BUILDING

Building an Epic Salad

An Epic Salad combines a balance of textures and flavours, creating a final product that is greater than the sum of its parts. It can be something you create from scratch, or a way of giving new life to leftovers. Embrace the following five guiding principles when coming up with your own salad creations, but remember: flexibility is key and rules are made to be broken.

Leaf

Leafy greens and herbs are known for being nutritional powerhouses that bring texture and visual appeal to the beloved salad. Think loose leaves, lettuces, cabbages, herbs, microherbs and sprouts.

Protein

The backbone of sustenance in many dishes, protein is the element that makes a salad robust and fulfilling. The salads in this book call on tofu, eggs, legumes and dairy for their protein hit. While meat and fish are also sources of protein, you won't find them in this book but you can absolutely substitute them in or serve on the side.

Dressing

A good dressing is the quintessential element that ties all the ingredients in your salad together. There are some kickass recipes on pages 39–43 but sometimes a dollop of hummus, guac, mayo or tahini is all you need. Likewise, a squeeze of lemon, lime or balsamic with a drizzle of olive oil can take your salad to the next level.

Body

The body is the heart of your salad, the components that lend heft and nutrition, transforming your leaves from a side dish to a hearty, satisfying meal. Think raw, pickled, roasted or sautéed veg, fresh or dried fruit, grains, pastas and noodles.

Crunch

While fresh veg lends a wonderful crunch in its own right, adding an additional crunch factor brings a whole extra layer of textural magic, flavour and moreishness. Think roasted and toasted nuts and seeds, crispy croutons and even fried tortillas – tiny additions that will make your salad *sing*.

Leaf

Leafy greens and herbs are known for being nutritional powerhouses that bring texture and visual appeal to the beloved salad. My go-to leafy greens are rocket (arugula), spinach and kale due to their accessibility, flavour and texture. You will notice I use them interchangeably throughout this book alongside my go-to herbs – dill, parsley, coriander (cilantro) and basil. Cos (romaine), iceberg, cabbage, radicchio, beetroot (beet) leaves, silverbeet (Swiss chard), microgreens and sprouts all get a look-in here too, as do slightly harder-to-find herbs such as Vietnamese mint, Thai basil and sorrel.

Washing, drying and storing leafy greens

Washing your greens as soon as you get them home can set you up for ease and success during the week, as it means one less step at mealtime. Some people recommend *not* washing ahead of storing as it can make the leaves go slimy. However, if you dry and store your greens correctly, this will not be a problem and, in fact, will usually ensure they last longer than they would in the bags or containers you brought them home in. The exceptions to this are cabbage, iceberg and cos. While you can wash ahead (and yes, I am sorry, but you really do need to wash them), they will usually last more than a week tucked away in their packaging in your veg drawer.

Wash
Fill a large bowl with water, or the bottom of your salad spinner, or even your kitchen sink if you're washing a lot of things at once (give it a scrub and wipe out with white vinegar before you begin). Pop the greens in, leave for a moment, then swish them around a little to remove any dirt or sediment. Rub any stubborn bits of dirt away with your thumb, then lift the greens *out* of the water and into the spinning basket, rather than pouring the greens and water into a strainer (and pouring the sediment back onto the clean greens).

When swishing the greens around in the water, keep an eye out for any rotten or disintegrating leaves. Discard these – they can sully an entire bunch of good leaves if left to mingle.

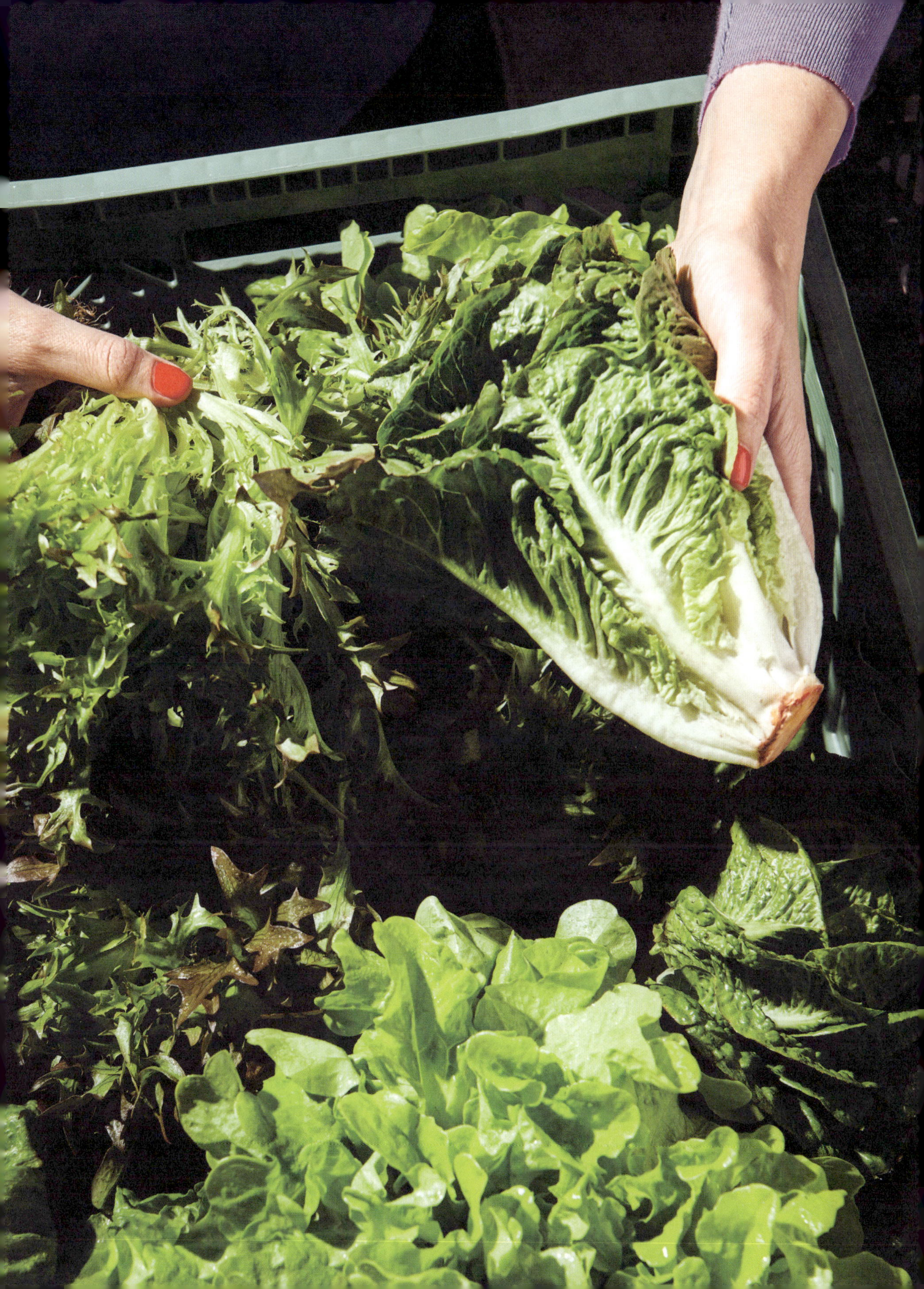

Dry

Drying your greens not only extends their life, but also ensures that the dressing has something to stick to.

For years I avoided owning a salad spinner, but I can honestly say it's one of the most used pieces of equipment in my kitchen; it's well worth the amount of cupboard space it takes up. Good ones can be pricey, but they will save you time and money over the years. You can also use them to dry berries (except raspberries), tinned beans and washed chopped veggies such as broccoli and cauliflower. Some salad spinners can even be used to store your greens once you've washed them!

I recommend spinning your greens twice, pouring out any water that's collected in the bottom of the salad spinner and giving the leaves a little shake between spins. Do this in batches if you need to, rather than overcrowding the spinner.

If you don't own a salad spinner, the next best thing is to lay your greens flat on a clean tea towel (dish towel), gently roll it up, hold both ends together and then swing it around like a helicopter to dry.

An exception to this is cabbage – I like to leave it alone until I am ready to use it then give it a soak and a spin after slicing. This ensures it's properly clean, keeps the cabbage crisp and mellows its pungent aftertaste.

Store

Storing washed and dried greens is a balancing act between keeping them moist enough to stay crisp without becoming slimy or mouldy. The trick is to achieve the perfect humidity and air flow. What you are storing, what you have on hand, how much fridge space you have and when you are planning to use them all come into play here. When stored correctly, your washed leaves should last up to a week.

I like to use paper towels and lidded glass containers, as the paper towels seem to strike that perfect moisture-wicking/humidity balance. Linen napkins and tea towels (dish towels) work a treat too. The key is to use something light that won't squash the greens once they are all wrapped up. You want to cover the top with the lining as well as the bottom to ensure the leaves don't get slimy against the top of the container. You can also use paper towels and zip-lock bags, a produce bag or a produce saver – a nifty creation designed to prolong the freshness and lifespan of fruits and veggies by regulating airflow and humidity. For a more comprehensive guide, see opposite.

Kale

I feel like a real champ when I manage to wash, dry and chop kale in preparation for the days ahead. With kale, you don't need to line the container you are using, as the leaves are hardy enough to withstand any moisture they come into contact with.

Soft herbs

Soft herbs such as dill, parsley, coriander (cilantro) and chives can be laid flat in paper towel-lined glass containers, or wrapped in little bundles in a larger container, ready to use.

Whole cabbages and lettuces

When left intact these will usually last over a week tucked away in their packaging in your veg drawer.

Bigger lettuce leaves

Lay flat on a tea towel (dish towel), roll up, fold in half and gently place in the top of your veg drawer.

Loose leaves

Line a glass container with paper towel. Add washed and dried loose leaves, top with another paper towel, pop the lid on and place in the fridge (any shelf will do, it doesn't have to be the veg drawer).

Basil

Basil is best stored in a glass of water on the bench, either in the plastic it came in, or with a reusable zip-lock bag placed over it to keep it moist. I avoid buying basil plants and opt instead for the big leafy bunches with moist roots intact. You can store dill this way too.

A loose guide to storing leaves

Body

The body is the heart of your salad, the components that lend heft and nutrition, transforming your leaves from a side dish to a hearty, satisfying meal. Think raw or cooked veggies, fresh or dried fruit, legumes, grains, etc. One or two of these ingredients will usually stand out as the hero.

I also use a lot of pasta, noodles, grains and legumes, depending on what I'm making and how much time I have. If using legumes, these can either be cooked from scratch or straight from a tin.

Veggies

Prepping veggies
While my recipes involve a fair amount of chopping, I believe that the extra 5 minutes it takes to cut everything to be *truly* bite-sized is worth it for the eating pleasure this brings.

Hate chopping?
You're not alone. While chopping can be quite meditative, it can also be a source of sensory overwhelm, especially when using a knife that is too small, blunt or uncomfortable to hold, or when the chopping board is sliding all over the bench. If the latter is an issue, try placing a tea towel (dish towel) or a damp cloth underneath your chopping board and, if the former, make sure your knife is big enough that you can hold it without knocking your knuckles on the chopping board. It doesn't need to be expensive, it just needs to have a strong, sharp blade, a comfortable handle and enough depth in the blade so that you don't bang your knuckles (the worst).

Corn

Cooking veggies

While raw veggies have an important place in the salad world, I would argue that cooked veg is just as important. Sure, there are days when it's too hot to turn on the oven, but there are also days when at least one cooked element is essential, especially when it's cold, or if you have trouble digesting too much raw veg.

I mostly cook veg in the oven and/or on the stove, depending on the weather, how much I'm cooking, how much time I have and what state my kitchen is in. Many of the methods in this book are interchangeable – I have noted where this applies. If you have the barbecue cranking, many of the veggies in these recipes can be cooked on there too.

In recipes that use roasted veggies, you'll notice that I recommend tossing them in salt and oil before placing them on the roasting tray. This gives you an even coating of oil on your veggies – it's much more efficient than tossing them on the roasting tray and removes the sensory overwhelm of getting oily, salty hands.

Cooking corn

While most of my cooking methods are outlined in the recipes, I wanted to talk about cooking corn here as there really are so many ways you can do it, depending on whether you are working with fresh, tinned or frozen, and if you have a gas stove or barbecue, or not.

1 cob of corn yields approx. ¾ cup (150 g/5½ oz) kernels

There are two ways I generally cook corn – either by slicing the kernels from the cob (or using tinned or frozen kernels) and frying them with a tablespoon of oil and a pinch of salt in a hot frying pan, or by charring the entire cob on an open flame. This can be done on a gas stove or on the barbecue. Whichever way you cook it, the corn will pop and sizzle, which can result in oil splatter as the steam escapes the kernels.

Cooking the cob

Place an ear of husked corn over the flames of your gas burner or barbecue on medium–high heat. Turn the corn as the underside blackens, until it is charred on all sides to your liking, about 4–5 minutes in total. You can also place a cooling rack (for baking) over your gas hob and put a couple of pieces of corn on it at a time – just be conscious of potential chemicals/coatings on your rack that may transfer to your food when heated.

The art of salad building

That being said, this is my favourite way of cooking corn because you can just chuck it on and check on it intermittently while you prepare other things.

Alternatively, brush an ear of husked corn with oil and place on a hot barbecue or chargrill pan, turning as it starts to colour, until evenly cooked all over. If cooking in a pan, be careful not to overcrowd it as this will cause the corn to steam and will compromise the texture. You want a high heat and a quick char to ensure the kernels stay juicy and allow their natural flavours to shine.

Allow the cooked corn to cool, then slice the kernels from the cobs.

Cooking the kernels

Heat a tablespoon of olive oil in a large frying pan over a medium heat. If using canned/frozen kernels, squeeze any excess juices out, then add them to the hot pan with a pinch of salt and cook for 3–5 minutes, stirring frequently until golden brown, watching out for oil splatters. Remove from the heat and set aside.

Having a tub of cooked grains in the fridge or freezer can make a world of difference when you want to throw dinner together quickly or turn leftovers into a new and different meal.

Cooking grains

I like to use the absorption method for rice and quinoa, and the rapid boil method (see opposite) for all other grains. The rapid boil method makes them less starchy, which is what you want when using them in salads.

Absorption method

Rinse 1 cup of grain under cold running water in a fine-mesh sieve (strainer) until the water runs clear. Place in a small saucepan with 2 cups (500 ml/17 fl oz) of water and ½ teaspoon of salt. Stir, then cover with a lid. Bring to the boil then lower the heat and simmer, covered, for 20 minutes. Keep the lid on and do not disturb the grains while cooking.

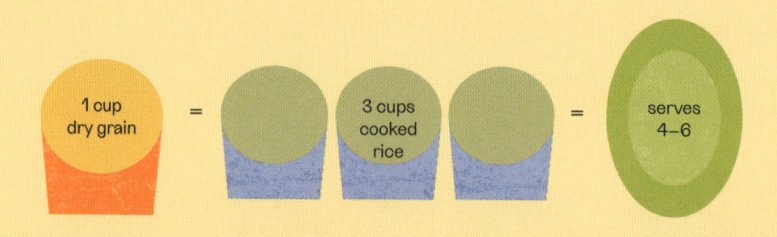

Grains

1 cup dry grain = 3 cups cooked rice = serves 4–6

The art of salad building

If you want to check that all of the water has been absorbed, use the handle of a spoon to pull back some of the grains and see if there is still water in the pan, rather than stirring them.

Once cooked, remove from the heat and allow to sit for 5–10 minutes. Remove the lid, add a light drizzle of olive oil (optional) and fluff the grain with a fork. Allow to sit, uncovered, for 10 minutes.

You can use the grain immediately if you want a warm meal, or spread it over a baking tray to help it cool more quickly.

Rapid boil method
Rinse 1 cup of grain under cold running water in a fine-mesh sieve (strainer) until the water runs clear. Fill a large saucepan with ample water – about 1–1.5 litres (4–6 cups/34–51 fl oz) – and add a generous pinch of salt. Bring to a boil. Add the rinsed grain to the boiling water and stir briefly to prevent sticking. Cook the grain for approximately 20 minutes, or until it reaches your desired level of doneness. To check, carefully remove a small amount of grain with a spoon and taste it. There's no need to keep the pot covered or to avoid stirring, as the grains are intended to cook freely in the water, much like pasta.

When it's cooked to your liking, drain into a large colander and rinse in lots of cold water. Drain again, and shake off any excess water before using.

Use warm, or allow to cool, depending on your needs and what your salad calls for. Store in an airtight container in the fridge for up to 4 days, or in the freezer for up to 3 months.

A note about puffed grains
You will notice I use puffed grains frequently throughout this book. While you can absolutely puff your grains at home, doing so requires you to cook and cool your grains before frying them in hot oil which encourages them to 'puff'. Store-bought puffed grains are different to homemade puffed grains in that they are puffed without oil, under a high heat and high pressure. While I love the homemade version, I almost always use store-bought as they are lighter and a whole lot less time consuming than homemade. You can find them at your local health food store.

Protein

The backbone of sustenance in many dishes, protein is the element that makes a salad robust and filling. Whether it's the hearty satisfaction of legumes, the flavour and satiety of tofu or the velvety decadence of a boiled egg, throughout this book, you'll find an array of plant-based proteins and ideas for how to use them. In an Epic Salad, the protein is not just an afterthought, but a star player that sings in harmony with the leaf, body, dressing and crunch of your salad, elevating every bite.

Legumes

Having beans cooked and ready to go means meals come together in a pinch, but I totally get that you may not always have the time or mental space for this (I certainly don't) which is why a large section of my pantry is dedicated to tinned beans and chickpeas.

You can add a tin of beans or chickpeas to pretty much anything. To maximise flavour, I recommend marinating them à la the salads on pages 78, 82, 107 and 121. If using butter beans, you can also fry them in a little salt, oil and garlic as per the recipe on page 105.

Cooking legumes

If you're cooking dried legumes from scratch, it's beneficial to soak them, both to reduce their cooking time and to break down their phytic acid, which is an enzyme that occurs naturally in legumes and can prevent the absorption of nutrients. It's also best to sift through any dried pulses before cooking, in case of the very slight chance there may be a rogue stick or stone in there.

All the recipes in this book are written with the below ratios in mind so you can swap home-cooked and tinned with ease.

1 x 400g (14 oz) tin of beans = 1½ cups cooked beans = ½ cup dried beans

The art of salad building

Cooking dried lentils

There are two main ways you can cook lentils on the stove – either by placing them in cold water and bringing the water to a boil with the lentils in it, or by bringing the water to a boil and then adding the lentils. While both work great, boiling the water first ensures a more consistent cooking temperature from the start, meaning your lentils will cook evenly and won't be mushy, which is what we want when making salads.

Soak 1 cup (185 g/6½ oz) of French green (Puy) or Beluga lentils* in a bowl or pot of water overnight.

Bring a pot of water to a boil. Once boiling, add the lentils and a big pinch of salt. Reduce the heat to a simmer and cook, uncovered, for 15–20 minutes, or until the lentils are tender but still holding their shape. Drain, rinse with cool water, then shake off any excess water and set aside.

Cooking beans

All of my recipes can be made with tinned beans, but if you prefer to cook your beans from scratch, here's how:

Soak 1 cup of beans in a bowl or pot of water overnight. Drain and rinse well (if cooking black beans, drain most of the water but leave the dark, sediment-filled water and don't rinse the beans, as this is where all the flavour is) then place in a large saucepan with 1 litre (4 cups/34 fl oz) of water. Cover, bring to the boil, then reduce the heat and simmer for 1–2 hours, checking the softness of the beans every 30 minutes or so by squishing them on the side of the pot. When they start to soften, add a teaspoon of salt and continue to cook until tender (the total amount of time they take will depend on how old and dry they are). Drain.

Cooked legumes can be stored in their cooking liquid in an airtight container for up to 1 week in the fridge, or 3 months in the freezer. Simply drain off the cooking liquid before using.

Epic tip

* French green lentils hold their shape best, followed by Beluga and classic green lentils. Brown, red and yellow lentils will break down as they cook, making them better suited to soups and stews, rather than salads.

Tofu

I used to think tofu was bad. Genetically modified, heavily processed, laden with cancer-causing estrogen, responsible for deforestation, etc. I have since learned that tofu is in fact a wholefood and that it's not causing deforestation. While it's true that soy cultivation is a significant driver of deforestation, most of that soy is used for animal feed. Those animals aren't meant to eat soybeans, which means they get sick and need antibiotics, and therein we have antibiotic resistance and a cascade of other global health and environmental issues to contend with.

But I digress. Tofu is great! It's environmentally friendly, high in protein, nowhere near as processed or high in estrogen as many household staples, and furthermore, is a blank canvas that you can use to create a myriad of flavours and textures, much like you would with chicken. You just need to know how to cook it. Let me show you.

Just as with animal-based proteins, the magic often lies in seasoning and cooking techniques.

Fresh tofu vs packaged tofu

If you're lucky enough to have access to fresh tofu that's come straight from the manufacturer without being packaged, then you can probably get away with eating it unseasoned – there's nothing quite like it! The same goes for you clever folks who make your own tofu at home. I've tried, but my results have been mediocre at best.

Unfortunately, most of us have to buy packaged tofu, and with that comes an array of preservatives and tastes. Some of the tofu available in Australia is so unbelievably bitter or metallic that even my own recipes can't help you.

If you've tried tofu once and sworn off it forever, I beg you to try again with a different brand, a different marinade, another cooking technique … I promise it's delicious – you just have to know what to do with it.

Major flavour

The best way to maximise marinade absorption isn't time, but freezing your tofu! Doing so gives it a spongy, more porous texture, allowing it to soak up even more delicious flavours from the marinade.

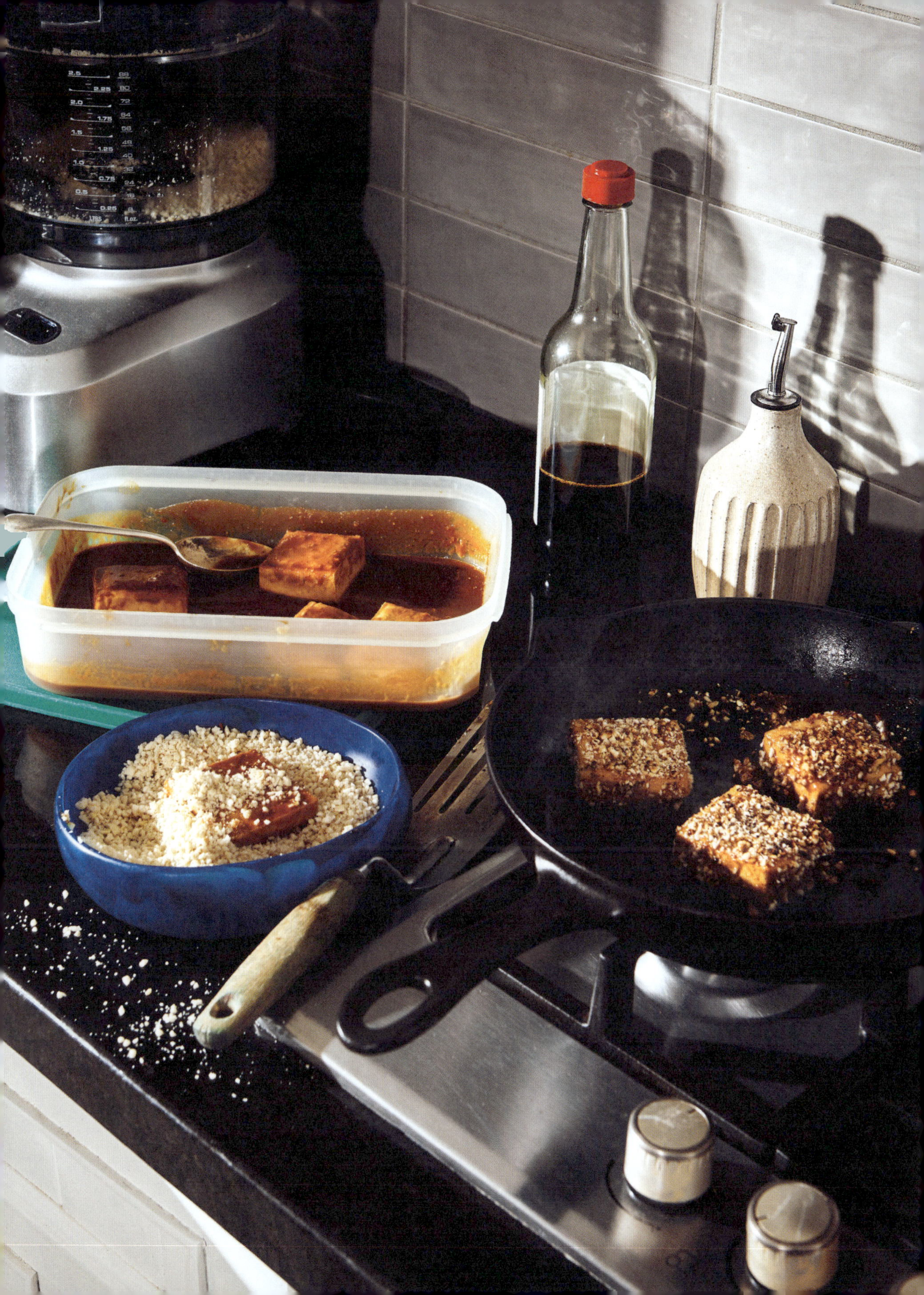

Choose your own tofu adventure

1
Pick your tofu

You want to use firm tofu for this recipe. Soft/silken can be used in a pinch, and can be delightful if done correctly, however it is too fragile for many folks' fingers.

2
Press your tofu

Either use a tofu press, or wrap your tofu in a clean tea towel (dish towel) and put it under something heavy. I put it between two chopping boards and then sit a heavy, cast-iron pot on top. Pressing the tofu removes excess moisture, creating space for the flavours to seep into.

4
Pick your marinade

Use any combination of the following:

- soy sauce
- strong veg/fake chicken stock
- lime juice
- microplaned ginger or garlic
- onion powder, garlic powder
- ground cumin, coriander, paprika
- sriracha/gochujang/chipotle

You can stop here and eat your tofu marinated and raw, or go to step 7, or you can crumb your tofu before cooking.

3
Pick your cut

Think about the shape your tofu will be when you cook it, and how you will cut it when it's cooked. For example, you might choose:

- big square steaks that can be cut into triangles
- slabs
- rods
- crumbled
- diced
- torn into nuggets

5
Pick your stick

- peanut butter
- tahini
- mayo
- aquafaba
- beaten egg (if using egg, you'll need to lightly coat the tofu in flour first)

If using peanut butter, tahini or mayo, mix in with the marinade. Aquafaba and egg should be put on after the marinade.

6
Pick your crumb

- cornflour (cornstarch) and nori flakes
- peanuts — raw, if possible, blitzed in food processor if you have one (a fine crumb is heaven)
- cornflour (cornstarch)/potato starch/regular flour (although cornflour crisps up the best)
- crushed cornflakes and spices
- panko crumbs
- no crumb – this is great if you marinated the tofu in stock

7
Pick your cooking method

A frying pan, oven and air fryer are all great for different reasons. Just choose what works best for you!

Frying pan – quick, oily, moreish. Can shallow-fry, or use just enough oil to prevent sticking.

Oven – this guarantees you a crisp result, and it means you can put it in and forget about it while you tend to other things.

Air fryer – great for when you want the crisp without the oil, and without the energy use of the oven.

If you want to do your own experiment, start with the ratio of 1 serve tofu: 1 teaspoon each of soy sauce and mayo, or see more detailed recipes as listed below:

Peanut tofu (page 86)
Tofu nuggets (page 162)
Tofu croutons (page 68)
Crispy nori tofu (page 72)
Panko tofu (page 67)

Two-minute tofu – four ways

This is by no means an original recipe but rather my take on Japanese Hiyayakko tofu or Chinese Liangban tofu – dishes that have been around for centuries. It's the perfect way to pump up the protein when you're seeking a light and no-fuss meal, especially on a hot day. This is a dish that's best served cold, but a few minutes out of the fridge doesn't do it any harm either. Serve with plain rice or noodles, and any of the salads featured in this book.

There are so many ways you can make this easy, light and fresh dish. It starts the same way every time – a block of silken tofu and a 2:1 ratio of soy sauce to sesame oil. Sometimes you add some spice, sometimes you add some crunch, or preferably both.

Sesame, soy and crunchy chilli (pictured on p. 80)

1 block soft or silken tofu
2 tablespoons soy sauce
1 tablespoon toasted sesame oil
1 heaped tablespoon of crunchy bits from a jar of chilli oil
2 spring onions (scallions), sliced

Sesame, soy and peanut

1 block soft or silken tofu
2 tablespoons soy sauce
1 tablespoon toasted sesame oil
1 heaped tablespoon of roasted peanuts, chopped
a few Vietnamese mint leaves

Gochujang

1 block soft or silken tofu
2 tablespoons soy sauce
1 tablespoon toasted sesame oil
1 teaspoon gochujang paste
1 heaped tablespoon fried onions
a few coriander (cilantro) leaves

Lemongrass (pictured on p. 181)

1 block soft or silken tofu
2 tablespoons panko crumbs
1 teaspoon minced lemongrass
2 tablespoons soy sauce
1 tablespoon toasted sesame oil
a few Vietnamese mint leaves

Place a block of soft or silken tofu in the bottom of a shallow bowl or dish. You can leave it whole, slice it, or cut it into bite-sized cubes. Just remember, silken tofu is delicate so handle it with care.

Choose your dressing, then whisk the ingredients together. Before dressing, check the tofu to see if any water has collected into the serving dish and if so, gently pour this away or pat with a paper towel.

For the lemongrass variation, fry the panko crumbs and lemongrass with a lick of oil over on a medium heat for a couple of minutes, transfer to a bowl and set aside.

Cover the tofu with the dressing, then add herbs and your crunchy bits. Enjoy.

Epic tips

1. There are endless ways to bring crunch to this humble dish. As well as the suggested chilli oil, roasted peanuts, fried onions and fried panko, you could use sesame seeds, spring onions, roasted slivered almonds or chopped roasted cashews.

2. You could also add fresh herbs like Thai basil, Vietnamese mint, coriander or shiso.

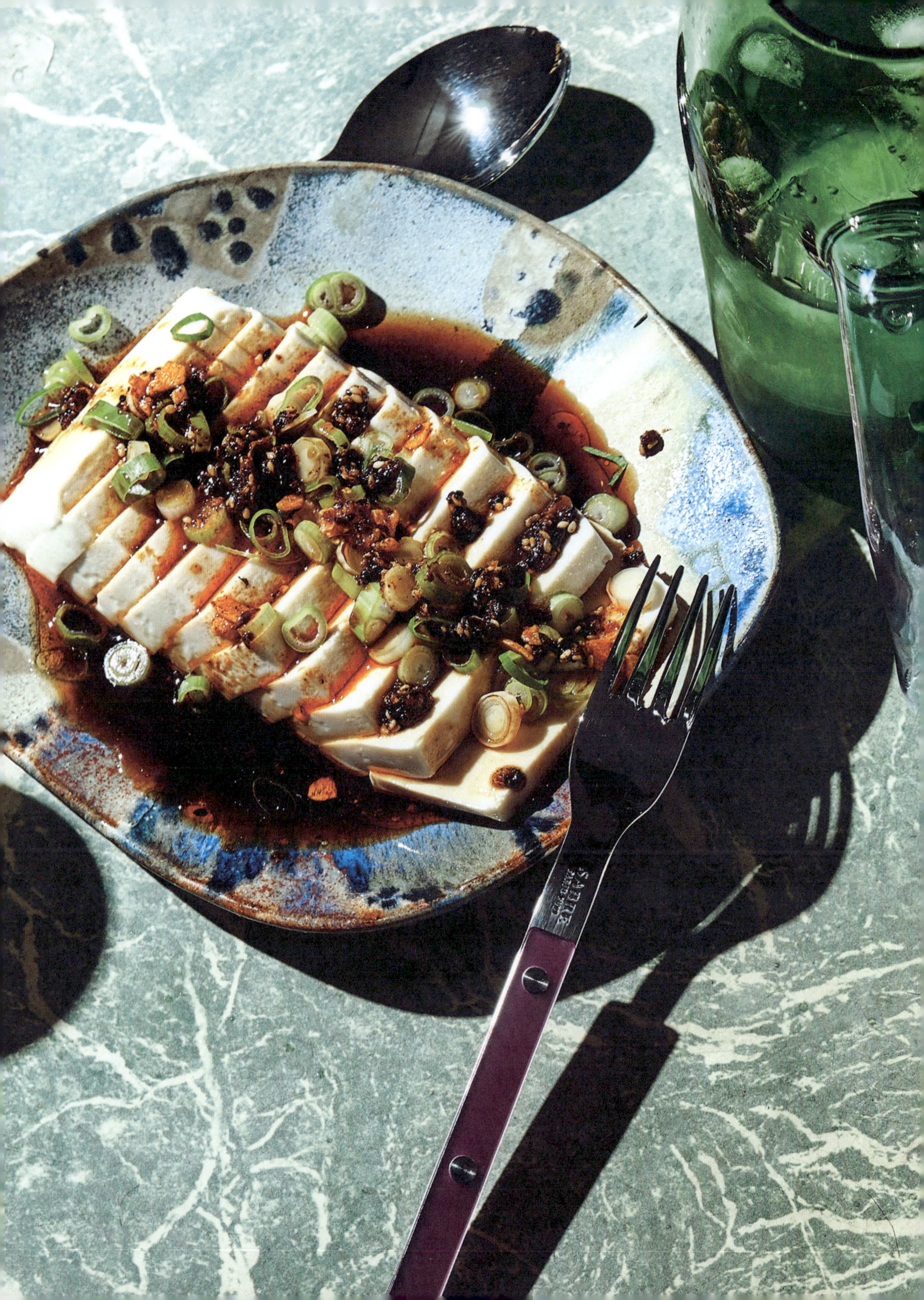
SABRE

The perfect boiled egg

Eggs are such an excellent way to add a pop of protein to basically any meal.

When making salads, I tend to reach for boiled eggs, as they have so many applications; they can be eaten hot or cold, prepped ahead of time, marinated, mixed or served on the side. I personally like mine with a well-cooked but not rubbery white, and a yolk that's not runny but still bright yellow.

For this guide I use 70 g (2½ oz) eggs. If yours are bigger or smaller, add or subtract a minute in cooking time for every 10 g (¼ oz) difference.

Bring a pot of water to a boil and prepare an ice bath. Prick the bottom of your eggs with an egg pricker if you have one, then, using a tablespoon, lower the eggs into the boiling water, one at a time. If cooking a few eggs at once, gently stir the water for the first 30–60 seconds of cooking time, to ensure the heat is evenly distributed through the water, then reduce the heat so the eggs don't bounce around. Cook for 7–12 minutes, depending on how runny you like your yolk.

Jammy yolks – 7 minutes
Perfect – 9 minutes
Hard-boiled – 12 minutes

Once cooked, drain the water and transfer the eggs to the ice bath for 5–10 minutes. You can also cool your cooked eggs under running water, but this method doesn't shock the membranes like the ice does, so the shell may not come away easily.

Once cool, roll the eggs on the counter, applying enough pressure to gently crack the shell all over. Starting with the indent at the base of the egg, break the shell and peel it off, rinsing the peeled egg under running water to remove any stubborn pieces of shell. Eat immediately, or pop in the fridge for later. Boiled eggs are also great marinated in soy, as per the recipe on page 36. Boiled eggs, both peeled and unpeeled, will last for up to 7 days in the fridge.

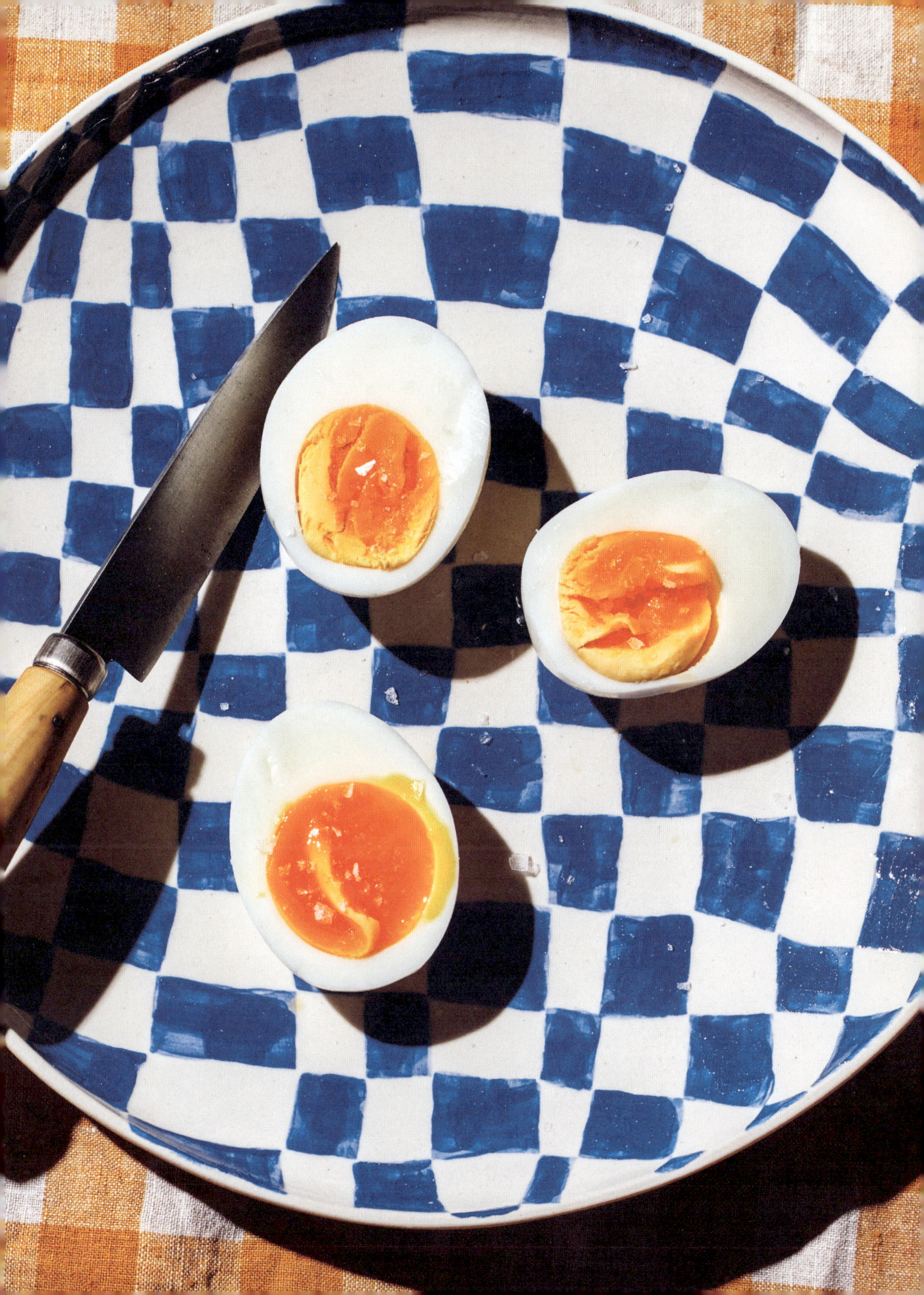

Soy sauce eggs

Makes 6 eggs

Before you begin this recipe, make sure you have a vessel that will fit six boiled eggs. You want them to be snug but not squashed, and able to be fully submerged. This can be a glass jar or dish, or a zip-lock bag.

---

6 eggs
1 tablespoon sugar
100 ml (3½ oz) boiling water
¾ cup (185 ml/6 fl oz) light soy sauce
¼ cup (60 ml/2 fl oz) black vinegar or rice vinegar
optional extras – chilli flakes/sauce/paste, minced garlic or shallots

Cook your eggs according to the instructions on page 34.

While the eggs are cooking, prepare the marinade. Dissolve the sugar in the boiling water, then pour into a glass jar or dish with the soy sauce and vinegar and stir to combine.

Gently transfer the peeled eggs to the marinade, ensuring they are fully submerged. Leave for 2–6 hours for soft eggs and 12–24 hours for harder eggs. Once marinated, you can refrigerate the eggs in an airtight container for up to a week (you can leave them in the marinade, but be warned: they will become increasingly salty over time). You can also re-use the marinade for another six eggs before discarding.

Other ways to pump up the protein

Tempeh
Look for a brand that uses whole soy beans and that isn't stored in water. The texture of water-packaged tempeh is different to the texture of vacuum-packed tempeh. You don't want it to be watery. If it does come in water, drain very well and pat dry before using. To cook, either thinly slice or crumble, cook in a little oil and then season with salt and pepper. Also excellent with a teaspoon of Chinese five-spice added during cooking, or a drizzle of sriracha added after cooking.

Edamame beans
While technically a legume, edamame get a special mention here because they are my absolute favourite beans to use when I need to boost my protein. In Australia, you can buy shelled edamame beans in the freezer section of your supermarket. All you need to do is defrost them and they are ready to eat – no cooking required! To defrost, you can leave them in the fridge overnight, on the bench for a few hours, or cover with boiling water for a couple of minutes. In the UK and USA you can find shelled edamame in the refrigerator section. Tinned, shelled edamame are also available at some supermarkets, however their consistency is a bit mushy.

Haloumi
Is there anything haloumi doesn't go with? For best results when cooking, ensure that the pan is hot before adding the haloumi. This helps to achieve a nice sear and keeps the cheese from sticking to the pan. Heating the pan first also allows the haloumi to start cooking immediately upon contact, creating a beautiful golden crust while keeping the inside soft and melty.

Whipped tofu
See the recipe on page 198 for a delightful, completely plant-based alternative to the whipped feta that features heavily in this book. It also happens to be high in protein, and is wonderful smeared on a piece of bread or cracker.

Tofu puffs
Find these in the refrigerator section of your Asian supermarket or wholefoods market. Some mainstream supermarkets carry them too. To heat, bake them in the oven and then slice however you wish – I usually do big triangles or thin squares.

Tofu noodles
Find them at your local Asian supermarket and use anywhere you would use regular noodles.

Omelettes
Great to serve alongside a side salad or leftovers for a simple meal. I love leftover cooked veg in mine. Some favourite combinations are:

- roasted pumpkin (squash), raw onion, Danish feta
- cheese, corn, spinach
- broccoli, pea, ricotta
- fried mushrooms, goat's cheese.

Dressing

While many ingredients shine with the simple combo of olive oil, lemon and salt, I believe that the key to a good salad often lies in its dressing; it's the quintessential element that ties all the ingredients together and a good dressing has the power to completely change the flavour profile of a bowl of humble veg.

By mastering a handful of versatile, flavourful salad dressings, understanding their perfect pairings and knowing when to bypass the dressing in favour of a simple squeeze of citrus, I have significantly lightened my mental load. I can cook without having to think, and I can often create a brilliant meal simply by combining whatever I've got in my fridge and pantry.

Dressings are also the one thing I can confidently meal prep. In fact, knowing I have a dressing in the fridge is often the difference between mustering up the motivation to make a salad or not.

Use these recipes as a guide; taste, test and adjust to your liking and the ingredients you have available. The brand of soy sauce, the age of your garlic and where your limes were grown, etc. will all play a part in the final flavour of your dressing, so follow your tastebuds more closely than the recipe. When making a dressing, I like to keep Samin Nosrat's concept of *Salt, Fat, Acid, Heat* in mind, except with dressings it's Salt, Fat, Acid, *Sweet*.

For best results, make your dressing before you start on your salad and set it aside. This will give your flavours time to mingle and will also make everything come together much more effortlessly at the end.

You'll find an 'alternative chapters' list on page 44, which groups the salads in this book according to their dressing, so you can make your dressings in bulk and meal plan your little heart out.

Basic balsamic

Makes 250 ml (8½ fl oz)

¼ cup (60 ml/2 fl oz) balsamic vinegar
1 French shallot, very finely diced
½ cup (125 ml/4 fl oz) extra-virgin olive oil
1 tablespoon Dijon mustard
1 teaspoon maple syrup
1 teaspoon salt flakes

Put the vinegar and shallot in a jar and set aside for 5–15 minutes to mellow its raw, sharp taste. Add the remaining ingredients, screw on the lid and shake until well combined.

Coconut satay

Makes 300 ml (10 fl oz)

⅓ cup (80 ml/2½ fl oz) smooth peanut butter
⅓ cup (125 ml/4 fl oz) coconut milk
3 teaspoons soy sauce
2 teaspoons maple syrup
¼ teaspoon salt
1 teaspoon grated ginger
1 teaspoon crushed garlic
2 teaspoons sriracha
2 teaspoons lime juice
2 makrut leaves, very thinly sliced
2 tablespoons water, plus extra if needed

Combine all ingredients, except the water, in a small saucepan over a low–medium heat. Bring to a simmer and cook, stirring often to prevent catching, for 5 minutes. Set aside until ready to use. This dressing is best served warm. It will thicken significantly in the fridge, so to serve, warm up then add water to thin.

Chilli lime

Makes 160 ml (5½ fl oz)

juice and pulp of 2 limes –
    approx. 75 ml (2½ fl oz)
3 tablespoons light olive oil
1 tablespoon maple syrup
1 teaspoon salt
1 bird's eye chilli, deseeded and very finely chopped
1 garlic clove, crushed

Combine all ingredients in a glass jar with a lid and shake to combine. Use immediately, or store in the fridge for up to 4 days.

Coriander pesto

Makes approx. 250 ml (8½ fl oz)

1 cup (30 g/1 oz) coriander (cilantro), including stalks
2 garlic cloves, roasted*
120 ml (4 fl oz) olive oil
2 tablespoons lime juice (1 lime)
½ teaspoon salt
2 tablespoons nutritional yeast (optional)
2 teaspoons maple syrup
½ cup (70 g/2½ oz) cashews, roasted

Wash, rinse and spin dry the coriander, and remove the skins from roasted garlic. Put all the ingredients, except the cashews, in a high-speed blender and blend until smooth. Add the cashews and pulse until combined but still a little chunky.

Epic tip

* I roast the garlic with other veg in the oven. Leave the cloves in their skins, rub with a little oil and roast for 10-15 minutes. You can also sautee the garlic in a little of the olive oil, then allow to cool before using.

Pictured overleaf →

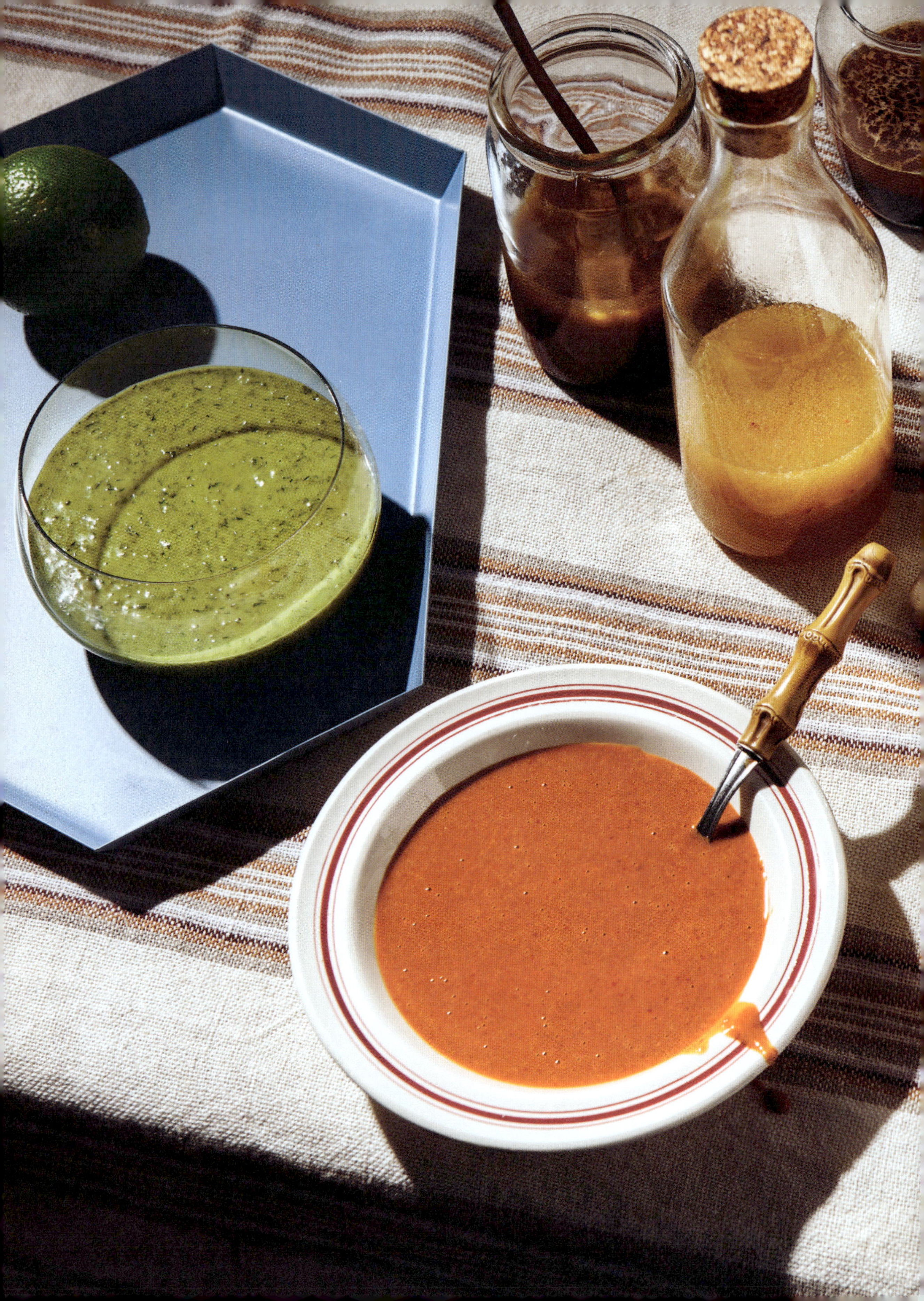

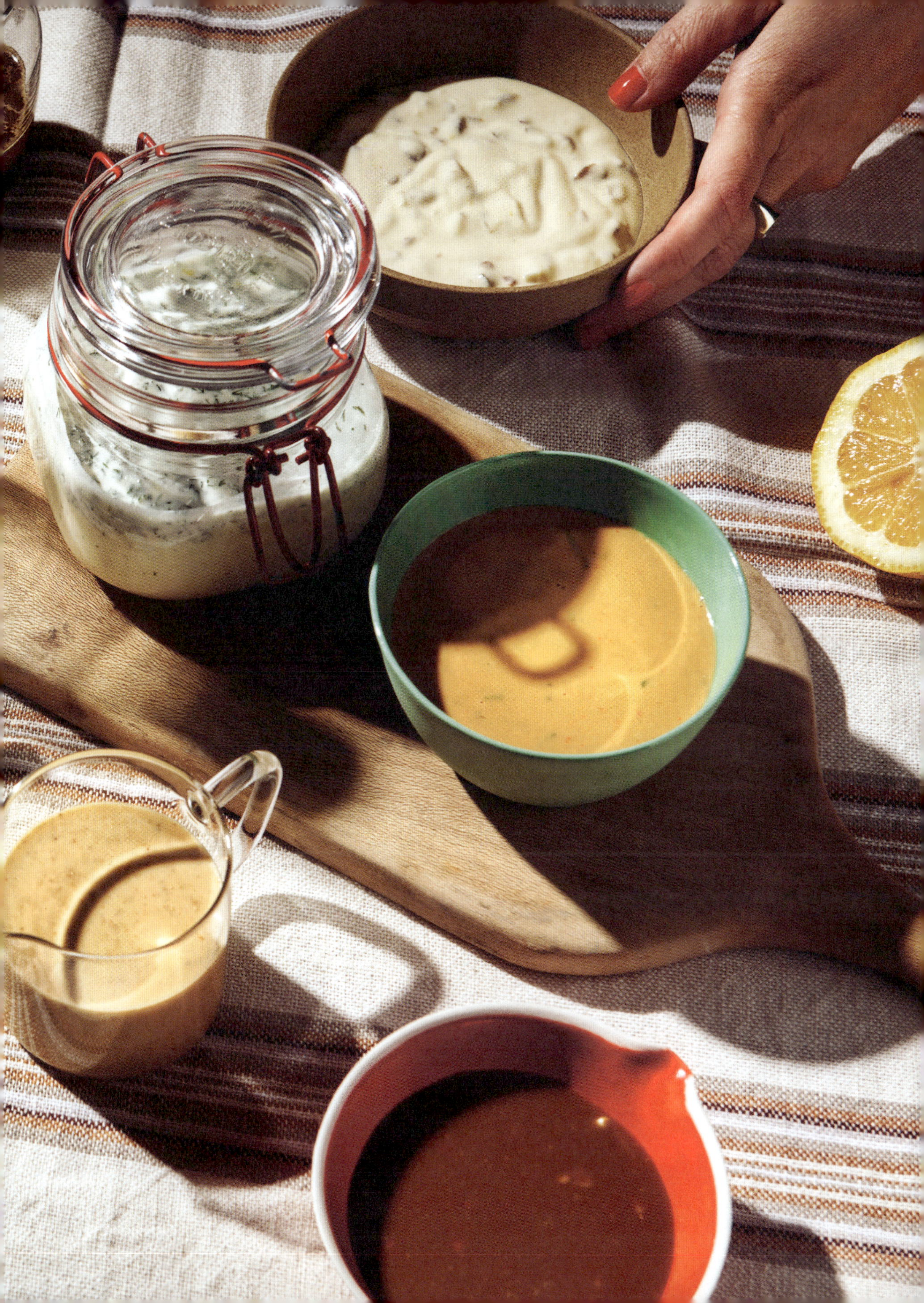

Lemon tahini yoghurt

Makes 300 ml (10 fl oz)

½ cup (125 g/4½ oz) Greek yoghurt
2 tablespoons tahini
1 tablespoon honey or maple syrup
2 tablespoons lemon juice
1 teaspoon lemon zest
½ garlic clove, microplaned
2 tablespoons olive oil
1 tablespoon very finely chopped pickles
1 tablespoon very finely chopped sultanas
½ teaspoon salt

Combine the yoghurt, tahini, honey or maple, lemon juice, lemon zest and garlic in a small bowl and whisk to combine. Add the oil, 1 tablespoon at a time, whisking well after each addition. Add the pickles and sultanas and stir. Transfer to a glass jar and allow to sit for at least 30 minutes. Stir well before using. Use immediately, or store in the fridge for up to 4 days.

Pomegranate

Makes 175 ml (6 fl oz)

⅓ cup (80 ml/2½ fl oz) olive oil
2 tablespoons (40 ml/1¼ fl oz) apple-cider vinegar
2 tablespoons (40 ml/1¼ fl oz) pomegranate molasses
1 teaspoon Dijon mustard
1 teaspoon sumac
½ teaspoon salt
½ teaspoon microplaned garlic

Combine all ingredients in a glass jar and shake to combine. Use immediately, or refrigerate for up to 1 week.

Sesame mayo

Makes 175 ml (6 fl oz)

2 tablespoons sesame seeds
⅓ cup (80 ml/2½ fl oz) Japanese mayo
1 tablespoon rice vinegar
2 teaspoons light soy sauce
2 teaspoons maple syrup
2 teaspoons sesame oil

Toast the sesame seeds in a dry frying pan over a medium heat, stirring and tossing frequently until lightly golden and fragrant. Transfer to a dinner plate and allow to cool, then blitz in a high-powered blender for approximately 10 seconds until finely ground but before a sticky, crumbly paste has formed.

Combine all the remaining ingredients in a bowl or measuring cup and whisk to combine. Add the ground sesame seeds and stir to combine. Use immediately, or store in an airtight jar for up to 4 days.

Spicy peanut

Makes 200 ml (6 fl oz)

2 tablespoons peanut butter*
2 tablespoons sriracha or sambal oelek
2 tablespoons soy sauce
1 tablespoon rice vinegar
1 tablespoon toasted sesame oil
1 tablespoon maple syrup
1 garlic clove, crushed
1 teaspoon grated fresh ginger

Combine all ingredients in a glass jar and shake to combine. Use immediately, or refrigerate for up to 1 week.

*For this recipe, you want peanut butter that's a pourable consistency. Substitute for tahini if you can't do nuts.

Spicy soy

Makes 150 ml (5 fl oz)

2 tablespoons sriracha
2 tablespoons soy sauce
1 tablespoon rice vinegar
1 tablespoon toasted sesame oil
1 tablespoon maple syrup
1 teaspoon tamarind paste
1 garlic clove, crushed (minced)
1 teaspoon grated fresh ginger

Combine all ingredients in a glass jar and shake to combine. Use immediately, or refrigerate for up to 1 week.

Supergreen

Makes 350–400 ml (12–13½ fl oz)

¾ cup (185 ml/6 fl oz) olive oil
⅓ cup (80 ml/2½ fl oz) lemon juice
1 teaspoon lemon zest
1 tablespoon maple syrup
2 teaspoons Dijon mustard
½ garlic clove, crushed
½ teaspoon salt
2 cups (60 g/2 oz) mixed herbs
1 tablespoon capers

Place all ingredients, except the herbs and capers, in a food processor and blitz to combine. Then add the herbs and capers and blitz until the herbs are finely chopped but not completely puréed.

You can also make this dressing in a lidded jar by very finely chopping your herbs and capers by hand and adding these in after you have emulsified the rest of your dressing.

This will keep in the fridge for up to 1 week and freeze for up to 1 month. It will go lumpy when chilled but will loosen up as it gets to room temperature. Shake before use.

The GOAT (greatest of all time)

Makes approx. 250 ml (8½ fl oz)

80 g (2¾ oz) soft goat's cheese
100 g (3½ oz) Greek yoghurt
3 tablespoons olive oil*
pinch of salt
1 teaspoon lemon zest
1 heaped tablespoon chopped dill
½ garlic clove, microplaned

Put the goat's cheese and yoghurt in a small mixing bowl and use a fork to break down the cheese and slowly work it into the yoghurt. Once combined, add the oil, a little at a time, stirring well after each addition to ensure the dressing doesn't split. Add the salt, lemon zest, dill and garlic, and stir to combine. Use immediately, or store in an airtight container in the fridge for up to 1 week.

Epic tips

If you're vegan, use unsweetened coconut yoghurt in place of the goat's cheese and Greek yoghurt, and add a few drops of lemon juice to taste. It's an entirely different dressing, but just as delish.

* The amount of oil you need will depend on how oily your cheese is and how wet or firm your yoghurt is. Feel free to thin it out with water if you are trying to avoid adding too much extra oil, but resist the temptation to use the lemon juice for this purpose. It will overpower the dressing and you won't taste the goat's cheese, dill or garlic, which is what makes this dressing sing. In this dressing, the zestie is your bestie.

Contents by dressing

Basic balsamic
Roasted pumpkin, maple walnut and blue cheese	126
Lemon ricotta pasta salad	150
Greens with avocado, pepitas and sesame seeds	170
Greens with radish, parmesan and garlic croutons	171

Chilli lime
Marinated chickpea, avocado and feta salad	82
Chilli lime pinto bean salad	109
Marinated black beans with crispy tortilla strips	121
Ever-versatile tomato and cucumber salad (swap)	180

Coconut satay
Gado Gado salad plate	76
Satay tofu and edamame bowl (swap)	90
Coconut-crusted pumpkin and chickpea salad	110

Coriander pesto
Coriander pesto and roasted pumpkin pasta salad	143

Lemon tahini yoghurt
Pomegranate, eggplant and cabbage	115
Roasted zucchini, crispy pitta and beans	130

Pomegranate
Roasted feta and grape fattoush	89
Three bean salad	107
Grain salad	114
Roasted cauliflower salad	129
Roasted eggplant and zucchini with pearl couscous	157

The art of salad building

Sesame mayo
Egg salad for one (swap)	64
Super salad	97
Warm greens noodle salad	165

Spicy peanut
Spicy peanut slaw with tofu croutons and almonds	68
Five-spice tempeh and cauliflower salad	113
Spicy peanut udon salad	154
Soba salad with edamame and corn	161

Spicy soy
Spicy tofu puffed rice salad	94
Spicy soy noodle salad with warm tofu puffs (swap)	162

Supergreen
Egg salad for one (swap)	64
Butter bean breakfast salad (swap)	105
Roasted zucchini and feta with sorghum	122

The GOAT
Chickpea, celery and walnut salad for one	64
Egg salad for one	64
Haloumi chickpea salad	118
Honey mustard carrot and chickpea salad	125
Root-to-leaf beet salad	133
Roasted tomato orzo salad	146
Charred broccoli and pea pasta salad	149
Cos, parmesan, fried pasta, basil	170
Kale and crouton side salad	171
Grilled iceberg lettuce with capers	179
Tomato salad with fried capers and pinenuts	185
Raw cauliflower and broccoli salad	186
Warm greens and toasted spelt	189

The art of salad building

Crunch

While you will often find crunch in the leaf or body of a salad, I like to add an additional crunch factor as a finishing touch, for texture, flavour and overall moreish-ness. On a textural level, crunch is important for satisfaction, but the kind of crunch I'm talking about uses the magic of heat to enhance natural flavours and create new ones.

The following are some go-to methods for bringing that extra crunch factor.

Crunchy bread bits

Whether it's pangratatto or croutons, frying stale bread is a culinary trick that's been used for centuries. There is a magic that happens when you combine bread (or breadcrumbs) with salt, olive oil, garlic and heat. This crunchy little flavour bomb is infinitely more than the sum of its parts and can be used to give life, crunch and extra depth to anything it touches.

I always find it tricky to get sourdough bread stale enough to turn into breadcrumbs. If you have the same problem, try slowly drying it out on a low heat in the oven for 10 minutes or so. Once it's no longer squishy, allow it to cool, then break into chunks and blitz in your food processor. If using pre-made breadcrumbs, I prefer panko crumbs to standard breadcrumbs because they are rougher and more jagged in shape.

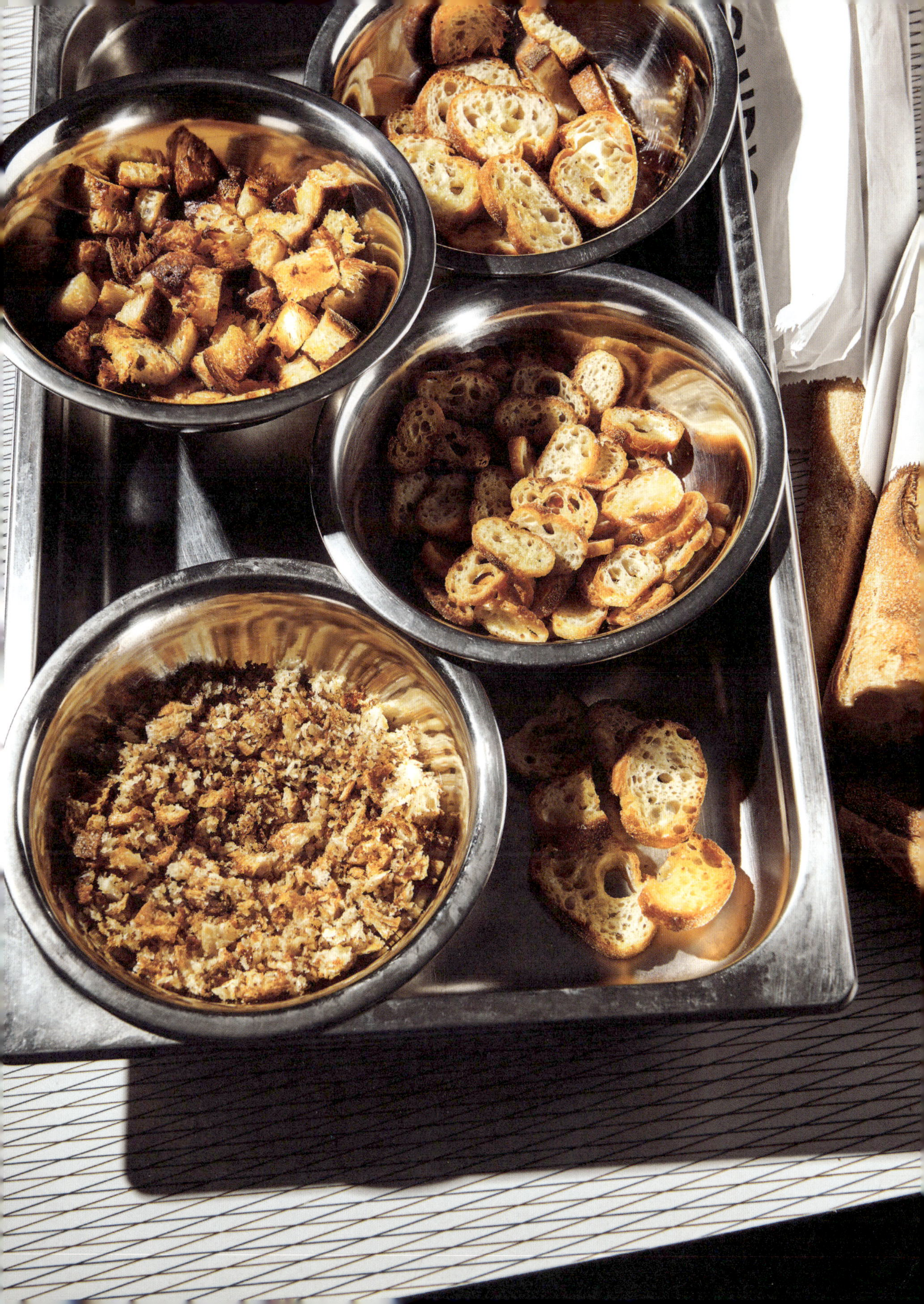

Choose your own crunch adventure

1 Pick your bread

For pangratatto
100 g (3½ oz) panko crumbs or 1 slice of stale sourdough (approx. 100 g/3½ oz), blitzed into breadcrumbs

For croutons
1 slice of stale sourdough (approx. 100 g/3½ oz), cut into cubes or
½ baguette or ficelle, thinly sliced
or 100 g (3½ oz) pitta bread, cut into squares

2 Combine in a mixing bowl with

- 1–2 tablespoons olive oil
- 1 teaspoon crushed garlic
- 1 teaspoon flaky sea salt

Use your fingertips to mix everything until well combined.

To make in the oven

Preheat the oven to 180–200°C (360–390°F). Spread the bread on a baking tray and bake for 5 minutes. Toss, then return to the oven for another 2–5 minutes, or until golden brown and crispy.

Use immediately, or store in an airtight jar for up to 6 months.

3
Pick your cooking method

To make in a frying pan

Place a large frying pan over a medium–high heat. Place half the bread in the bottom of the hot frying pan and cook for 2 minutes or until golden brown, tossing every 30 seconds or so (more frequently as the breadcrumbs start to brown).

Transfer the toasted breadcrumbs to a plate and repeat with the remaining mixture.

Pangratatto will take approximately 2 minutes.

Croutons will take about 10 minutes.

I personally find a light char quite delicious, so I like to let them go until slightly blackened in parts.

Roasting and toasting nuts and seeds

Roasting and toasting nuts and seeds enhances their flavours in a profound way. I can't think of a single nut or seed I would prefer to eat raw than roasted. While you can buy them already roasted and toasted, I prefer to do this just before eating to get the best flavour and most satisfying crunch.

Roasting nuts

Preheat the oven to 140–160°C (285–320°F).

Spread nuts on an oven tray in a single layer and place in the hot oven. Cook, keeping a close eye on them and giving them a toss about halfway through. I find chopped/sliced/slivered nuts are usually done within 5–10 minutes, while whole nuts usually need closer to 15.

Once the nuts are lightly brown, remove them from the oven and allow to cool until ready to use. They will continue to cook on the hot tray, so if they are a little dark, transfer to a dinner plate and allow to cool there. They will become crunchier as they cool.

If using in a recipe where you are roasting vegetables, you can also chuck them straight on the tray with the veg for the final 5–15 minutes of cooking time, depending on their size. Just keep a close eye on them, as the oven will be running at a higher temperature than you would usually roast nuts in.

Toasting seeds

Place a large frying pan over a medium–high heat. Once hot, add 1–2 handfuls of seeds (ideally, you want a single layer, but this can be tricky with sesame seeds) and cook, stirring or tossing constantly, until they are fragrant and start to pop. Transfer to a dinner plate and allow to cool. Pine nuts can go either way – oven or stove – depending on whatever else you are doing in the kitchen.

Storing the little morsels of joy

I try and use any roasted and toasted nuts and seeds within 2 weeks. To prolong their shelf life, store in an airtight container in a cool, dark place – this will slow oxidation. However, be wary of roasted nuts that you find lurking in the back of your pantry – roasted or toasted nuts or seeds tend to go rancid more quickly than their raw counterparts. I recommend giving them a sniff before eating. If they smell plasticky, they're probably best avoided.

All this to say – while you *can* do this ahead of time, you're better off roasting and toasting as you need them.

Hazelnut dukkah

Makes 1 cup

1 cup (175 g/6 oz) hazelnuts
¼ cup (30 g/1 oz) sesame seeds
1 tablespoon cumin seeds
1 tablespoon coriander seeds
½ teaspoon sea salt
½ teaspoon freshly ground black pepper

I've been making this dukkah recipe for as long as I can remember. It's always a hit when served with good-quality olive oil and fresh bread, but it's incredible on salads too. Serve on top of whipped feta or tofu (see page 198) alongside an array of other bits and bobs.

Preheat the oven to 160–180°C (320–360°F).

Spread the nuts on a baking tray and place in the hot oven for 10 minutes. Remove and allow to cool.

If your hazelnuts have skins on them, transfer to a slightly damp tea towel (dish towel) while still warm. Fold the tea towel onto the nuts and then rub vigorously until most of the skins have come off.

Put a large frying pan over a medium–high heat. Add the sesame, cumin and coriander seeds and cook for 2–3 minutes until fragrant and starting to pop. Transfer to a plate and allow to cool.

When the nuts are cool, place in a food processor and blitz until lightly chopped. Add the seeds, salt and pepper and pulse until finely chopped and well combined.

Store in an airtight jar in the fridge until ready to use.

This can also be made with almonds; there's no need to remove the skins if you do this.

Maple walnuts

Makes 1 cup

1 cup (100 g/3½ oz) walnut halves
2 tablespoons maple syrup
1 tablespoon salted butter

Lightly frying walnuts in a little maple syrup and salted butter is the perfect way to transform any salad from average to epic.

Place the walnuts, maple syrup and butter in a large frying pan over a medium heat and cook for 5 minutes, stirring often, until the walnuts are golden brown. I like to use a silicone spatula to move all the maple butter goodness around and over the walnuts, ensuring they're really well coated. Spread in a single layer on a piece of baking paper and scrape all the excess maple butter over the top of them. Allow to cool for 10 minutes.

Assemble

While I love a salad that I can throw together and eat straight from the bowl, I also love hosting and taking photos of my food. And with that comes the joy of good presentation.

Presentation plays a significant role in the way we experience food; we eat with our eyes first, after all. When a meal is visually appealing, it not only creates excitement and anticipation about the eating experience, but also conveys the love and care that's gone into a meal, while showcasing its hero ingredients.

There are a variety of ways you might choose to assemble and present your salads and, of course, different types lend themselves to different presentations. Here are my favourite options.

Big bowl salads

These are salads where everything is mixed together before serving. As a general rule, when making big bowl salads, I usually keep a portion of any crunch factor or herbs aside to use as a garnish.

Platter salads

These are salads where you prep the individual elements and then build the salad in layers, to showcase and ensure an even distribution of hero ingredients and crunch.

Presentation-wise, it's nice to use a large, flat platter with a raised edge or lip, but you can absolutely use a large bowl if that's all you have.

Serving bowl salads

There are also salads that benefit from being assembled directly in the bowl you are eating from, whether for structural integrity, to ensure even distribution of hero ingredients or to minimise dishes — or all of the above!

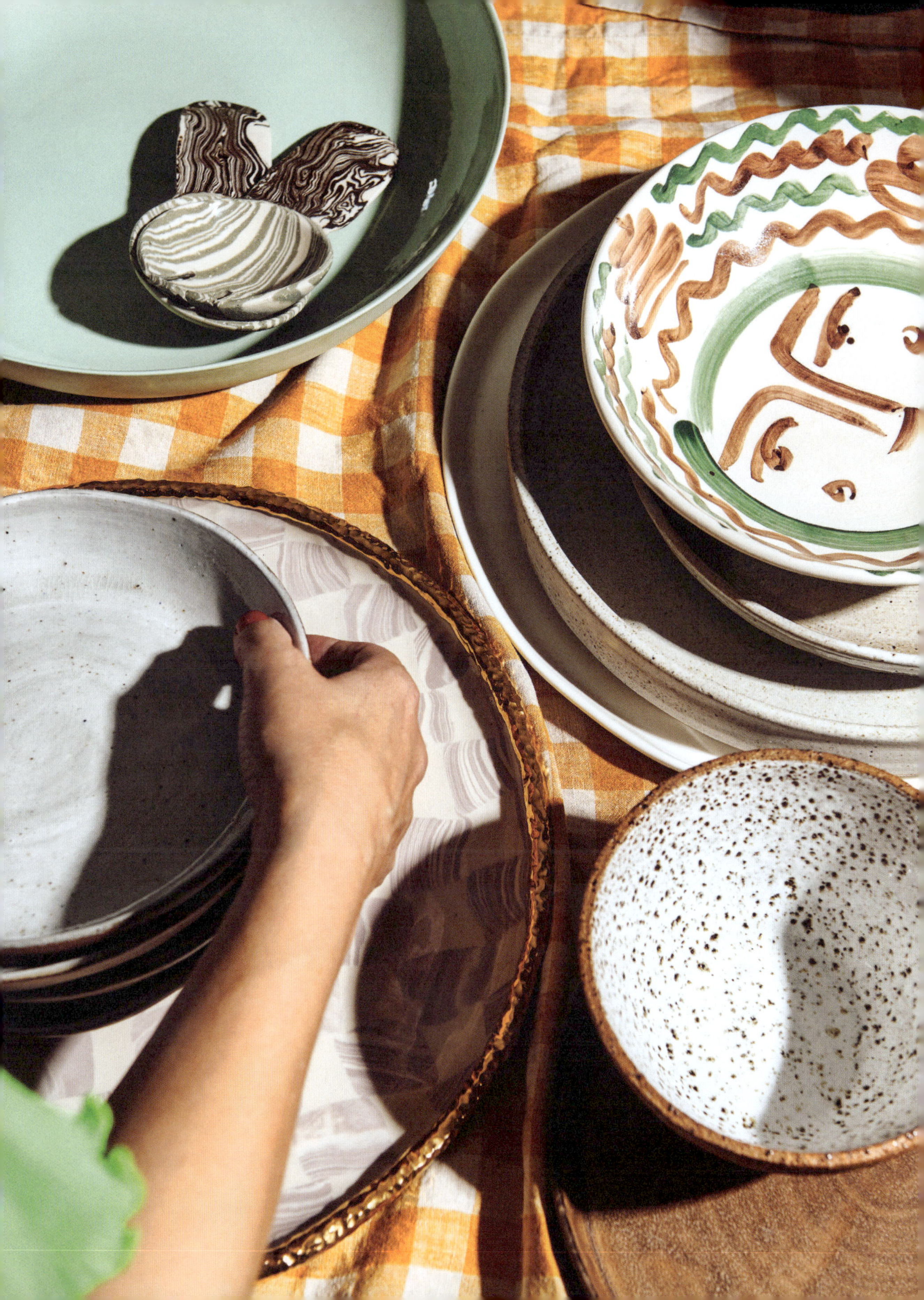

Epic salads pantry list

The following is a list of salad-specific ingredients that you will find in my kitchen at any given point in time. While this list may seem excessive, it's important to me that the ingredients I use in my recipes are easily accessible. You will find most (if not all) of these ingredients at your local supermarket, but I also want to encourage and inspire you to shop at independently owned produce stores and local farmers' markets too; an important step in cultivating community and keeping your money in the local economy.

Quality ingredients

I've always had a soft spot for a fancy ingredient. It can be hard to splurge on such things when you have multiple mouths to feed, but I do believe in buying the best quality you can afford — it will make a big difference in the flavour of your meals. I absolutely understand how this varies from home to home, and according to which season of life you are in or even what day of the week it is. Budget, convenience and mental load all come into play here.

I find that my local market and Asian supermarket are the most affordable options, which makes it easier to splurge on organic ingredients where necessary/possible. That being said, sometimes the quickest and easiest option is my local supermarket — the veggies aren't as good, but the payoff is convenience, and sometimes that convenience is the difference between a cooked meal and takeout.

GOOD
BALSAMIC
NAKHIL®
طحينة
اكسترا
SGAMBARO
MOLINO E PASTIFICIO
100% ITALIANO
DAI CAMPI AL CUORE

The ultimate pantry list

1
Leaf

- Baby spinach
- Basil
- Butter lettuce
- Cabbage
- Coriander (cilantro)
- Cos (romaine)
- Dill
- Iceberg
- Kale
- Microherbs
- Mint
- Parsley
- Radicchio
- Rocket (arugula)
- Seaweed
- Sprouts
- Thai basil
- Vietnamese mint

2
Body

- Apple
- Asparagus
- Avocado
- Barley
- Beetroot (beets)
- Black barley
- Brown onion
- Capsicum (bell pepper)
- Carrot
- Celery
- Cherries
- Corn
- Cornichons (baby pickles)
- Couscous
- Cranberries
- Cucumber
- Currants
- Egg noodles
- Eggplant (aubergine)
- Farro
- Goji berries
- Jalapeños
- Kimchi
- Lime leaves
- Orzo
- Pasta
- Pearl couscous
- Pickled gherkins
- Pumpkin (squash)
- Quinoa
- Red onion
- Rice
- Rice noodles
- Sauerkraut
- Soba noodles
- Spelt
- Spring onion (scallion)
- Sultanas
- Sweet potato
- Tomato
- Zucchini (courgette)

3
Protein

- Beluga lentils
- Black beans
- Boiled egg
- Cannellini beans
- Chickpeas
- Cottage cheese
- Edamame beans
- Feta
- Free-range eggs
- Goat's cheese
- Greek yoghurt
- Haloumi
- Parmesan
- Puy (French green) lentils
- Ricotta
- Tempeh
- Tofu

4
Dressing

- Apple-cider vinegar
- Balsamic vinegar
- Brown-rice vinegar
- Chilli oil
- Coriander seeds
- Cumin
- Dijon mustard
- Extra-virgin olive oil
- Garlic
- Ginger
- Granulated garlic
- Lemons
- Light olive oil
- Limes
- Maple syrup
- Peanut butter
- Pepper
- Pomegranate molasses
- Red-wine vinegar
- Salt
- Sesame oil
- Shallots
- Sherry vinegar
- Soy sauce
- Sriracha
- Tahini
- Tamari
- Tamarind paste
- White-wine vinegar
- Wholegrain mustard

5
Crunch

- Almonds (flaked, slivered and whole)
- Barley rusks
- Cashews
- Corn chips
- Flatbread croutons
- Pangratatto
- Peanuts
- Pepitas (pumpkin seeds)
- Pine nuts
- Pistachios
- Sesame seeds
- Sourdough croutons
- Walnuts

Tools of the trade

While I have always said that all you need to make a good meal is a chopping board and a sharp knife, there are some other basic kitchen tools available that can make all the difference to your experience in the kitchen. Some of the ones I swear by are:

- High-speed blender
- Jars for making dressings in
- Juicer/citrus squeezer
- Mandoline
- Measuring cups
- Microplane
- Peeler
- Pots and pans
- Roasting trays
- Salad spinner
- Silicone spatula
- Stainless-steel bowls – I have so many of these in so many different sizes
- Whisk.

Overwhelmed by mess?

Setting myself up properly before I start cooking is key to not getting overwhelmed by mess. I always have a big bowl out for veggie scraps and another for rubbish, as well as a designated rubber band zone. I also have a bazillion small stainless-steel bowls that I use to pop prepped ingredients in. They are a godsend. Having a sponge on hand and giving your area a wipe-down periodically is also an obvious way to keep things clean and tidy.

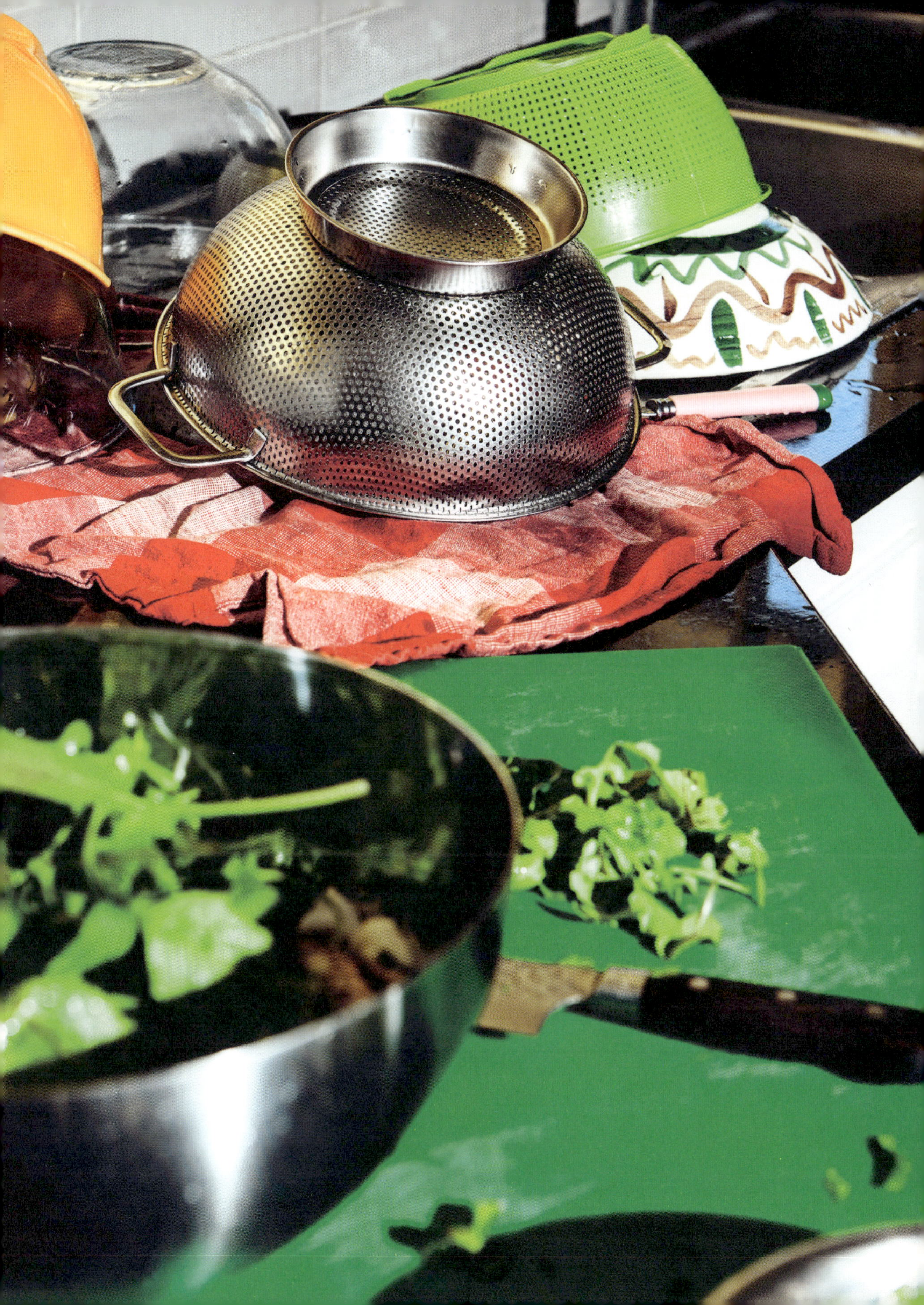

LIGHT

AND FRESH

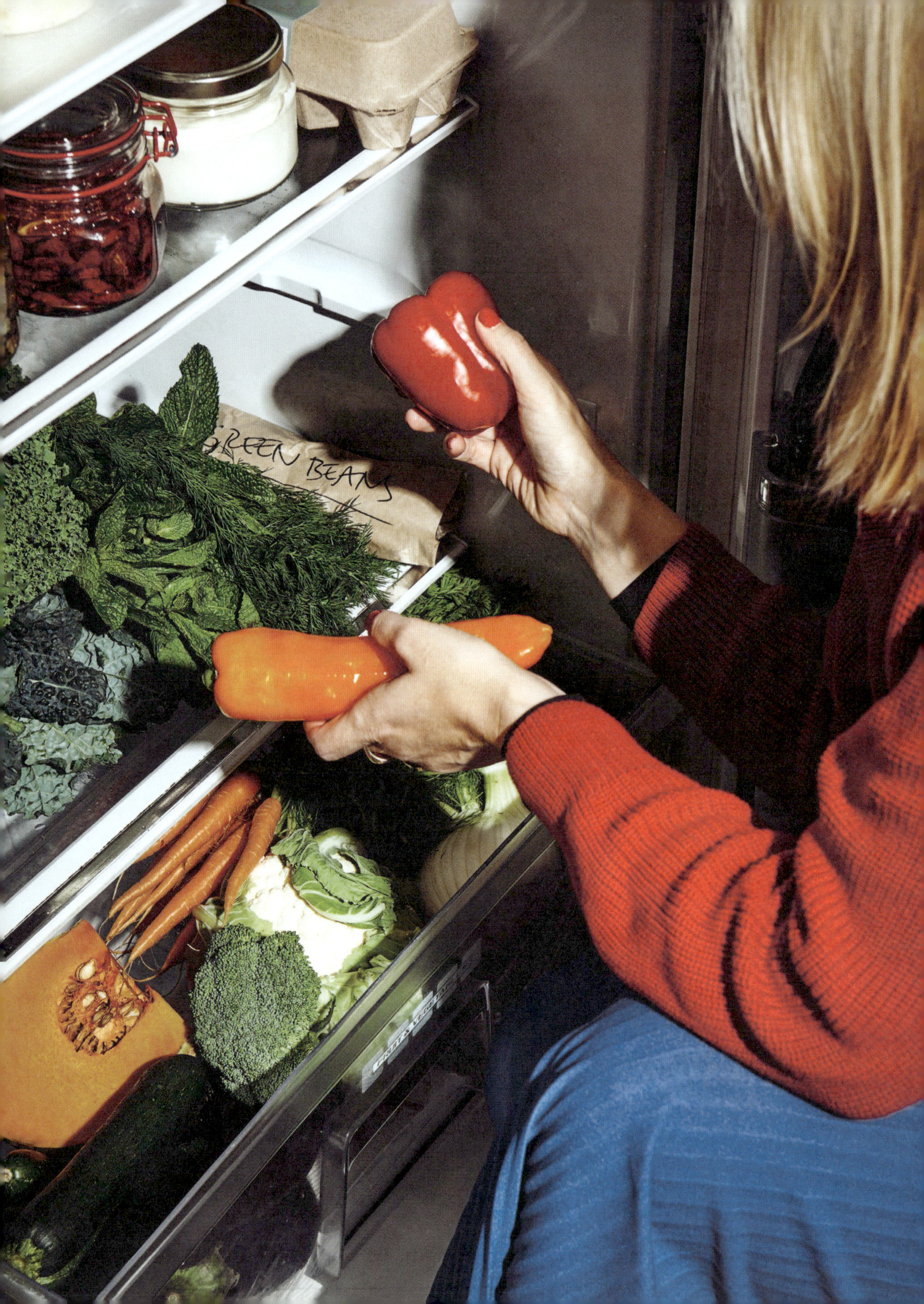
GREEN BEANS

The salads in this chapter are the epitome of zest and vitality. This is where crisp greens, juicy tomatoes and a rainbow of fresh veggies come into their own, dressed in light, zingy vinaigrettes and citrus-infused dressings. These salads focus on ingredients that are crunchy, raw, tender and as close to their natural state as possible – an homage to the textures and tastes that make eating a pleasure.

These are the salads that sing of summer days and springtime freshness, reminding us that sometimes the simplest ingredients can give rise to the most memorable and enjoyable meals.

The salads in this chapter are perfect when you crave something that's light, fresh and rejuvenating, and provide the perfect remedy when you have over-indulged. Most are quick to assemble, require little or no cooking, and can be mixed and matched to suit your mood and what you've got to hand.

Chickpea, celery and walnut salad for one

Serves 1

½ quantity of The GOAT (page 43)
1 × 400 g (14 oz) tin chickpeas, drained and rinsed
2–3 stalks celery, diced
¼ red onion, finely chopped
small handful walnuts (50 g/1¾ oz), roasted and chopped
small handful capers
small handful flat-leaf parsley, finely chopped
small handful baby spinach or rocket (arugula)
lettuce cups, to serve (optional)

This is a quick throw-together lunch, perfect for when you're working from home. The blend of crunchy walnuts, hearty chickpeas and crisp celery comes alive with the creamy tang of my beloved GOAT dressing in a salad that's perfectly portioned for one.

Combine all ingredients in a mixing bowl and stir to combine. Eat immediately, or transfer to an airtight container and refrigerate until ready to eat.

Egg salad for one

Serves 1

2 eggs
½ quantity of The GOAT (page 43)
2 pickled cornichons, sliced
1 spring onion (scallion), finely chopped
small handful spinach or rocket (arugula) leaves, sliced
toast, wraps, seeded crackers or lettuce cups, to serve (optional)

This is a great meal to make when you're working from home or need a quick, easy and protein-rich lunch. You can whip up the dressing while waiting for the eggs to cook, and reserve the other half for the Chickpea, celery and walnut salad, opposite.

Boil the eggs according to the method on page 34 and then drain, cool and peel.

While the eggs are cooking, put the dressing in a small mixing bowl and add the other ingredients. Once the eggs are peeled, chop or mash them and add to the mixing bowl. Stir to combine and serve, either as is, with a side of buttered toast, in a wrap with hummus or avocado, piled onto a seeded cracker or loaded into lettuce cups.

Swaps
Parsley, red onion, shallots, chilli flakes and fried capers all make wonderful additions, as does the Supergreen dressing (page 43) or Sesame mayo (page 42) instead of The GOAT dressing.

Epic tip
This recipe is perfect for one, but you can easily double or quadruple it if you're feeding extra people or want to eat it over a number of days.

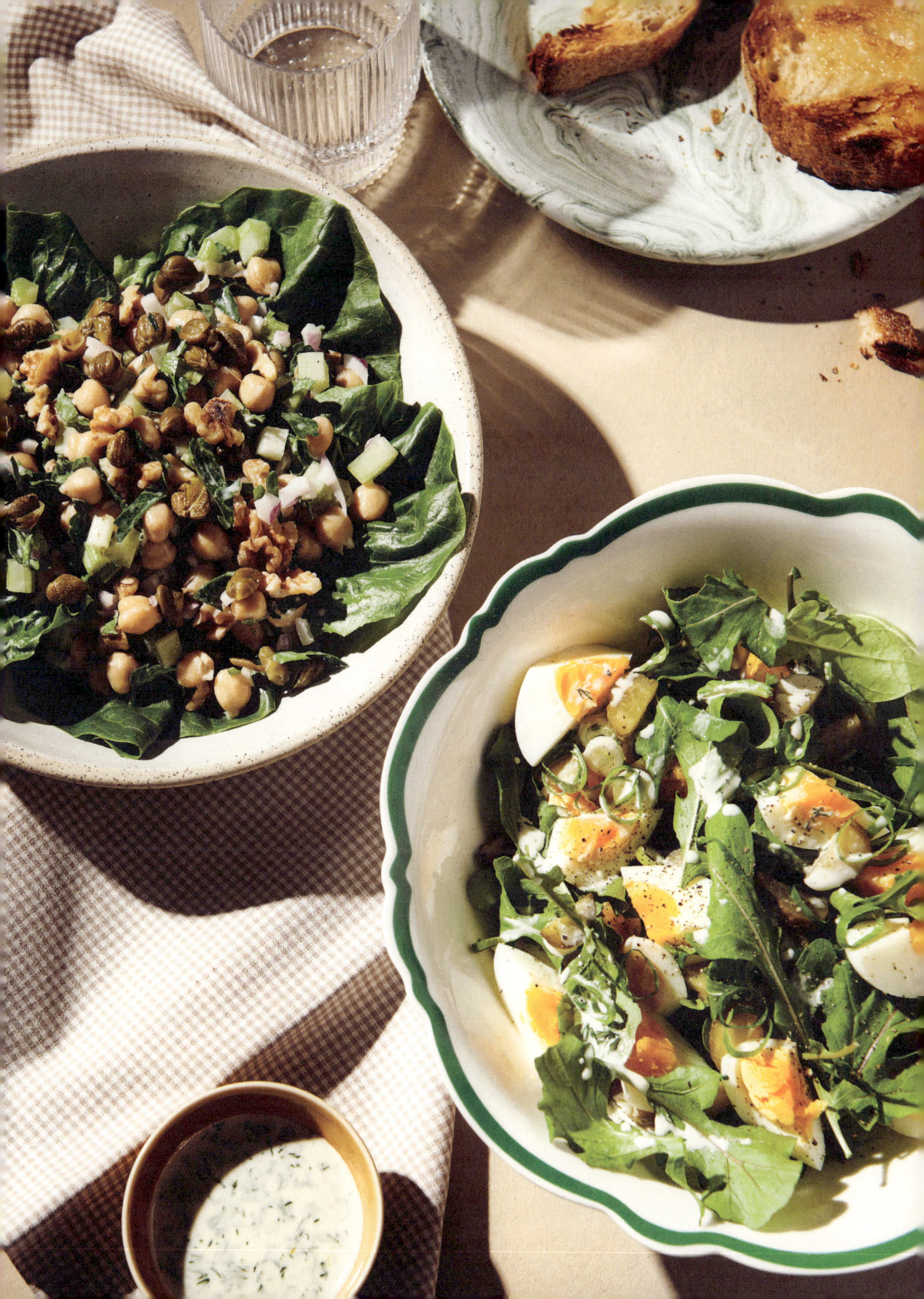

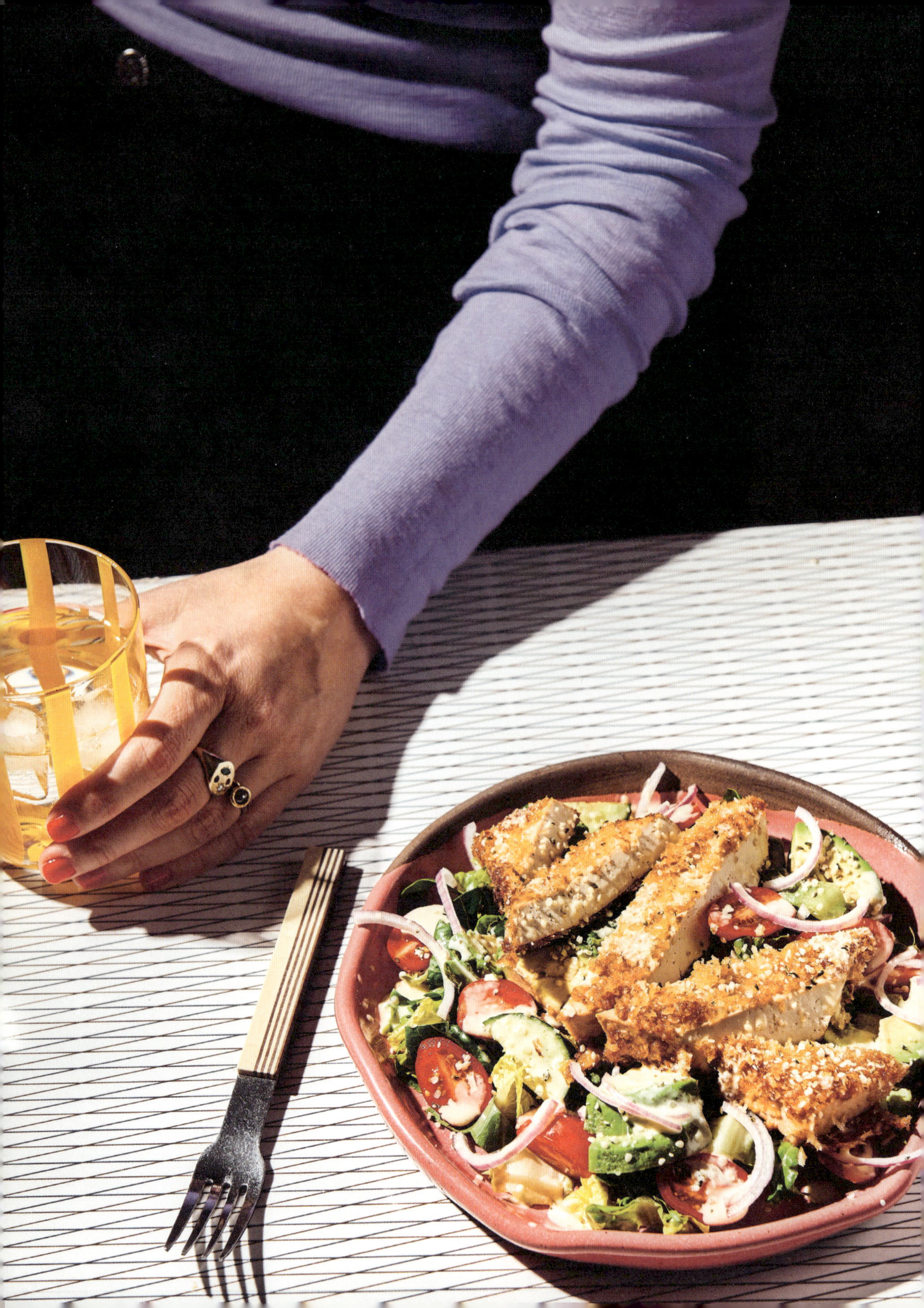

Panko tofu salad for one

Serves 1

I'm definitely not reinventing the wheel here but hot damn, this salad slaps. The light crunch of the lettuce, tomato and cucumber pairs perfectly with the tangy dressing and creamy avocado, and the warm panko tofu brings heart and flavour, making a salad that's both moreish and filling.

Use this recipe as a guide, increasing or decreasing the quantities depending on hunger.

Dressing

1 tablespoon mayo
1 teaspoon Dijon mustard
juice of ½ a lemon

Panko tofu

100–150 g (3½–5½ oz) firm tofu, drained and pressed
1 teaspoon soy sauce
1 teaspoon Japanese mayo
2 tablespoons panko crumbs
oil, for cooking

Salad

3 cos (romaine) lettuce leaves, washed, spun, sliced
6–8 baby roma tomatoes, halved
2.5 cm (1 in) chunk of cucumber, halved and sliced
½ avocado, sliced
⅛ red onion, sliced
1 tablespoon hemp seeds

To make the dressing, combine all the dressing ingredients in a small bowl and stir until well combined.

Start with a big slab of tofu. You will cut it once it's cooked. Lay flat between a clean tea towel (dish towel) or paper towel and squeeze out as much water as possible.

Combine the soy sauce and mayo in a flat-bottomed dish. Pat the tofu dry and add to the dish, coating it in the marinade, then leave it to sit for at least 30 minutes.

Pour the panko crumbs onto a dinner plate and gently place the tofu in the panko, lightly pressing it into the crumbs and then flipping and coating the other side. Press the crumbs into the sides of the tofu too.

Warm 1 tablespoon of cooking oil in a large frying pan over a medium–high heat. Add the tofu and cook for 2–3 minutes, until lightly golden on the underside. Flip and cook for another 2–3 minutes, until golden and crispy all over. Transfer to a lined plate and slice on the diagonal – as pictured – when ready to use.

Arrange the lettuce leaves in a bowl and drizzle with half of the dressing. Follow with the remaining ingredients and top with the tofu and the remaining dressing.

Serve immediately.

Epic tips

1. This salad is great piled into a wrap that's been schmeared with hummus.
2. To pump up the protein, add feta, a boiled egg or a serve of quinoa.
3. For a lighter version, swap the Panko tofu for the marinated tofu on page 68 or page 154 and bake it, rather than pan frying.
4. Not sure what to do with the rest of the tofu? Freeze it or marinate it. I often cook with a 400 g (14 oz) block of tofu and prep three serves of this to eat it over 3 days. Lunch, sorted.

Spicy peanut slaw with tofu croutons and almonds

Serves 4

This is one of my favourite ways to make tofu. Marinating it in a strong vegan chicken (or veggie) stock overnight gives it a delicious flavour that is milder than my usual marinades, but unbelievably moreish. Once baked, the tofu takes on a dry and crunchy texture that pairs perfectly with a rich dressing.

In this salad, cos lettuce and red cabbage form a fresh base for the spicy peanut dressing, which is complemented by fresh cucumber, herbs and flavoursome tofu. Slivered almonds and toasted white sesame round it all off with essential crunch, bringing you a salad that is light, fresh and filling.

Dressing
- 1 quantity Spicy peanut dressing (page 42)

Tofu croutons
- 2 vegan chicken bouillon cubes (enough to make 4 cups/1 litre/34 fl oz)
- 2 cups (500 ml/17 fl oz) water
- 1 tablespoon soy sauce
- 1 block tofu, pressed and cut into 1 cm (½ in) cubes

Salad
- 30 g (1 oz) slivered almonds
- ¼ red cabbage, very finely sliced
- 1 head cos (romaine) lettuce, leaves washed, spun dry, and diced
- 1 Lebanese (short) cucumber, halved, seeds scraped, and cut into half-moons
- 3 spring onions (scallions), sliced
- 1 tablespoon toasted white sesame seeds
- small handful coriander (cilantro), roughly chopped

To prepare the tofu, dissolve the bouillon cubes in the water. Add the soy sauce and stir to combine. Place the cubed tofu in a large, flat-bottomed dish. Pour over the stock and soy sauce marinade, cover, and place in the fridge to marinate overnight or for at least a few hours.

Preheat the oven to 180–200°C (360–390°F).

Place the tofu on a baking tray and bake for 20 minutes, tossing halfway through cooking time. If your almonds aren't already toasted, add them to the baking tray for the final 5 minutes of cooking.

To prepare the salad, combine the cabbage and lettuce with half the dressing. Toss to combine, then add the cucumber, spring onions, sesame seeds and most of the coriander and lightly toss again.

To serve, place half the salad on a serving platter. Top with half the tofu and almonds and a drizzle of dressing. Repeat with remaining salad, tofu, almonds and dressing, then top with reserved coriander.

This is best served when the tofu is still warm.

Swaps

1. If you can't do nuts, swap the peanut butter in the dressing for tahini and the almonds for pepitas (pumpkin seeds).

2. This slaw recipe is outrageously good with the Peanut tofu (page 86), and this tofu recipe works well with any of the coleslaw or noodle recipes in this book that call for tofu.

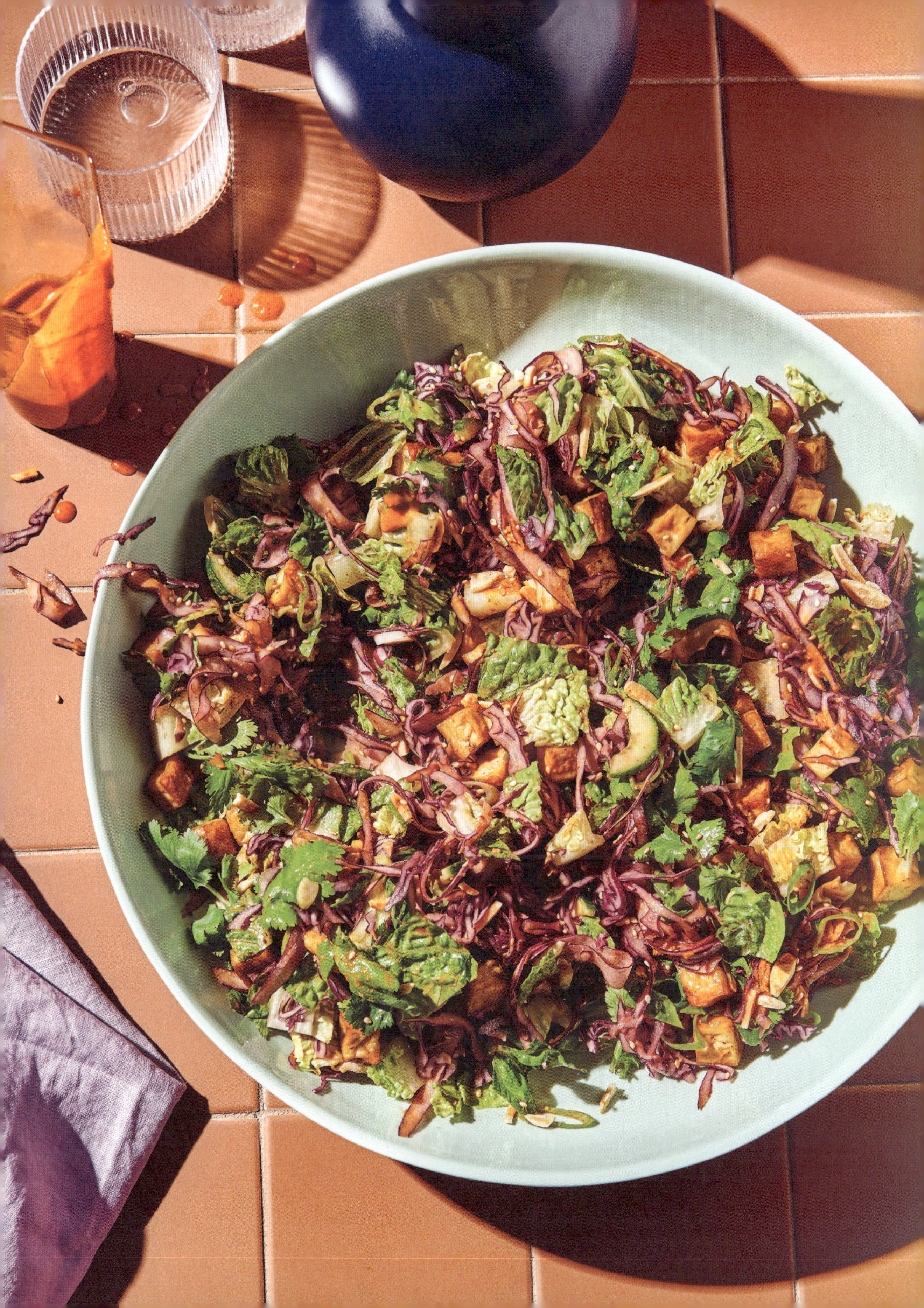

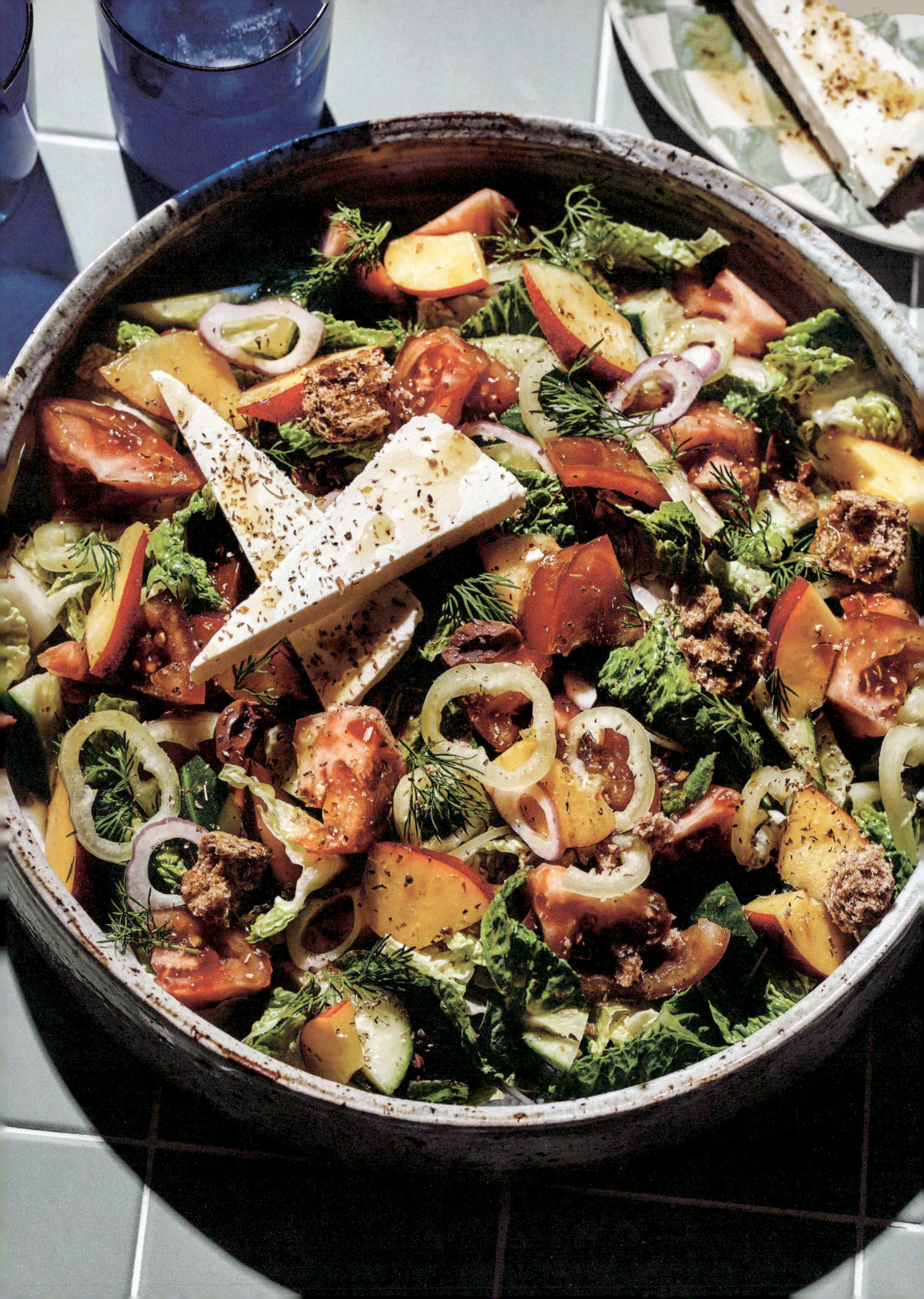

Greek salad

Serves 4

A true classic, Greek salad never fails to hit the spot when you are craving something light and fresh. This version uses sweet nectarines and yellow peppers to complement the vibrant combination of juicy tomatoes, crisp cucumbers and lettuce, sharp shallots and creamy feta cheese, bringing you a burst of freshness and rich flavours. With the addition of barley rusks, this salad is perfect as a standalone meal when you are languishing on a hot day, or as a side at a barbecue or other gathering.

Dressing

¼ cup (60 ml/2 fl oz) olive oil
1½ tablespoons (30 ml/1 fl oz) red-wine vinegar
¼ teaspoon dried oregano
¼ teaspoon salt

Salad

1 baby cos (romaine) lettuce, leaves washed, dried and diced
3–4 heirloom tomatoes, cut into 2 cm (¾ in) dice
1–2 Lebanese (short) cucumbers, cut into 2 cm (¾ in) dice
1 French shallot, finely sliced
large handful of pitted kalamata olives, halved
1–2 nectarines, stone removed and sliced into half-wedges
1 sweet yellow capsicum (bell pepper), thinly sliced
100 g (3½ oz) barley rusks, lightly crushed
200 g (7 oz) feta, cut into triangles
a drizzle of honey (optional)

Put dressing ingredients in a large jar with a screw-top lid and shake to combine. Set aside.

Combine all the salad ingredients, except the feta and honey, in a large mixing bowl. Pour over most of the salad dressing and toss to combine. Transfer to a serving dish, top with feta, then drizzle with the remaining dressing, and honey, if using.

Garnish with another pinch of dried oregano and serve immediately.

Epic tip

This is very good stuffed into a pitta or wrap with hummus and a chopped (veggie) sausage. Also good alongside hummus or Dreamy creamy loaded bean dip (page 201).

Swaps

1. Radishes, avocado, red capsicum (bell pepper) and dare I say, the ever-divisive green capsicum (bell pepper) all make excellent additions or substitutions.
2. If you can't find barley rusks, make some chunky croutons à la the recipe on page 48 or fry some torn up pieces of sourdough, as you would in a panzanella.

Crispy nori tofu with simple slaw

Serves 2–3

Hot diggety damn, for a recipe so simple, this slaw is *good*! The combination of cabbage and lettuce with the tangy lime and mayo dressing makes a perfect base for the addition of spring onion (scallion), corn and crispy nori tofu, giving you a salad that's full of flavour as well as protein. Serve this as an easy weeknight dinner, or in tacos smeared with a bit of avocado when you're looking for something that little bit extra.

Dressing
2 tablespoons Japanese mayo
juice and zest of 1 lime

Tofu
1 × 400 g (14 oz) packet firm tofu, drained and pressed
1 tablespoon soy sauce
2 tablespoons Japanese mayo
3 tablespoons cornflour (cornstarch)
1 teaspoon nori flakes
oil, for cooking

Slaw
2 ears of corn, husks removed and kernels cut from cob
4 cups (250 g/9 oz) white cabbage, sliced paper thin
8 cos (romaine) lettuce leaves, sliced
4 spring onions (scallions), sliced
1 tablespoon toasted sesame seeds
2 handfuls herbs such as Vietnamese mint, Thai basil and coriander (cilantro)

Slice the tofu into squares, or batons, approximately 1 cm (½ in) thick. Combine the soy sauce and mayo in a flat-bottomed dish and add the tofu, turning to coat it in the marinade and allowing it to sit for at least 30 minutes.

Combine the cornflour and nori flakes on a dinner plate, then place the marinated tofu on top in a single layer. Gently turn each piece of tofu so they are all coated in cornflour and nori flakes.

Cook the corn kernels in a hot frying pan with a tablespoon of oil and a pinch of salt and cook for 2–3 minutes. Allow to cool.

Cook the tofu in the same pan, giving it a wipe first if necessary. Warm a tablespoon of cooking oil in the frying pan over a medium–high heat. Add the tofu and cook for 2–3 minutes, until lightly golden on the underside. Flip and cook for another 2–3 minutes until golden and crispy all over. Transfer to a paper towel-lined plate until ready to use.

To make the slaw, put the cabbage and lettuce in a large mixing bowl. In a separate bowl, combine the mayo and lime. Whisk until smooth, then pour over the cabbage and lettuce and stir to combine. Add the cooled corn, along with the spring onion, sesame seeds and herbs.

Toss to combine really well, then transfer to serving dishes and top with cooked tofu. Alternatively, serve in tacos with a smear of avocado, chipotle mayo, or both.

Swaps
This slaw is great with the Peanut tofu on page 86, or you can serve this tofu as a standalone snack or sandwich filling, or with any coleslaw or noodle recipe in this book.

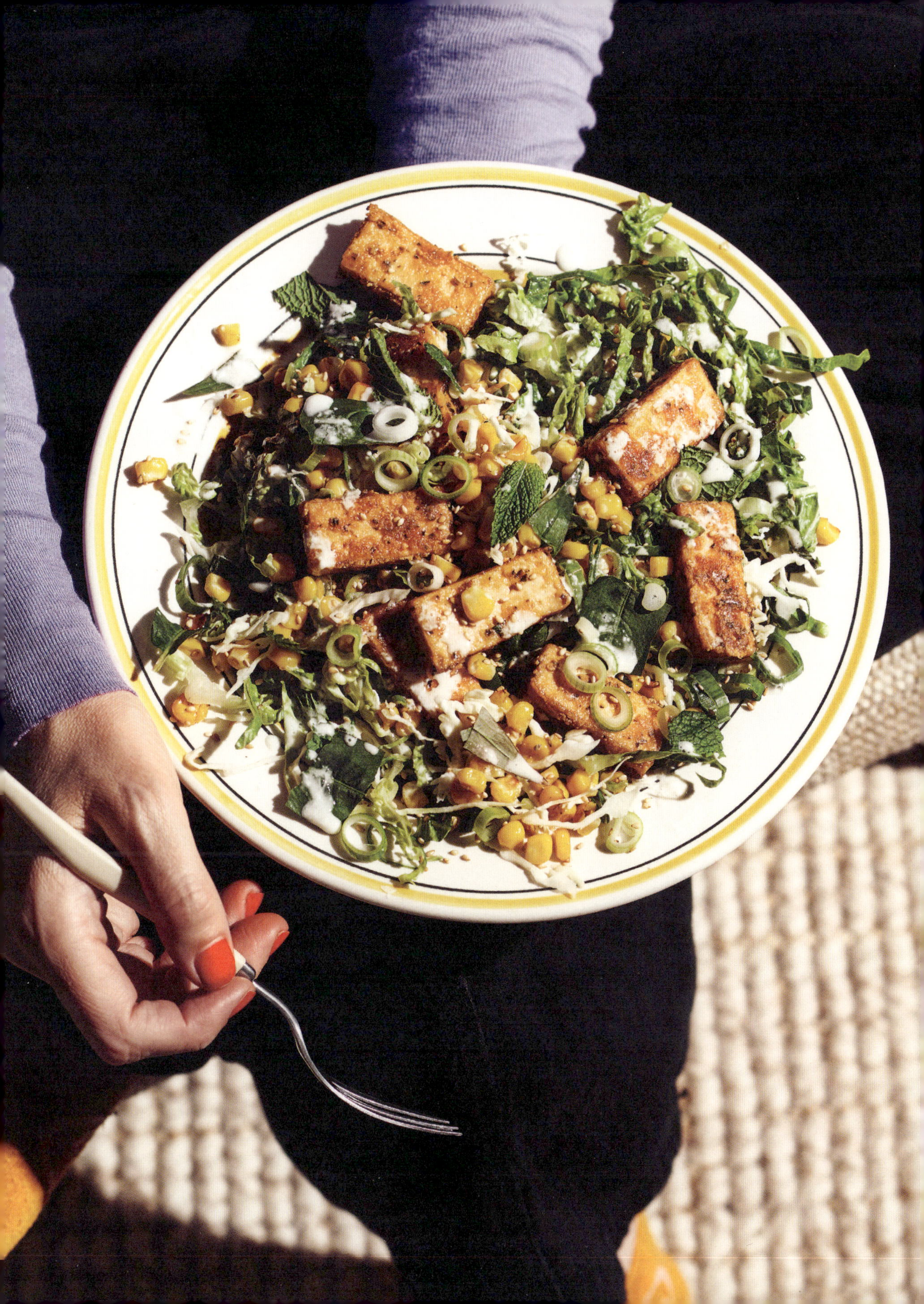

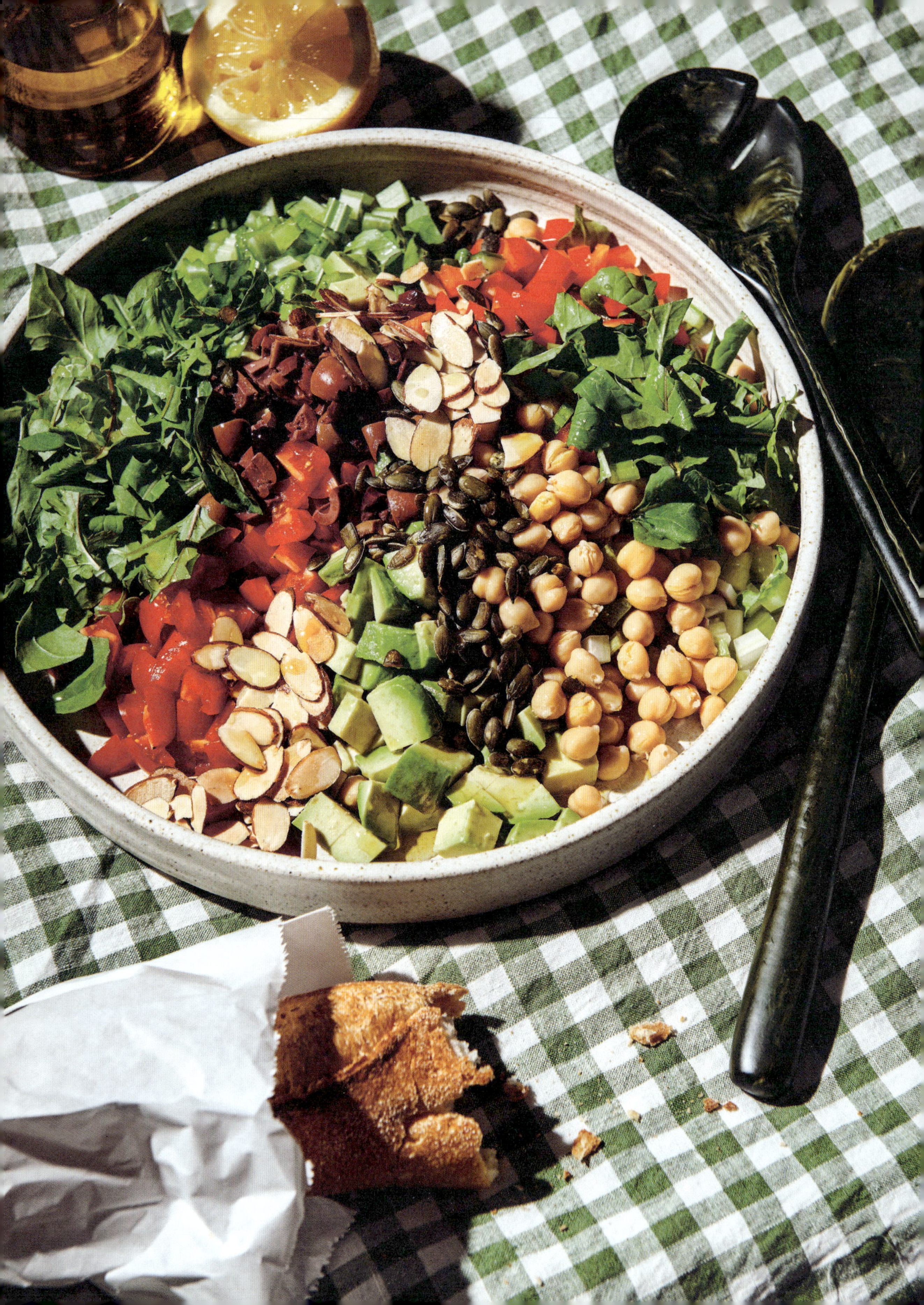

Forever favourite chopped salad

Serves 2–4

This is one of my most regularly made recipes. The key to its greatness is chopping everything quite small, so you get a little bit of everything in every mouthful. It's fresh and full of flavour, and filling while also being light, making it the perfect weekday lunch or dinner for post-indulgent times.

While it doesn't use a dressing per se, the red onion and olives pair perfectly with the lemon and olive oil to enhance the natural flavours of the fresh veggies the way a dressing would. It's really something.

---

1 × 400 g (14 oz) tin chickpeas, drained and rinsed
1 small red onion, finely chopped
2–3 celery stalks, finely chopped
1 red capsicum (bell pepper), seeded, finely chopped
large handful of baby roma tomatoes, finely chopped
small handful of pitted black olives, finely chopped
2 large handfuls of rocket (arugula), chopped
1 ripe avocado, diced
juice of 1 lemon
drizzle of olive oil
60 g (2 oz) toasted pine nuts, flaked almonds, pepitas (pumpkin seeds) or sunflower seeds

Put the chickpeas in a large mixing bowl, then add the onion, celery, capsicum, tomatoes and olives. Give it all a big stir.

Add the rocket and avocado to the bowl along with the lemon juice, olive oil and most of the toasted nuts or seeds. Use a spoon to give the salad a light mix, then top with the remaining nuts or seeds and serve.

This will keep in the fridge for up to 3–4 days.

Epic tip

To pump up the protein, add a boiled, chopped egg and 100 g (3½ oz) of crumbled Danish feta or goat's cheese. Alternatively, try 1½ cups (275 g/9½ oz) of cooked quinoa. Allow the quinoa to cool before combining with the salad – the heat will cause the ingredients to wilt slightly, and leftovers won't keep as well.

Light and fresh

Gado Gado salad plate

Serves 2–4

Gado Gado is an Indonesian dish that translates to 'mix mix'. It's usually a mixture of raw and cooked veggies and proteins, but what many people tie the name to is the coconutty, peanutty sauce that makes literally anything taste like heaven. I often find myself making this simplified version of Gado Gado, where I pair raw veggies with cooked proteins, which packs a heavy protein punch.

Dressing
1 quantity Coconut satay dressing (page 39)

Salad
4 eggs
200 g (7 oz) tempeh, thinly sliced
oil, for frying
salt
¼ iceberg lettuce
1 Lebanese (short) cucumber, sliced into rounds
1 heirloom tomato, diced
3–4 radishes, halved or quartered

Bring a small pot of water to a boil and prepare an ice bath. Once the water is boiling, prick the bottom of the eggs with an egg pricker (if you have one) and lower the eggs into the boiling water with a spoon. Lower the heat to a simmer and cook for 7–12 minutes depending on how runny you like your yolks. Once the eggs are cooked, remove from the heat and place in the ice bath for 5 minutes.

Roll the egg on your benchtop using a medium amount of pressure to create little cracks all over the shell without squashing the egg. Remove the peel and rinse any stubborn bits away under cold water.

Meanwhile, heat a small amount of neutral cooking oil in a frying pan. Add the tempeh and cook for 2 minutes, then use tongs to turn and cook for another 2 minutes. Transfer to a paper towel-lined sheet and sprinkle generously with salt. Set aside.

When ready to eat, cut the cooled eggs into quarters. Arrange all ingredients on a large serving platter or in individual bowls. Drizzle with half the dressing and serve the remainder on the side with a spoon. Devour.

Epic tip
For a heartier and more traditional version of this recipe, boil some potatoes and green beans, or use any leftover cooked veggies that are begging to be smothered in this delicious dressing.

Swaps
Use store-bought tofu puffs instead of tempeh and heat in the oven or air fryer.

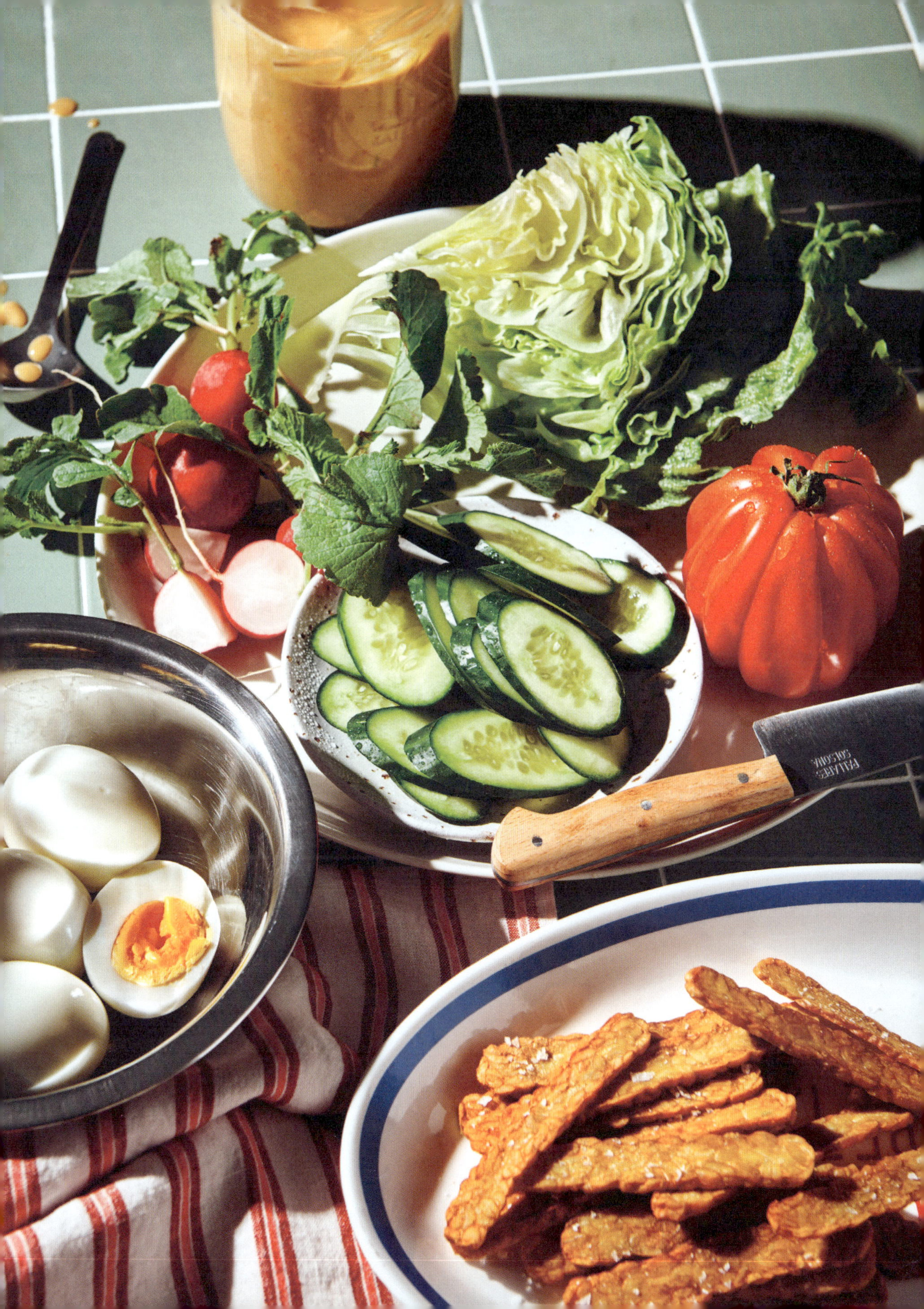

Late summer rusk salad

Serves 2–4

Rusk salad is one of my favourite Greek foods. I make this at the end of summer, when tomatoes and figs are in abundance and it's too hot to cook. I've included marinated beans in this version to make it a meal rather than a side. I prepare this in the morning so the flavours have all day to mingle, and so it comes together in a pinch when you are ready to eat.

Dressing

- ½ cup (125 ml/4 fl oz) olive oil
- ¼ cup (60 ml/2 fl oz) apple-cider vinegar
- 2 tablespoons runny honey or maple syrup
- 2 teaspoons wholegrain mustard
- 1 garlic clove, minced
- ½ teaspoon salt

Salad

- 1 × 400 g (14 oz) tin cannellini beans, drained and rinsed
- 600 g (1 lb 5 oz) tomatoes, cut into bite-sized pieces
- 100 g (3½ oz) olives, halved if you can be bothered
- 1 tablespoon baby capers, finely chopped
- 1 large or 2 small French shallots, very thinly sliced
- 100 g (3½ oz) rusks, crushed
- 60 g (2 oz) baby spinach
- 30 g (1 oz) fresh basil leaves, torn into bite-sized pieces
- 4–5 fresh figs, torn in half (optional)

To make the dressing, combine all ingredients in a glass jar with a lid and shake to combine. Use immediately, or store in the fridge for up to 4 days.

In a large mixing bowl, combine the dressing, beans, tomatoes, olives, capers and shallots, and stir to well combine. Cover with a dinner plate and allow to sit for at least 30 minutes, stirring every now and then if you remember.

When you're ready to serve, add the crushed rusks and stir so they are well coated in the dressing and tomato juices.

Add the spinach, basil and figs (if using). Toss gently and serve immediately.

Epic tip

If you have stale bread at home that you would like to use in place of rusks, tear it into pieces, coat with olive oil and bake for 10 minutes in an oven preheated to 160°C (320°F) until crispy and beginning to turn golden.

Grilled corn and edamame salsa

Serves 2–4

This is one of those recipes that comes together in a pinch. It can be served as a starter, or alongside an assortment of other dishes or salads. Paired with fried wonton wrappers or corn chips, it makes a showstopper of a starter; paired with jasmine rice and a side of tofu, or a boiled egg, it makes a wholesome and filling lunch or dinner. Take it to a potluck and it will pair with almost anything.

Dressing
2 tablespoons Japanese mayo
juice and zest of 1 lime

Salsa
1 tablespoon olive oil
2–3 ears of corn
200 g (7 oz) shelled edamame
1 large red capsicum (bell pepper), diced to about the size of corn kernels
½ red onion, finely chopped
large handful of Vietnamese mint leaves, roughly chopped
large handful of coriander (cilantro) leaves, roughly chopped
1 tablespoon toasted sesame seeds
corn chips or fried wonton wrappers, cut into small squares, to serve

Combine the mayo and lime juice and zest in a mixing bowl and whisk until smooth.

Cook the corn according to any of the methods on pages 23 and 24. Allow to cool, unless serving immediately.

Put the cooked corn, edamame, capsicum and red onion in the bowl with the lime mayo and stir to combine. Taste, season, then toss with the herbs and sesame seeds, and serve with corn chips or fried wonton wrappers on the side to scoop it all up. Yum!

Epic tip
Got leftovers? My husband Andy has been known to pile this on top of corn chips that have been nuked in the microwave with grated cheese on top, to make a sort of nacho fusion dish. He rates it!

Swaps
1. Serve with a side of rice for a wholesome meal. If you prefer, cook the corn on a barbecue or over an open flame, following the method used in the Dreamy creamy loaded guac (page 202).
2. For added protein, serve with any of the Two-minute tofu recipes (page 32).

Pictured overleaf with Two-minute tofu (page 32) →

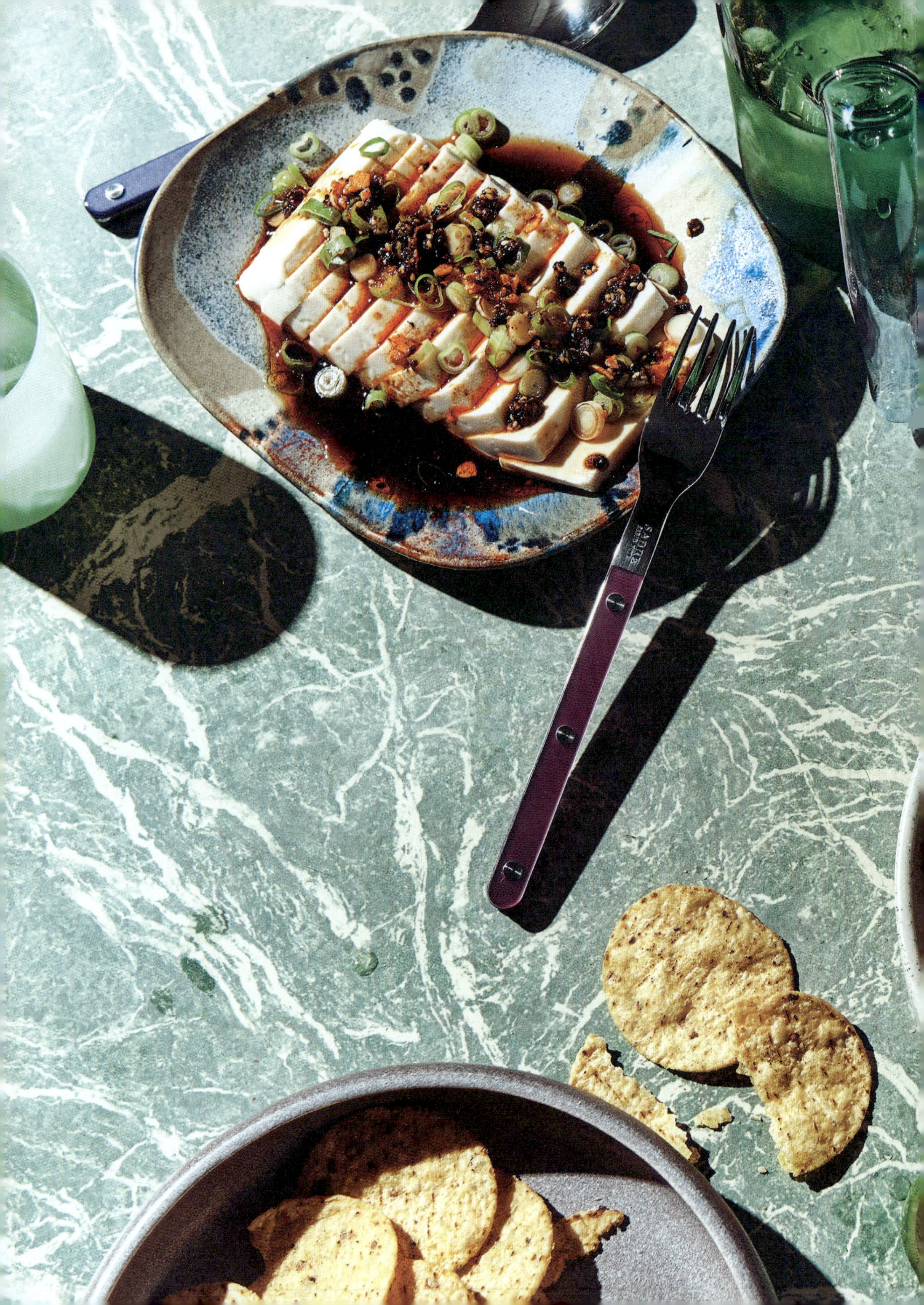

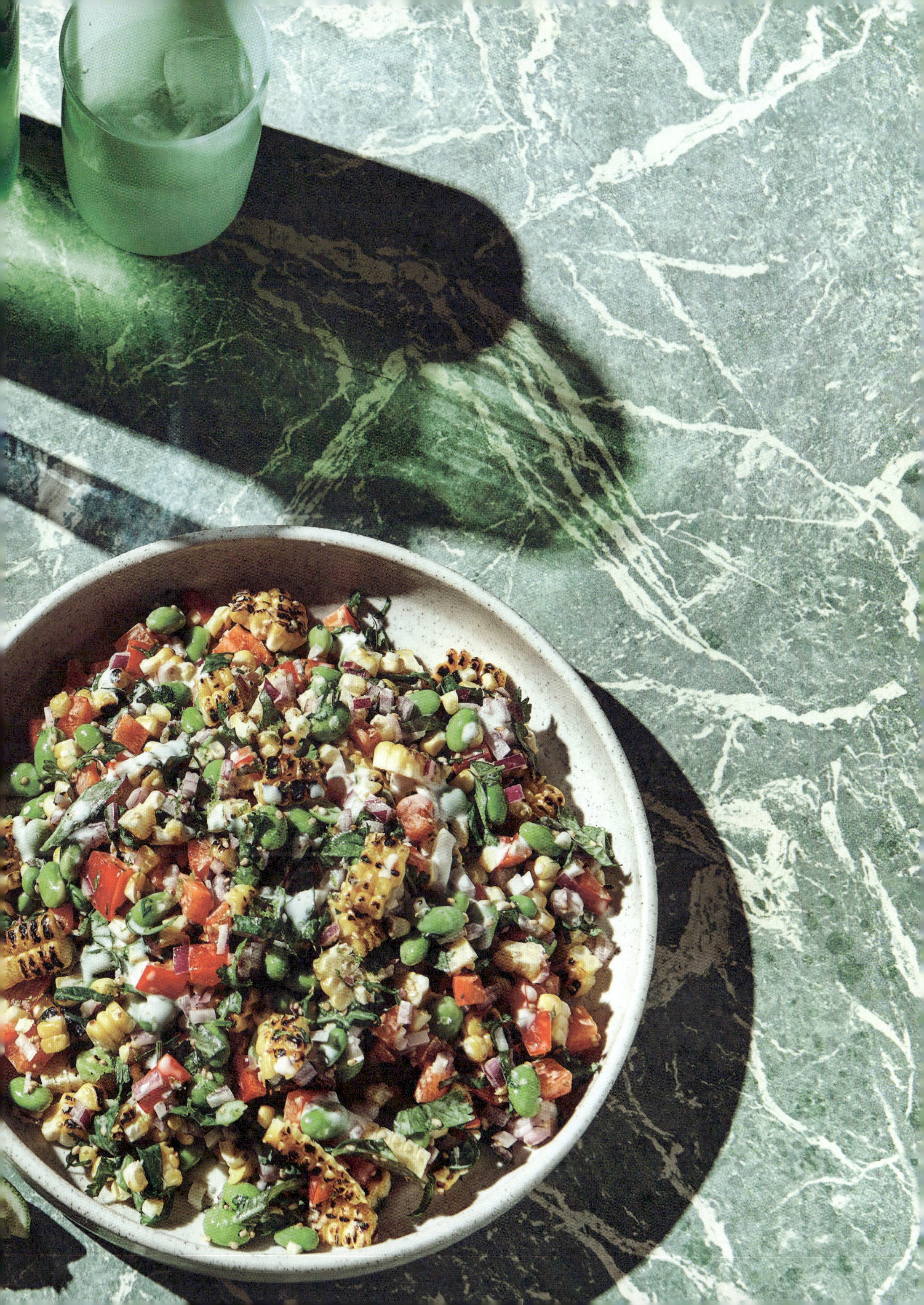

Marinated chickpea, avocado and feta salad

Serves 4

This simple salad is perfect to make when avocados are cheap and the weather is mild. It makes a great weekday lunch or dinner, and also holds up surprisingly well as leftovers (opt for a hardier green such as kale if you want to make it stretch longer than a day). The flavours get better the longer you let them mingle, so if you have time, marinate the chickpeas a day or two ahead. Just give them a stir/shake whenever you open the fridge. While the dressing is insanely good, you can also throw this together with just a squeeze of lemon and a drizzle of oil in a pinch.

Dressing

1 quantity Chilli lime dressing (page 39)

Salad

2 × 400 g (14 oz) tins chickpeas, drained and rinsed
¼ red onion, thinly sliced
6 celery stalks, thinly sliced
2 large or 4 small pitta breads, to serve
2 large ripe avocados
100 g (3½ oz) feta
frisée, rocket (arugula), spinach or kale
small handful coriander (cilantro) or flat-leaf parsley, roughly chopped

Combine chickpeas, red onion and celery. Stir, cover (I use a plate to save on plastic wrap) and pop in the fridge for at least 1 hour, or up to 2 days if you are prepping ahead.

When you are ready to eat, preheat the oven to 200–220°C (390–430°F).

Cut the pitta bread into 2 cm (¾ in) squares, toss with a little olive oil and salt, then spread on a baking tray and pop in the oven for 5–10 minutes, or until golden brown.

Cut the avocados into generous cubes and combine with the marinated chickpeas, feta, leafy greens and coriander or parsley, reserving a little coriander or parsley and feta as a garnish.

Place half the toasted pitta in the bottom of a serving bowl. Top with half the salad, then add the remaining pitta and salad. Garnish with extra feta and coriander, and serve.

Epic tips

1. You can also cut the pitta into wedges and serve on the side, if preferred. Or use pre-made pitta chips if it's too hot to turn the oven on.
2. To pump up the protein, add marinated, grilled tofu and serve in a wrap instead of in a bowl with pitta.

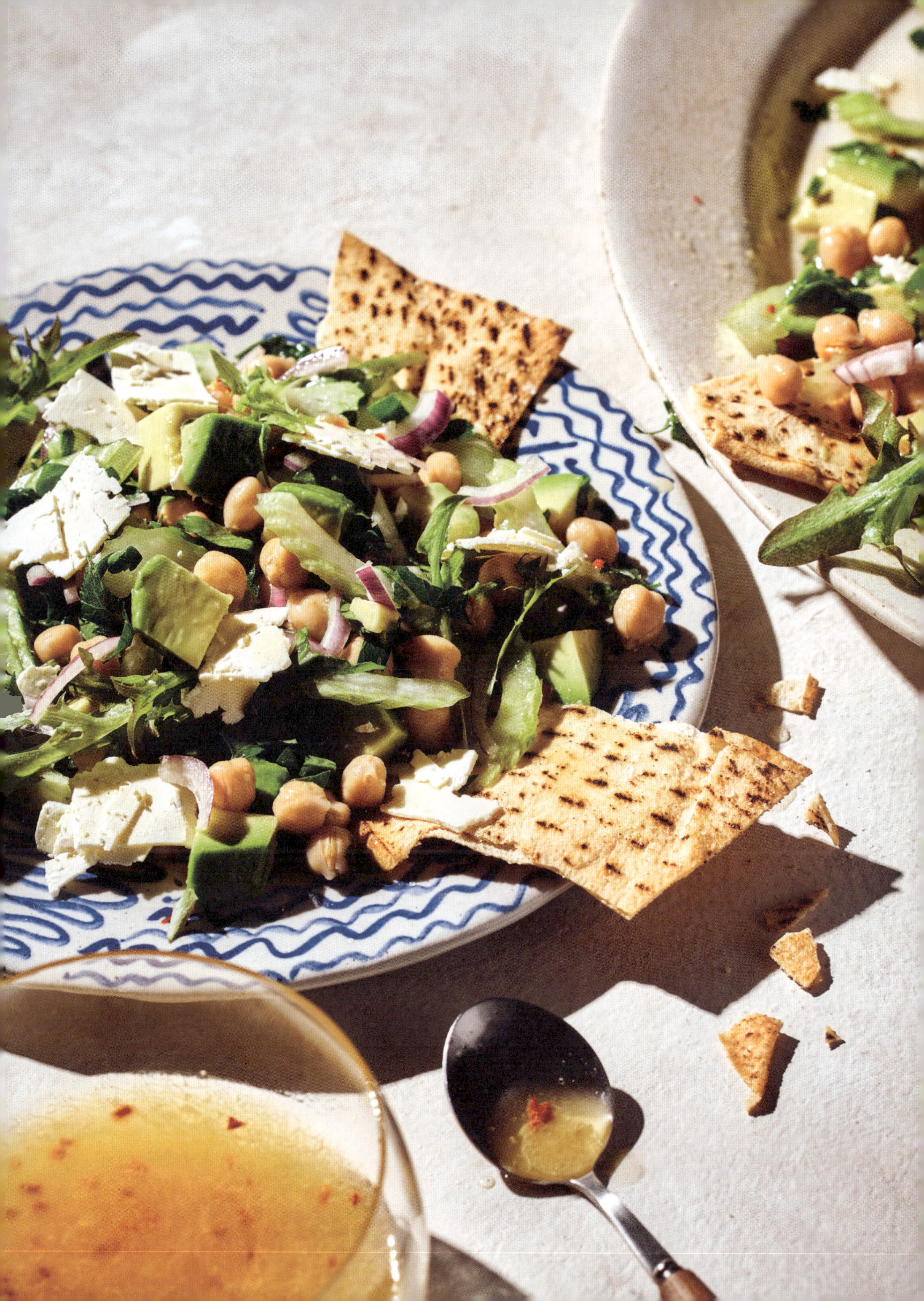

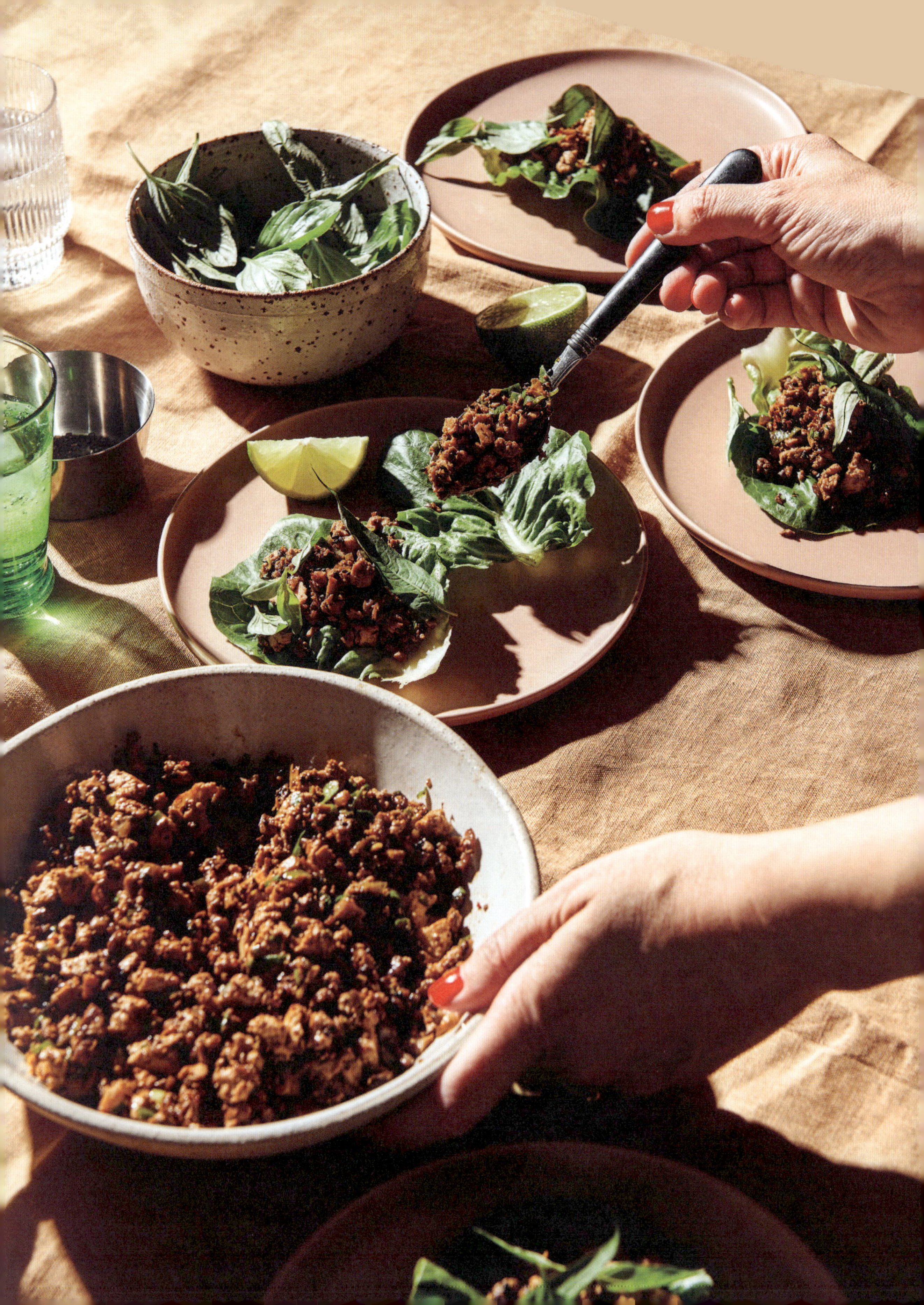

Mushroom and tofu laab

Serves 2–4

Laab is the perfect summer food and is something I crave when I want a meal that is warm and filling, but still refreshing and light. The flavoursome mushrooms and tofu are cooked with a powerful punch of ginger and garlic, then spooned into lettuce cups and laden with fragrant herbs, bringing you a South-East Asian flavour bomb that is irresistibly moreish.

If you haven't cooked with Thai basil or Vietnamese mint before, I implore you to try them as their flavours really make this recipe.

Sauce
- 1 tablespoon toasted sesame oil
- 1 tablespoon rice vinegar
- 1 tablespoon sambal oelek
- 1 teaspoon maple syrup
- ⅓ cup (80 ml/2½ fl oz) soy sauce

Filling
- 3 tablespoons olive oil
- 3 spring onions (scallions), trimmed, white parts cut into thin rounds
- thumb-sized piece of fresh ginger, peeled and finely chopped
- 2 garlic cloves, finely chopped
- 150 g (5½ oz) assorted mushrooms, cleaned and finely chopped (no need to be too exact in the chopping)
- 450 g (1 lb) firm tofu, drained and pressed, then crumbled
- 1 tablespoon toasted black sesame seeds

To serve
- 2 heads gem (bibb) or baby cos (romaine) lettuce; leaves separated, washed and dried
- handful each of fresh Asian herbs such as Thai basil, Vietnamese mint and coriander (cilantro), leaves picked

To make the sauce, mix all ingredients together in a small cup or jar and then set aside.

For the filling, heat the olive oil in a large frying pan over a medium–high heat. Add the spring onions and ginger and cook for a couple of minutes until fragrant, then add the garlic, mushrooms and tofu and cook for 5–10 minutes, stirring frequently, until all the liquid from the mushrooms has been released and has evaporated.

Stir in the sauce and cook for a further 5 minutes until the tofu starts to brown. Stir in the sesame seeds, remove from the heat and spoon the filling into lettuce cups. Garnish with fresh herbs to serve.

Epic tip
Any leftover tofu mixture will keep well in the fridge for up to 2 days. It also makes an excellent dumpling filling.

Light and fresh

Peanut tofu with green slaw

Serves 4

The combination of savoy cabbage, celery and apple makes for a moreish, juicy and crunchy slaw that is elevated by the addition of parsley, sesame seeds and sultanas. This slaw can be paired with pretty much any protein, or taken to a potluck or barbecue to be served with an array of other dishes. Here, I've paired it with peanut tofu, which is an outrageously delicious creation in its own right. While both the slaw and the tofu can be made separately, the peanut flavours work so well with the celery and apple in the slaw, I highly recommend making them together.

Tofu
- 400 g (14 oz) firm tofu, drained and patted dry
- 1 tablespoon soy sauce
- 2 tablespoons peanut butter
- 1 cup (160 g/5½ oz) raw peanuts, blitzed to a crumb
- 1 tablespoon coconut oil

Green slaw
- ½ savoy cabbage, core and outer leaves removed, sliced paper thin, soaked in water
- 6 celery stalks, thinly sliced
- 1 granny smith apple, julienned
- 1 spring onion (scallion), white part sliced
- 2 tablespoons toasted sesame seeds
- large handful (30 g/1 oz) sultanas
- small handful flat-leaf parsley, very finely chopped
- juice of 1 lime
- 2 tablespoons Japanese mayo

Cut the tofu into eight squares.

Combine the soy sauce and peanut butter and mix until well combined. Coat the tofu in the marinade and allow to sit for at least 30 minutes.

When ready to eat, preheat the oven to 180–200°C (360–390°F) and heat a large frying pan over a medium heat.

Place the peanut crumbs in a wide, shallow dish and melt the coconut oil in the frying pan.

Coat the tofu in the peanuts, then pop in the hot frying pan and cook for 2–3 minutes each side, until golden brown. Transfer to a baking tray and place in the hot oven for 15 minutes.

When you're ready to make the slaw, remove the sliced savoy cabbage from the water and spin it dry. You may need to do this a couple of times to get it bone dry.

Combine the cabbage with celery, apple, spring onion, sesame seeds, sultanas and parsley. In a separate bowl, combine the lime juice and mayo, whisk until smooth, then pour over the slaw and use your hands to combine.

Place the salad in individual serving dishes. Cut each tofu square on a diagonal through the middle, and place four triangles on top of each serving bowl.

This is best made right before eating, but leftovers are fine.

Epic tip
If you're taking this to a barbecue, serve both elements in individual dishes, side by side.

Swaps
Five-spice tempeh also works a treat here – see page 113.

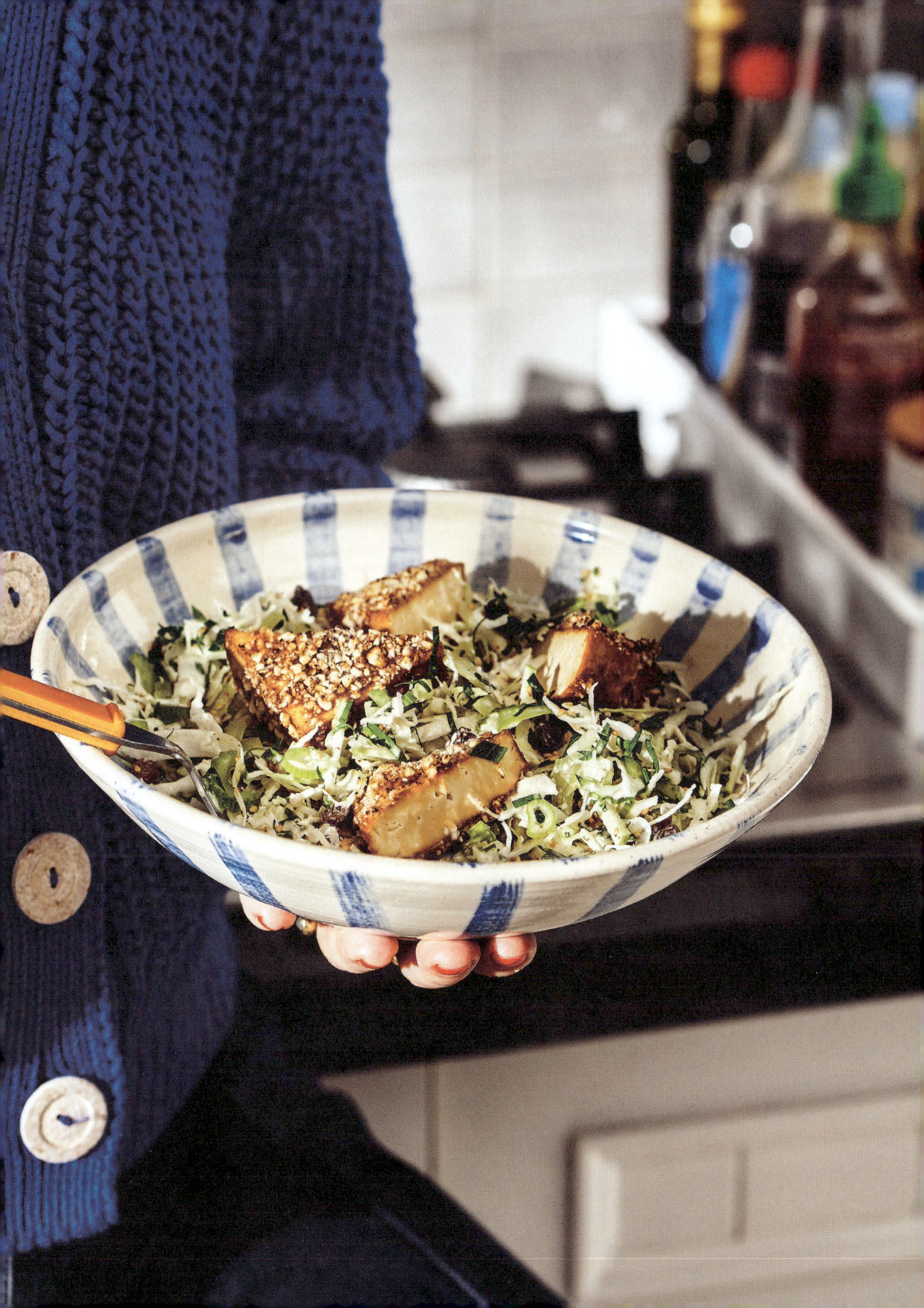

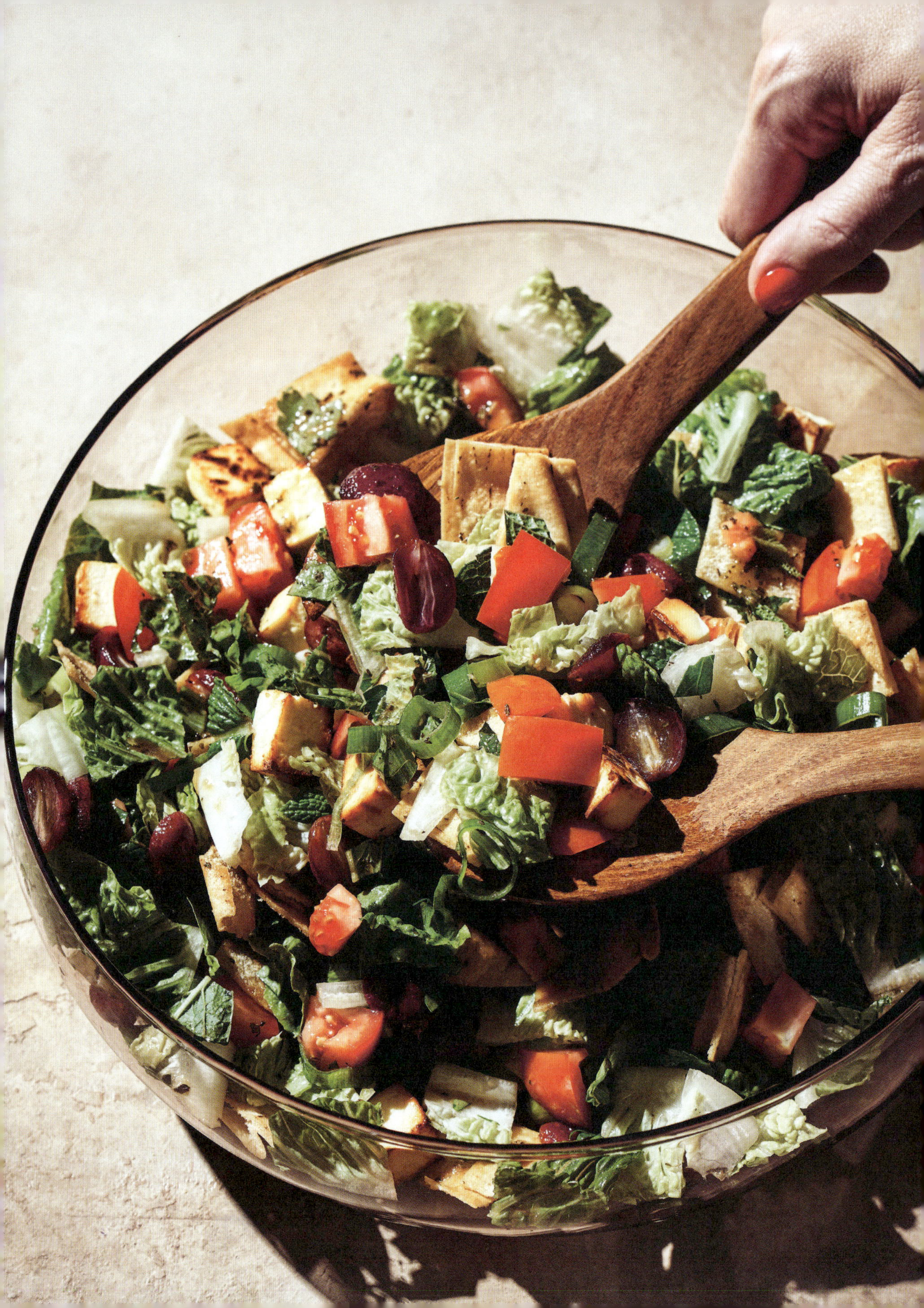

Roasted feta and grape fattoush

Serves 4

Fattoush is a Levantine dish that is based on the centuries-old tradition of frying stale bread to give it new life. You can add basically any combination of chopped raw veggies to it with lettuce, tomato, cucumber and radish being the traditional go-tos. This version adds a millennial twist by adding roasted grapes and feta, which bring a pop of sweetness and tang to round out the dish. It's a goodie!

If you can, make the dressing and add the mint, then let it sit overnight to maximise the minty flavour.

Dressing

1 quantity Pomegranate dressing (page 42)

Fattoush

1 teaspoon dried mint
180 g (6½ oz) block feta, cut into 1 cm (½ in) dice
1 generous cup (200 g/7 oz) red seedless grapes, washed thoroughly and halved
2 large pitta breads, cut into 2 cm (¾ in) squares
2 tablespoons olive oil
1 large or 2 small heads of cos (romaine) lettuce, chopped
2 large vine tomatoes, cut into 1 cm (½ in) dice
2 Lebanese (short) or 1 telegraph (long) cucumber, cut into 1 cm (½ in) dice
4–6 radishes, thinly sliced
4 spring onions (scallions), thinly sliced
large handful flat-leaf parsley, finely chopped
1 teaspoon sumac, to serve

Add the dried mint to the dressing, then set aside overnight or until ready to use. The mint flavour will become more pronounced when the dressing has time to sit.

Preheat the oven to 180–200°C (360–390°F) and line a baking tray with baking paper.

Put the feta on a lightly oiled baking tray and scatter the grapes around it, cut side up. Cook in the oven for 30 minutes while you prepare the rest of the ingredients.

Toss the chopped pitta bread in olive oil and salt, and spread on a baking tray. Add to the oven for the final 10 minutes of the cooking time, keeping an eye on it and tossing halfway through.

Combine the lettuce, tomato, cucumber, radish, spring onion and parsley in a large mixing bowl, reserving some parsley to garnish, then toss with the dressing. Transfer half to a serving dish and top with half the roasted pitta, grapes and feta. Repeat with the remaining salad, pitta, grapes and feta, then garnish with parsley and sumac.

Epic tips

1. To pump up the protein, add a tin of cannellini beans, butter (lima) beans or chickpeas.
2. Too hot to turn the oven on? Cut the grapes in half lengthwise, and pop them and the feta straight in the salad cold.

Light and fresh

Satay tofu and edamame bowl

Serves 3–4

Bowls are a wonderful way to blend the five key salad elements – leaf, body, protein, dressing and crunch – either by following a recipe such as this one, or simply using up what's in your fridge. In this version, warm rice with hardy red cabbage, carrots, tofu and edamame create a delicious and nourishing base, which is pulled together by the perfection of the spicy satay dressing.

Dressing
1 quantity Spicy peanut dressing (page 42)

Bowls
200 g (7 oz) shelled edamame
1 cup (200 g/7 oz) jasmine rice
¼ red cabbage, very finely sliced
2 carrots, julienned or grated
small handful coriander (cilantro), sliced
black sesame seeds, to garnish

Quick pickled cucumber
1 large cucumber, thinly sliced
2 tablespoons rice vinegar
1 tablespoon soy sauce
½ teaspoon maple syrup
½ teaspoon sesame oil
1 teaspoon black sesame seeds

Tofu
1 × 400 g (14 oz) block tofu, drained and pressed
1 tablespoon soy sauce
1 tablespoon sesame oil
½ teaspoon garlic powder
1 tablespoon cornflour (cornstarch)

If your edamame aren't already defrosted, place them in a heatproof bowl, cover with boiling water and allow to sit for 2 minutes. Drain, refresh with cold water, then drain again and set aside.

To prepare the cucumber, combine all ingredients in a small mixing bowl and allow to sit while waiting for the rice and tofu to cook. Stir occasionally to ensure even coating in the marinade.

Place the rice in a small pot with 2 cups (500 ml/17 fl oz) of water. Cover, bring to a boil, then lower the heat and cook for 15 minutes. Remove from the heat, fluff the grains and allow to cool, or use immediately if you want a warm meal. For more detailed cooking instructions, see page 24.

Preheat the oven to 180–200°C (360–390°F).

To prepare the tofu, first tear it into bite-sized cubes, then put it in a mixing bowl with the soy sauce, sesame oil and garlic powder. Toss to combine, then add the cornflour and toss again.

Spread on a baking sheet and bake in the hot oven for 20 minutes, tossing once during that time.

Once the tofu is cooked, assemble the rice and veggies in serving bowls. Drain the cucumber and add. Add the tofu and coriander, then drizzle with the dressing and sesame seeds, and serve.

Swaps
1. You can use Coconut satay (page 39) instead of the Spicy peanut dressing if you prefer.
2. While this particular assortment of ingredients really hits the spot, you could put anything with this dressing and it would be delicious. Go wild with veggies – use up what's on hand, or bring new life to sad veggies that have gone floppy in your fridge by roasting them, then adding them to these bowls.

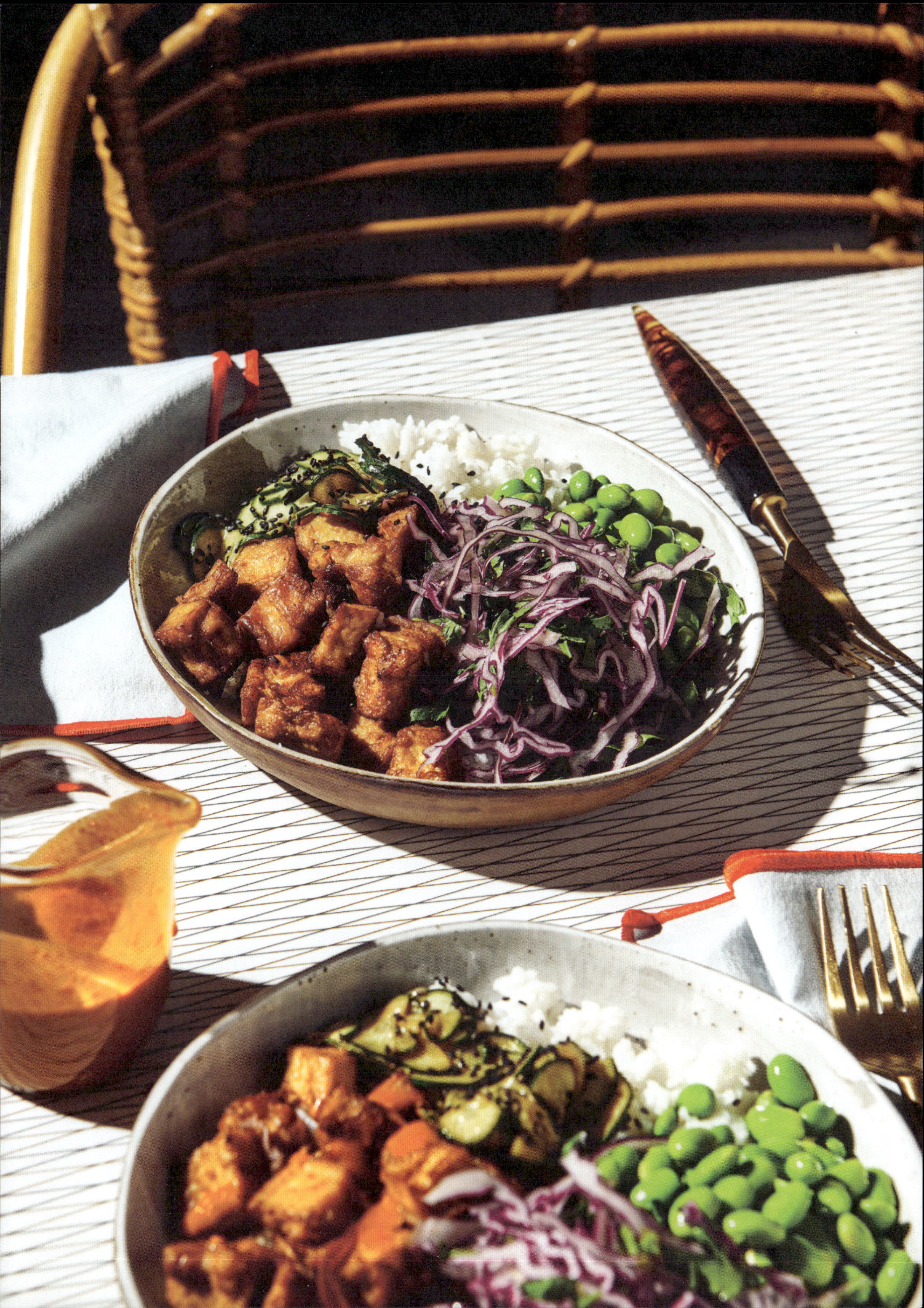

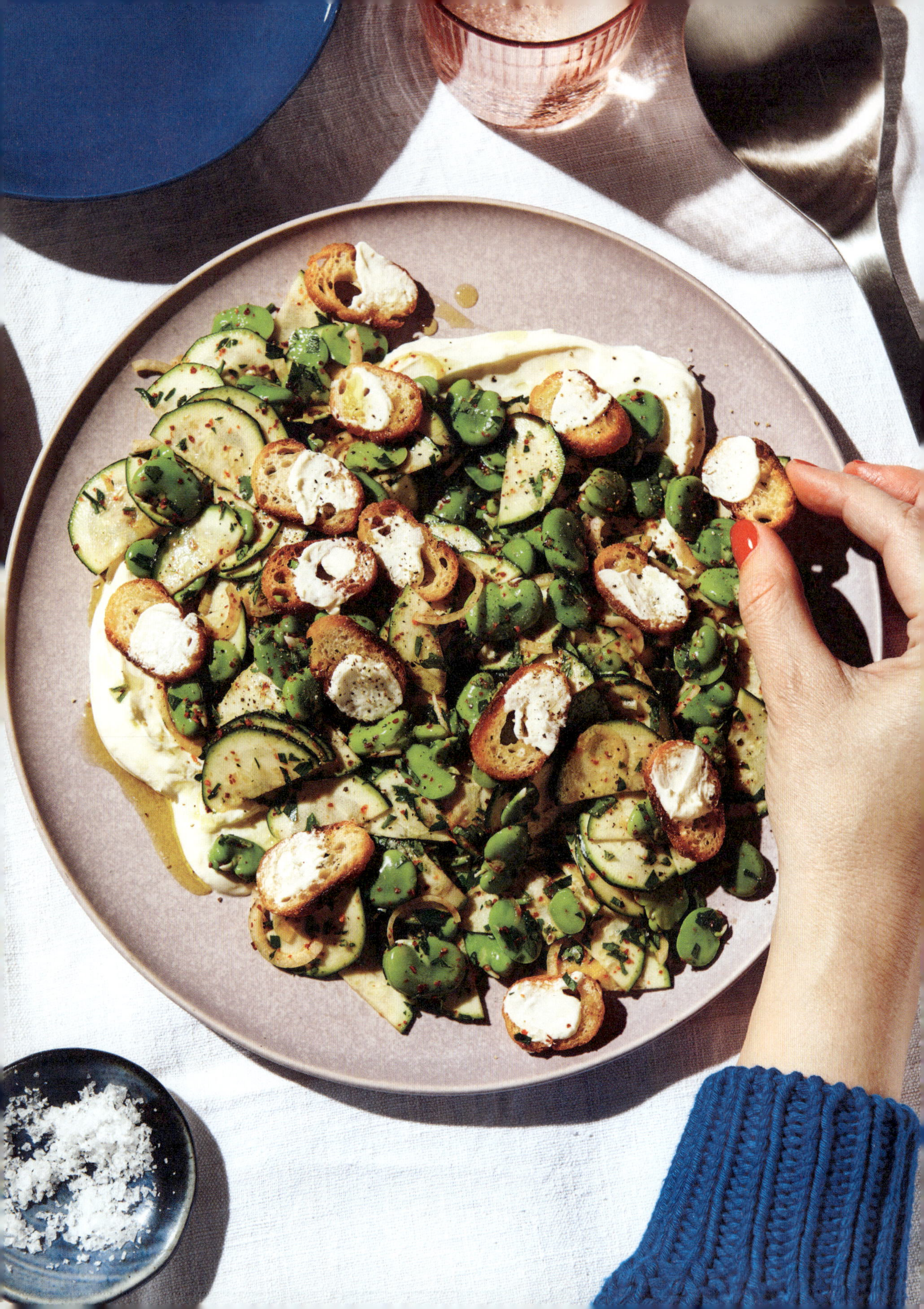

Super simple broad bean salad

Serves 2

The moment I first see broad beans in my local produce store, I buy them and make this salad. Broad beans are a labour of love to prepare, but they are perfect in all their tender simplicity; there's a reason so many people are willing to invest time and effort in shelling, cooking and podding these morsels of joy. Paired with the zestiness of the lemon, the creaminess of the feta and the slight heat from the chilli flakes, this salad strikes a harmonious balance of flavours that never fails to conjure the feeling of spring. It's perfect as a light meal for two, or as a side with an array of other dishes.

Dressing

juice and zest of 1 lemon
olive oil, to taste (approx. 20 ml/¾ fl oz)

Salad

450 g (1 lb) fresh broad beans, or 250 g (9 oz) podded fresh or frozen broad beans (aiming for about 1 cup of beans after the second podding)
1 zucchini (courgette), very finely sliced on a mandoline
1 French shallot, very finely sliced on a mandoline
small handful (30 g/1 oz) fresh flat-leaf parsley leaves, finely chopped
dried chilli flakes
Whipped feta (page 198)
100 g (3½ oz) Ficelle croutons (page 48)

Bring a saucepan of water to a boil and prepare an ice bath.

Blanch the broad beans in boiling water for 3 minutes, then drain and immerse them in the ice bath. Set yourself up with two bowls – one for the beans and one for their pods. Give each bean a squeeze and a small, tender and vibrant green bean should slip out of the skin.

Once you have podded your beans, toss them in a bowl with the zucchini, shallot and parsley. Add a drizzle of olive oil, lemon juice and zest, then sprinkle over salt, pepper and chilli flakes to taste.

Smear two-thirds of the whipped feta onto the bottom of a serving dish. Top with the broad beans, then smear each crouton with half a teaspoon of whipped feta and nestle among the beans and zucchini.

For a vegan version, use whipped tofu instead of whipped feta.

Spicy tofu puffed rice salad

Serves 4

This is another go-to recipe for when it's too hot to cook. The tofu marinade packs an incredible punch that has been known to sway even the most devout tofu-hater, and it doubles as the salad dressing, which is a genius move, if I do say so myself. Paired with the fresh burst of colours and flavours from capsicum (bell pepper), cucumber and South-East Asian herbs, the lightness of puffed rice and the salty punch of the roasted peanuts, this is the perfect thing to make when you're craving something light and fresh.

Dressing

1 quantity Spicy soy dressing (page 43)

Salad

1 × 450 g (1 lb) packet firm tofu, drained, pressed and cut into 1 cm (½ in) dice
3–4 spring onions (scallions), trimmed and finely chopped
1 Lebanese (short) cucumber, halved lengthways, watery core removed and flesh finely diced
1 red capsicum (bell pepper), seeded and finely diced
½ cup (80 g/3 oz) roasted peanuts, roughly chopped
1 cup (60 g/2 oz) firmly packed leafy Asian herbs such as coriander (cilantro), mint, Thai basil or Vietnamese mint, finely chopped
3½ cups (100 g/3½ oz) puffed brown rice
2 tablespoons sesame seeds
1 lime, halved

Put the dressing and tofu in a large mixing bowl and coat the tofu in the dressing. Allow to sit at room temperature for at least 30 minutes for the tofu to marinate, or all day if possible (cover the bowl with a plate and pop it in the fridge if that's the case).

When ready to serve, give the tofu a stir, then add the remaining salad ingredients (except the lime). Stir to combine, add a squeeze of fresh lime and serve immediately.

Epic tips

1. Got leftovers? Even though the puffed rice goes soggy, it's still surprisingly good the next day.
2. You can find puffed brown rice at health food stores and some supermarkets.

Swaps

Iceberg lettuce, edamame, corn, bean sprouts and avocado are all excellent additions to this salad.

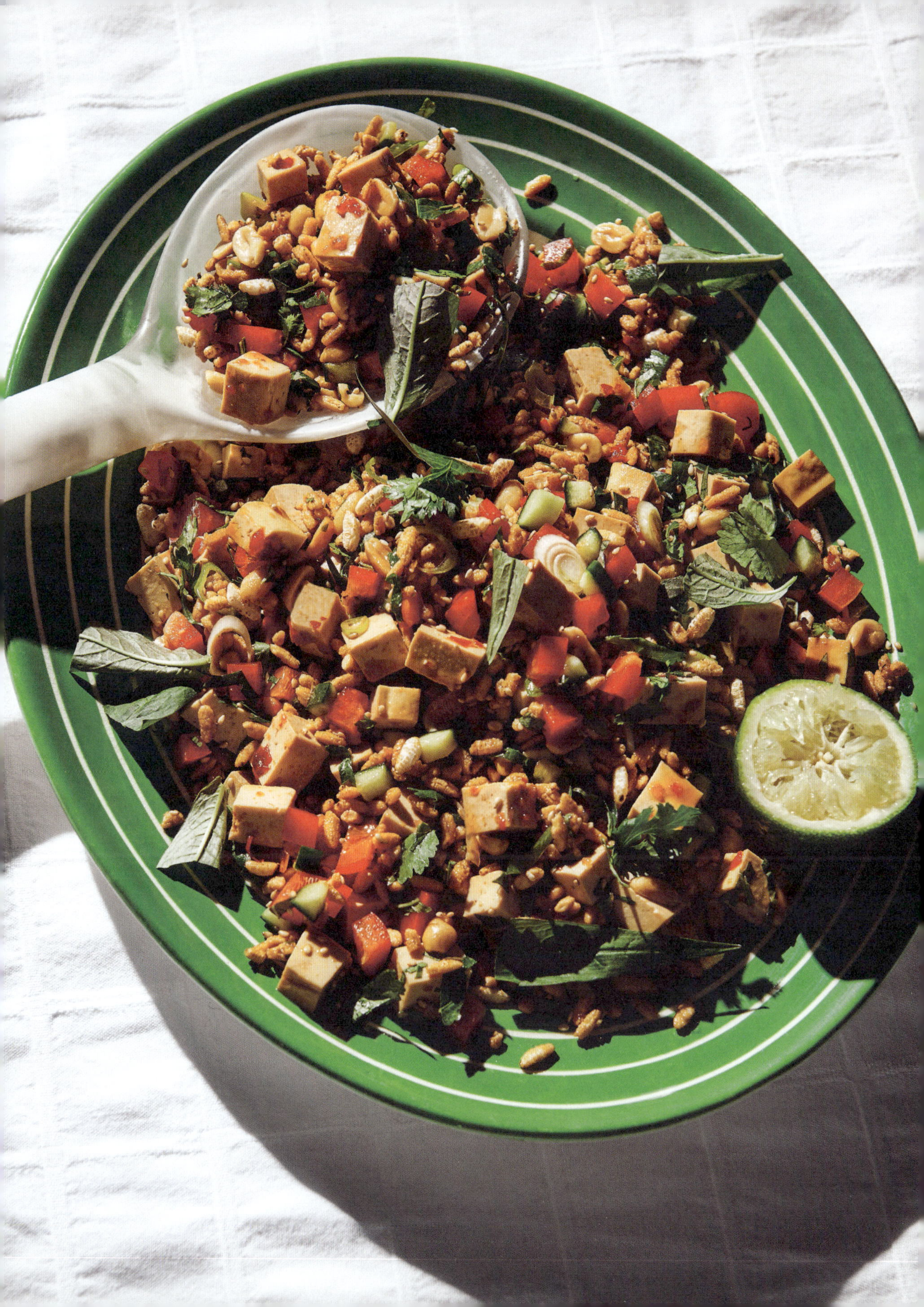

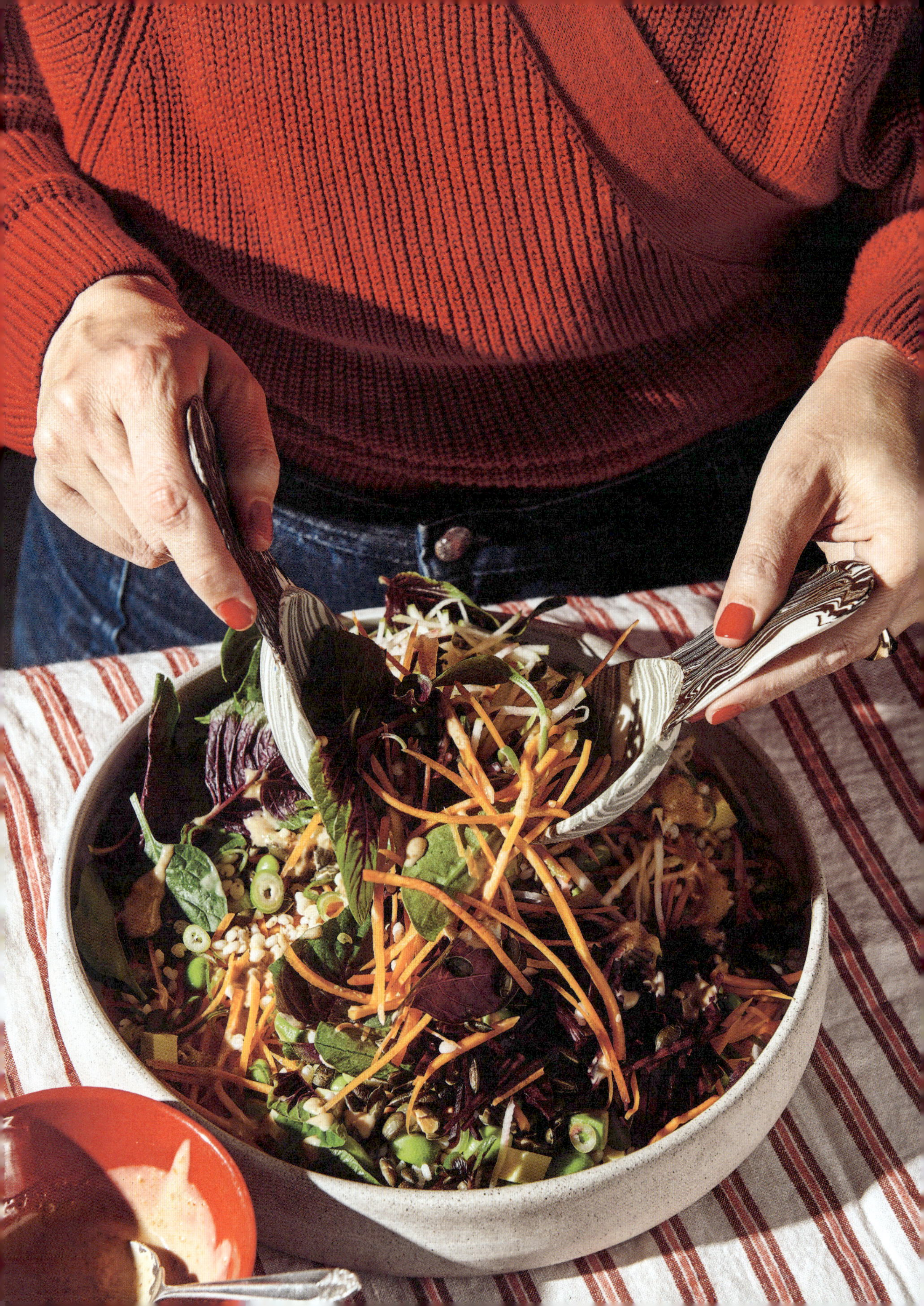

Super salad

Serves 3–4

This salad channels the wholesome charm of a salad bar with its array of fresh and vibrant ingredients, offering a burst of colours, textures, flavours and nutrients with every bite. The tender baby spinach serves as the leafy foundation, while the sorghum, beetroot (beet), carrot and avocado build the hearty body, with the edamame bringing a pop of protein. The moreish sesame mayo envelops each ingredient, while the toasted pepitas (pumpkin seeds) bring the essential crunch factor.

Dressing
1 quantity Sesame mayo dressing (page 42)

Salad
200 g (7 oz) shelled edamame
1 beetroot (beet), peeled and grated
1 teaspoon rice vinegar
½ cup (100 g/3½ oz) sorghum, rinsed
1 carrot, peeled and julienned
2–3 spring onions (scallions), sliced
60 g (2 oz) baby spinach
30 g (1 oz) Chinese spinach (amaranth)
1 avocado, diced
1 apple, julienned (nice, but not essential)
large handful (30 g/1 oz) pepitas (pumpkin seeds), toasted

If your edamame aren't already defrosted, place them in a heatproof bowl, cover with boiling water and allow to sit for 2 minutes. Drain, refresh with cold water, then drain again and set aside.

Combine the grated beets with the rice vinegar and stir to combine, then set aside. This will set the colour.

Put the sorghum in a saucepan with 1 cup (250 ml/8½ fl oz) of water. Bring to a boil, then reduce to a low heat and cook for 15 minutes. Remove from the heat, fluff the grains and allow to cool – or use immediately if you want a warm meal. For more detailed instructions, see page 24.

Combine the beetroot, carrot, edamame and spring onions and stir to combine. Add most of the Sesame mayo and give the mixture a good stir, then add the spinach, avocado, apple and pepitas and toss to combine. Drizzle with remaining dressing.

Eat immediately or store in the fridge for up to 3 days.

Epic tips
If you own a food processor, I highly recommend using it to grate your veg and save your wrists.

Light and fresh

Avocado salsa

Serves 2–4

This is one of those dishes I make when the weather is warm and the avocados are plentiful. The base makes a perfect snack or light meal, but you can easily double it if feeding a crowd, or bulk it out with beans and greens to turn it into a heartier meal.

Dressing
juice of 1 lime

Salsa
100 g (3½ oz) tomatoes
1 avocado, diced
2 ears of corn, husks removed
1 avocado, diced
¼ small red onion, sliced
chilli flakes, to taste
coriander (cilantro) leaves, to garnish
salted ricotta, to taste
corn chips, to serve

Cut the tomatoes into bite-sized pieces. If using baby roma tomatoes, I like to cut them in half. Heirloom tomatoes can be cut into chunks, about the same size.

Cook the corn, following any of the methods outlined on page 23, then remove the kernels from the husks and set aside.

Combine the tomato, corn, avocado, red onion and lime juice with a generous pinch of salt and chilli flakes, to taste. Garnish with coriander leaves and a cloud of salted ricotta (use a microplane for this). Serve with a side of corn chips.

Epic tips
Pair with Roasted capsicum dip (page 203), Marinated black bean salad (page 121), Grilled corn and edamame salsa (page 78).

Swaps
You can use an assortment of tomatoes here, and if you don't have access to salted ricotta, crumbled feta makes a great substitute.

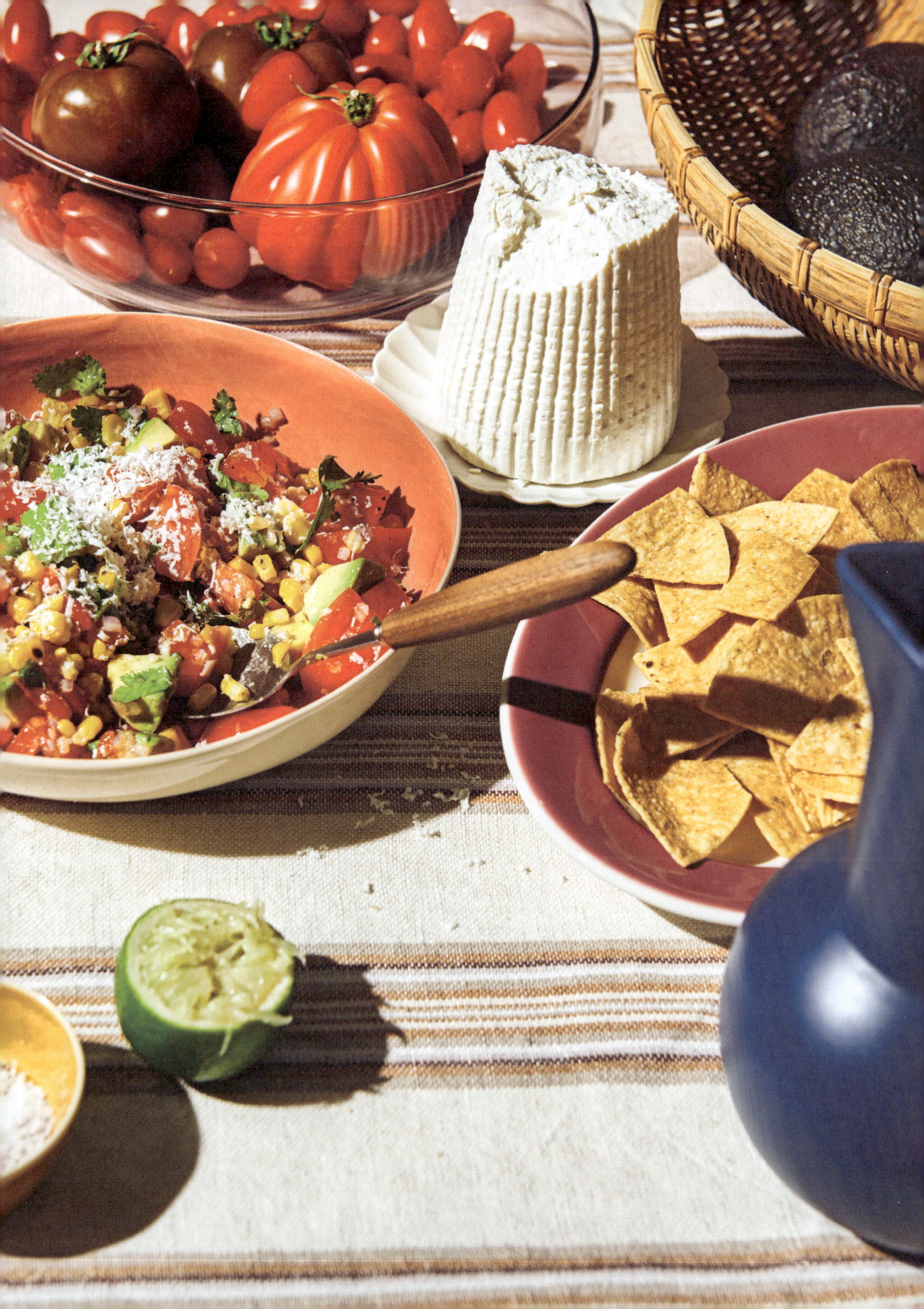

GRAINS AND

LEGUMES

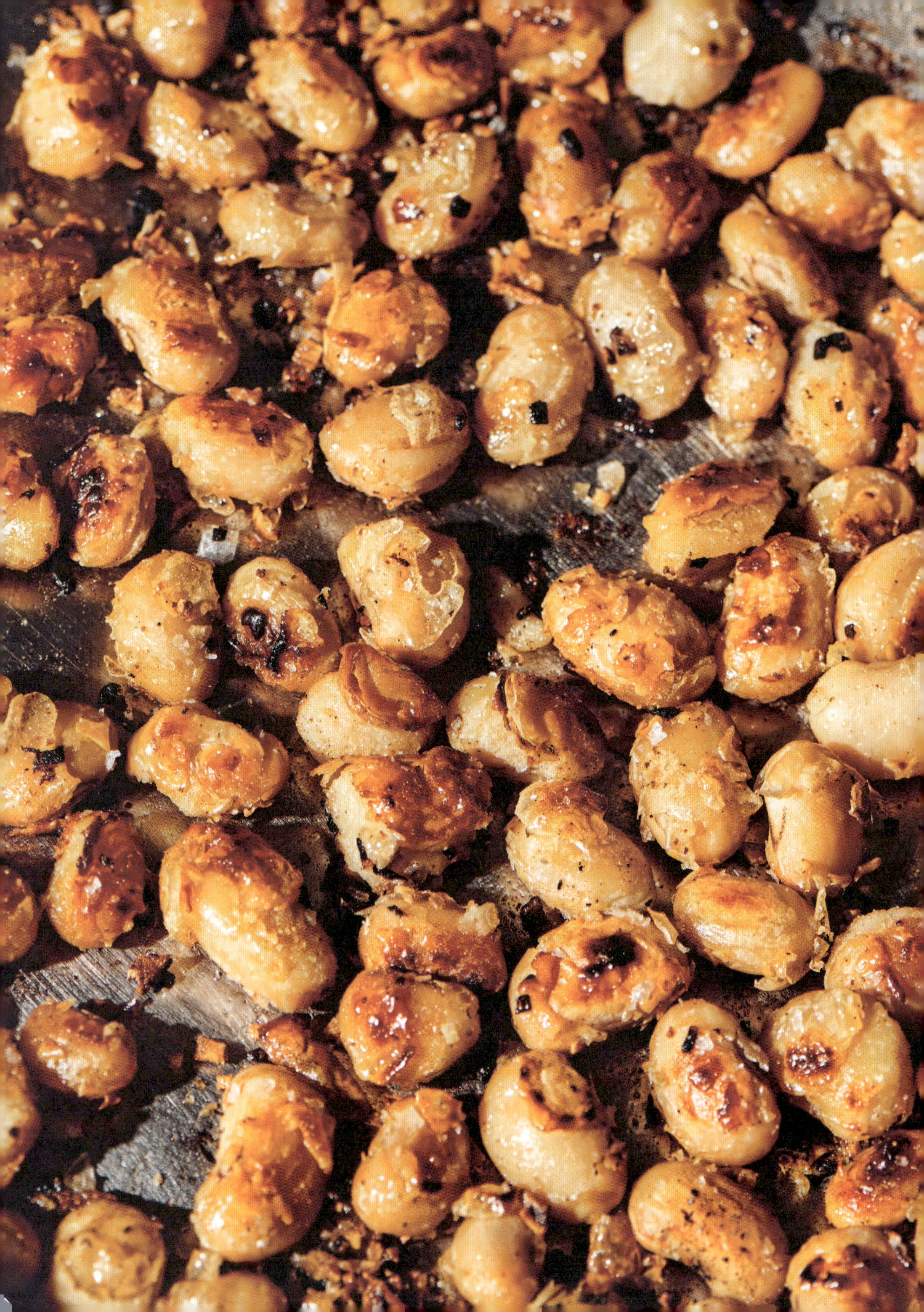

Here you will find salads with heft and heart. Filling, nutritious, delicious, year-round dishes, brimming with nutrition, that can be enjoyed as full meals. These recipes showcase the earthy comfort of cooked grains and legumes, and offer clever but simple ways to use up those veggies lurking in the bottom of your veg drawer.

Roasted vegetables add caramelised depth, while fresh vegetables, herbs and leafy greens lend vibrancy and crunch. Pull it all together with a vibrant dressing and what's not to love?

Whether you're prepping for a busy week ahead or you want to impress a crowd, these salads are your steadfast allies. They are the make-ahead marvels that wait patiently in your fridge, their flavours melding and maturing, ready to be enjoyed at a moment's notice. Their leftovers last for days, and can be served with your favourite protein for a perfect meal the following day. Dress them down for a humble, nourishing dinner, or go all-out with the trimmings (and sides!) on special occasions. These salads are a testament to the versatility and staying power of grains and legumes — true staples in any salad lover's pantry.

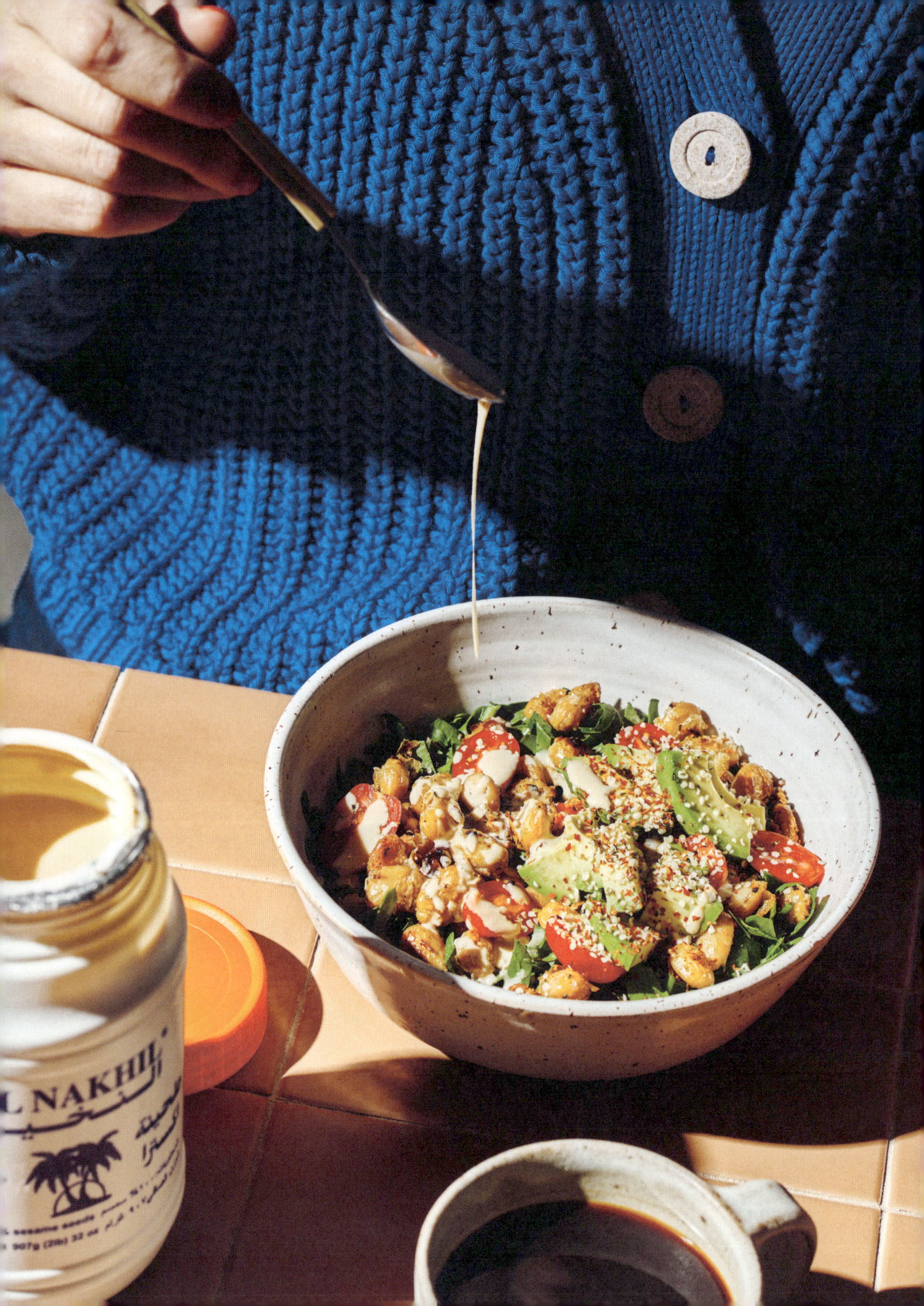
L NAKHIL

Butter bean breakfast salad

Serves 1

This breakfast salad is the perfect thing to eat when you need an extremely filling, nourishing and flavour-packed start to your day. The butter beans are *the thing* here. They are crispy on the outside, creamy on the inside and perfect in every way. The other ingredients can be pulled together in the amount of time it takes to make the beans – creamy avocado, fresh spinach, a burst of tomato and a nutty drizzle of tahini or hummus. A dream combo!

Dressing

lemon, to squeeze

Salad

1 teaspoon olive oil
1 × 400 g (14 oz) tin butter (lima) beans, drained, rinsed and dried
1 garlic clove, chopped
handful baby spinach leaves, sliced
handful baby roma tomatoes, halved lengthways
½ avocado, diced
hemp seeds and chilli flakes, to serve
2 tablespoons good-quality, runny tahini

Heat the oil in a large frying pan over a medium–high heat.

Add the beans to the pan and let them sit for 5 minutes – don't move them at all, as they need this time to crisp up properly. Add the garlic and a generous pinch of salt, then give the mixture a little toss and cook for another minute or so.

While the beans are cooking, place the spinach leaves in the bottom of a serving bowl and squeeze some lemon juice over them.

Once the beans are cooked, place them on top of the spinach along with the tomato, avocado, hemp seeds, chilli flakes and a drizzle of tahini. Season to taste.

Swaps

If you find straight-up tahini too much, use hummus instead. If you have any leftover Supergreen dressing (page 43), this also works a treat. Pepitas (pumpkin seeds) and sesame seeds are great additions, as is goat's cheese, haloumi or an egg (fried, boiled, poached, however you like).

Monday salad

Serves 4

This isn't so much a recipe as it is a life hack. Every Monday, I chop the following ingredients and store them in an airtight container in my fridge. Then I'll scoop a portion out each day and (sometimes begrudgingly) eat it in any myriad of ways – with an egg, with feta, with some leftover cooked grains or pasta, or any kind of legume (lentils, chickpeas and cannellini beans all work great). Sometimes I will dress it in nothing but salt, lemon juice and olive oil, other times I'll reach for one of the dressings in this book. My husband Andy likes to put it in a wrap with hummus and falafel. It's a great way to make sure I reach for veggies when I am exhausted, hungry and would otherwise find myself snacking on crap.

Salad
- 3 celery stalks, sliced
- 1 Lebanese (short) cucumber, seeds scraped out with a teaspoon, and diced
- 1–2 large tomatoes, diced
- 1 red capsicum (bell pepper), diced
- 1 carrot, thinly sliced
- 1 avocado, diced
- 2 large handfuls rocket (arugula), spinach or kale, chopped

Finely chop all ingredients and store in an airtight container. Scoop a portion out every day to enjoy in any way you desire. Thank yourself for having the foresight to prepare this ahead of time.

Swaps
Use any veg you have handy.

Three bean salad

Serves 4-6

It's fresh, it's bold, it's filling, it's dependable. You can make it ahead and its flavours only get better with time. It's a great one to take to summertime potlucks but it's also great to have on hand in the fridge, to add a pop of protein to any meal.

Dressing

1 quantity Pomegranate dressing (page 42)

Salad

1 × 400 g (14 oz) tin cannellini beans, drained and rinsed

1 × 400 g (14 oz) tin chickpeas, drained and rinsed

1 × 400 g (14 oz) borlotti (cranberry) beans, drained and rinsed

½ red onion, diced

2 tomatoes, diced

1 telegraph (long) cucumber, seeds removed and diced

½ cup (15 g/½ oz) fresh parsley, leaves picked and chopped

dried chilli (hot pepper) flakes, to taste

Make the dressing in a large mixing bowl. Add the drained beans and chickpeas, veggies and herbs and stir to combine. Add black pepper and chilli flakes to taste.

You can eat the salad immediately but it is much better if you let it sit in the fridge for a couple of hours, stirring it every now and again if you remember, so the flavours can mingle and the onion softens.

Swaps

This salad also works well with the Honey mustard dressing on page 78.

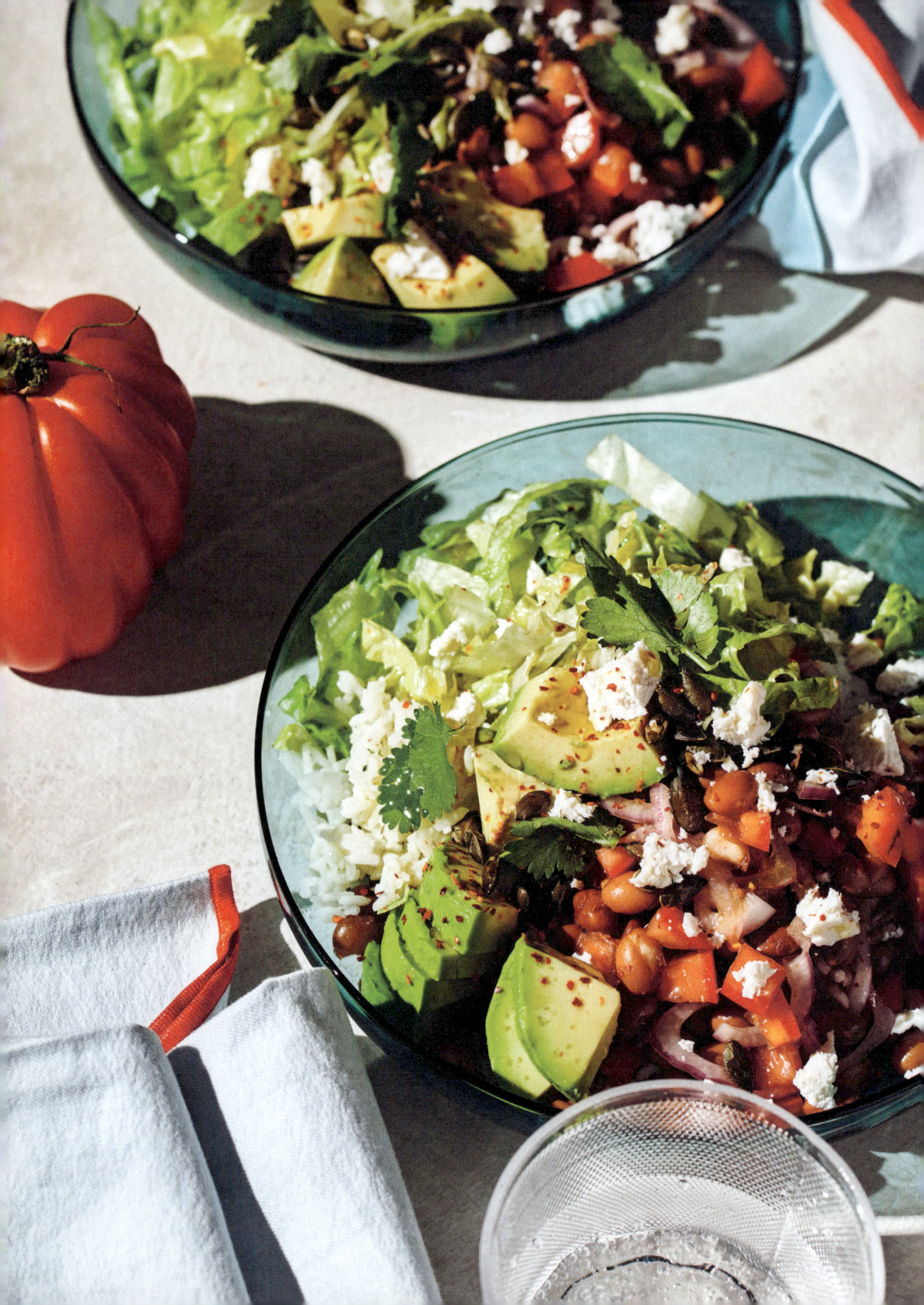

Chilli lime pinto bean salad

Serves 4

This salad takes the iconic duo of rice and beans and adds a burst of tomato, crispy lettuce, creamy avocado and crunchy pepitas (pumpkin seeds), creating a nutritious and filling salad that is perfect for casual get-togethers or weeknight dinners.

Dressing
1 quantity Chilli lime dressing (page 39)

Salad
2 × 400 g (14 oz) tins pinto beans, drained and rinsed
1 red onion, thinly sliced
1 teaspoon cumin seeds, lightly crushed in mortar and pestle
2 tomatoes, diced
1 cup (220 g/8 oz) short-grain rice
1 avocado, diced
⅛ iceberg lettuce, shredded (approx. 2 cups)
salted ricotta, to serve
handful pepitas (pumpkin seeds), toasted, to serve
coriander (cilantro) leaves, to garnish
hot sauce, to taste

Combine the dressing with the pinto beans, onion, cumin and tomatoes. Stir to combine well, and then place in an airtight container and refrigerate for at least a couple of hours, but preferably overnight, giving it a stir (or simply turning the container upside down) when you remember/when you open the fridge.

Place the rice in a small pot with 2 cups (500 ml/17 fl oz) of water. Cover, bring to a boil, then lower heat and cook for 15 minutes. Remove from the heat, fluff the grains and allow to cool, or use immediately if you want a warm meal. For more detailed cooking instructions see page 24.

To serve, place the cooked rice in serving bowls with the bean mixture and lettuce. Top with avocado, a dollop of salted ricotta, and a sprinkling of pepitas. Garnish with coriander and hot sauce, if using.

Swaps
I find the iceberg lettuce provides enough of a crunch, but if you need more, corn chips or crispy fried tortilla strips (see page 121) work a treat. You can also use black beans or borlotti (cranberry) beans instead of pinto beans, or add feta, sour cream, cashew cream or Roasted capsicum dip (page 203) in place of salted ricotta.

Coconut-crusted pumpkin and chickpea salad

Serves 4

This salad tastes like summer; the flavours of the coconut, makrut and peanut dressing are so tropically moreish, I could drink it. The crunchy cashews and hearty chickpeas complement the lightness of puffed rice, spinach and herbs, while coating the pumpkin in coconut before roasting it makes this a real showstopper of a dish.

Dressing
1 quantity Coconut satay dressing (page 39)

Salad
500 g (1 lb 2 oz) kent pumpkin (winter squash), seeds and skin removed and cut into 1 × 2 cm (½ × ¾ in) wedges
1 tablespoon olive oil
¼ cup (25 g/1 oz) desiccated (shredded) coconut
100 g (3½ oz) raw cashews
2 × 400 g (14 oz) tins chickpeas, drained and rinsed
2 large handfuls (60 g/2 oz) spinach, sliced
2 cups (30 g/1 oz) puffed brown rice
2 spring onions (scallions), thinly sliced
small handful coriander (cilantro), to garnish (optional)

If you've made the dressing ahead of time, take it out of the fridge and stand it in a bowl of warm water, stirring every so often, until it is smooth and runny.

Preheat the oven to 180–200°C (360–390°F).

Put the pumpkin in a large mixing bowl with the olive oil and a pinch of salt. Toss to combine, then add coconut and toss again so the pumpkin is evenly coated in the coconut. Spread the pumpkin on a baking tray (line with baking paper first if you wish), being mindful not to pour the loose bits of coconut onto the tray, as these will burn. Cook in the oven for 25 minutes, turning once about halfway through the cooking time.

Place the cashews on another baking tray and roast for the final 10 minutes or so of cooking time (keep an eye on them, as the oven will be a little hotter than is ideal for cashews). Once cooked, allow to cool on baking tray for 10 minutes.

Combine the chickpeas, spinach, puffed rice and spring onions in a large mixing bowl along with most of the dressing, reserving a little to garnish.

Place half the spinach and chickpea mixture on a serving dish. Top with half the pumpkin and cashews. Repeat with the remaining chickpea mixture and finish off with the remaining pumpkin and cashews. Drizzle with the reserved dressing, garnish with coriander, and serve. Alternatively, build the salad straight into serving bowls, as pictured.

This is best served warm, but leftovers are great, and the puffed rice is totally delish and fine when soggy.

Swaps
Swap the puffed brown rice for cooked jasmine rice if you want something warming and heartier.

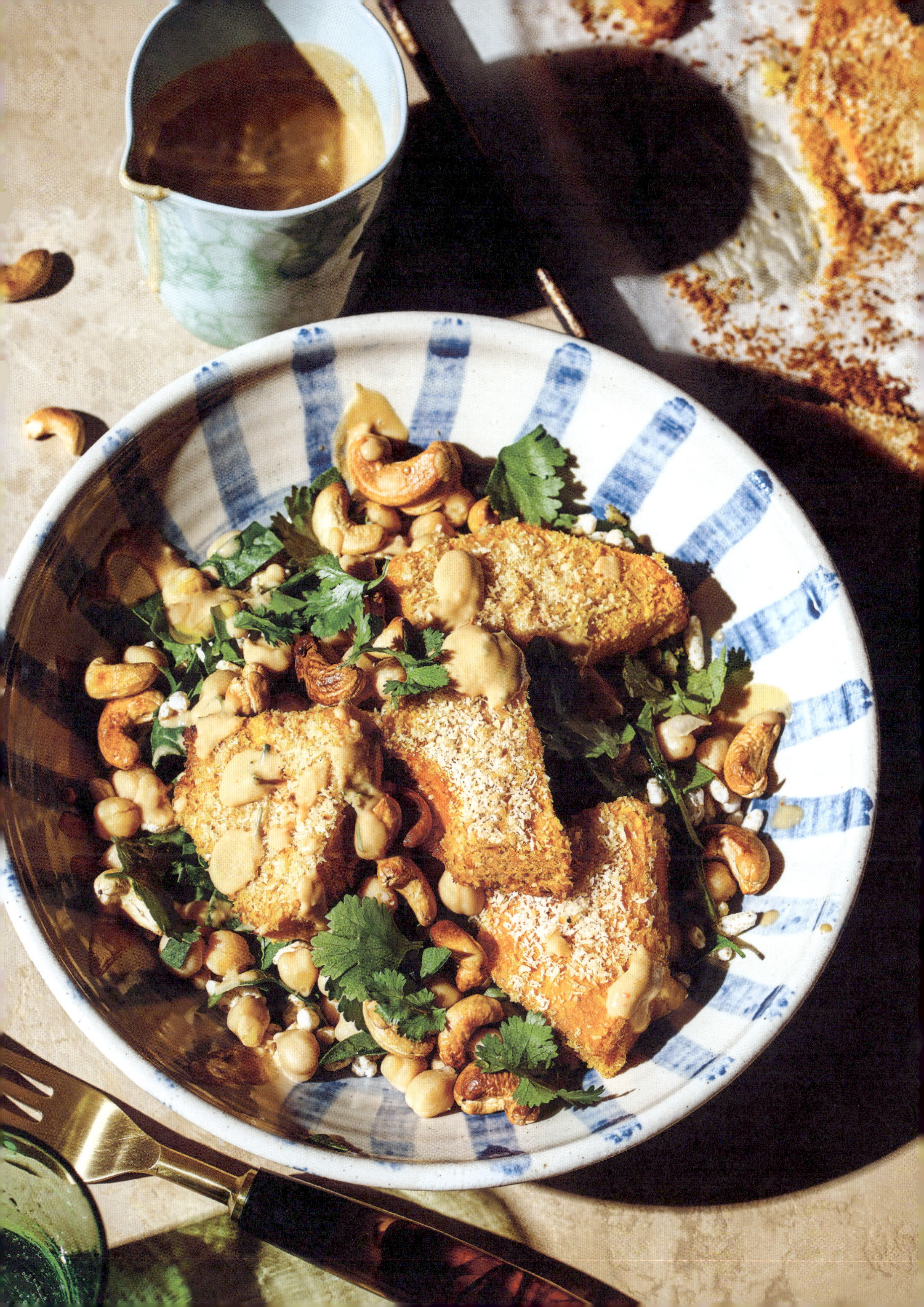

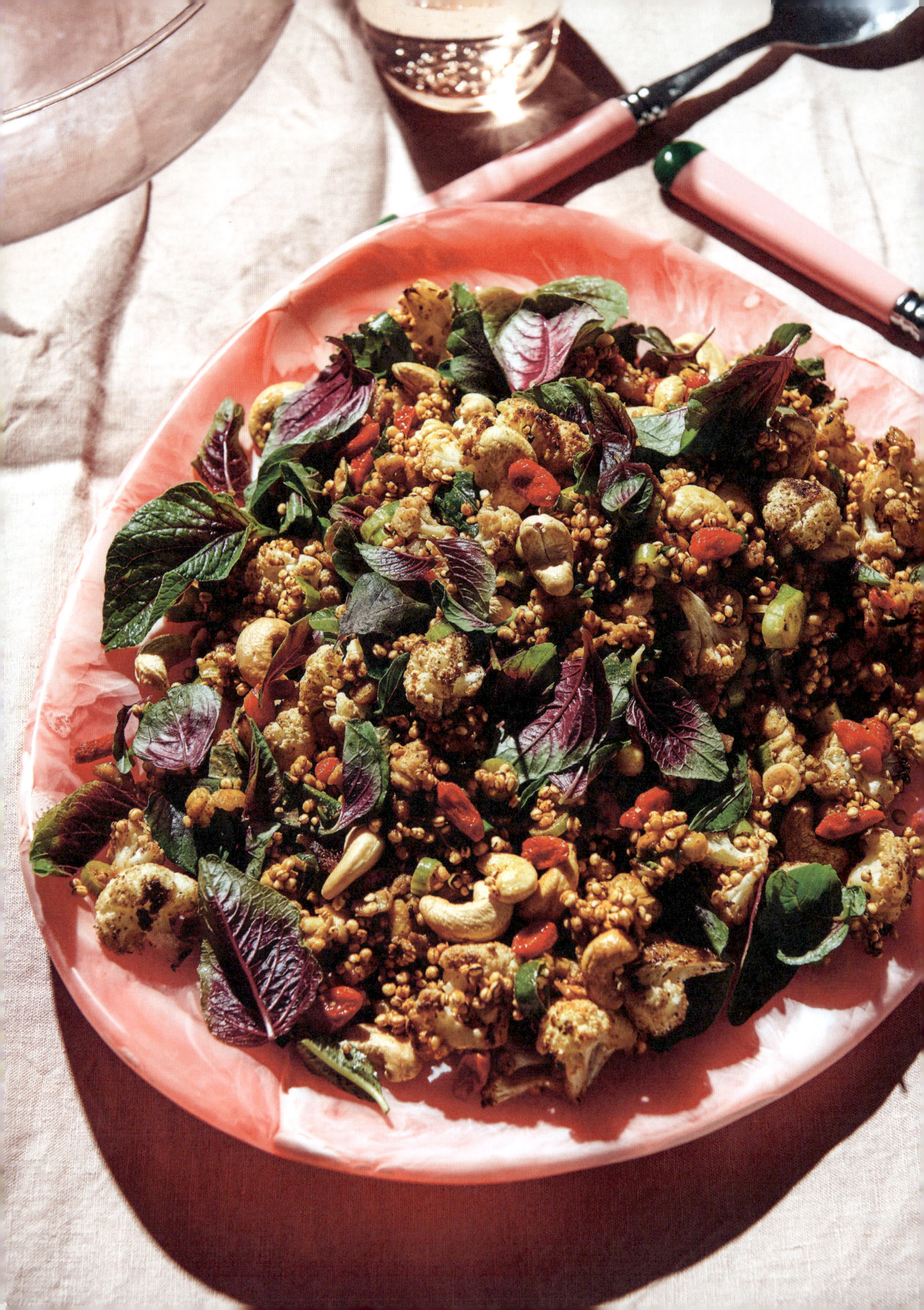

Five-spice tempeh and cauliflower salad

Serves 4

This salad is a celebration of flavour with five-spiced cauliflower, puffed grains, sweet goji berries and a kick from the Spicy peanut dressing. Tossed with quinoa, cashews and fresh herbs, it's a vibrant plate full of texture and taste that will have you coming back for more.

Take the extra time to cut your cauliflower pieces to be truly bite-sized. This will maximise the surface area for all that delicious five spice and spicy peanut dressing to stick to. Ideally, you want to be able to eat this salad without needing a knife.

Dressing
1 quantity Spicy peanut dressing (page 42)

Salad
1 whole cauliflower, cut into florets, stalk trimmed and cut into bite-sized pieces
2 tablespoons olive oil
1 teaspoon salt
2 teaspoons Chinese five-spice
generous handful of cashews
225 g (8 oz) tempeh, crumbled into approx. 1 cm (½ in) pieces
1 tablespoon goji berries, soaked in hot water
4 cups (60 g/2 oz) puffed quinoa or puffed brown rice
2 handfuls Chinese spinach (amaranth)
2 spring onions (scallions), finely chopped
1–2 handfuls Vietnamese mint, finely chopped

Preheat the oven to 180–200°C (360–390°F).

Place the cauliflower in a mixing bowl and drizzle with half the oil. Toss to coat the cauliflower in oil, then add half the salt and half the Chinese five-spice and toss. Spread the cauliflower evenly across a baking tray and cook for 25 minutes, or until the edges of the florets are slightly blackened, tossing once during the cooking time. Set aside to cool for 10 minutes. Meanwhile, roast your cashews in the oven for 10 minutes or so (keep an eye on them, as the oven will be a little hotter than is ideal for cashews).

Warm some olive oil in a large frying pan over a medium–high heat. Add the crumbled tempeh and cook for 5–10 minutes, tossing occasionally until lightly browned. Once brown, add the remaining Chinese five-spice and salt, and stir for a couple of minutes until fragrant, then remove from heat and set aside.

Check the goji berries for plumpness. If they are soft all the way through, they're ready to be drained. Combine the puffed quinoa, Chinese spinach, spring onions, Vietnamese mint and goji berries. Drizzle with half the dressing and lightly toss.

Place half the salad mixture on a serving dish. Top with half the cauliflower, cashews and tempeh. Repeat with the remaining salad mixture, cauliflower and cashews, then top with the remaining dressing and reserved herbs. Toss to combine, then devour while still warm.

Epic tip
This is super yummy even when the puffed rice gets soggy, which surprises yet pleases me every time there are leftovers.

Swaps
Use chopped baby spinach instead of Chinese spinach.

Grain salad

Serves 4–6

The original version of this grain salad by Hellenic Republic's Travis McAuley might just be Melbourne's favourite salad. It's had over one million hits on the Good Food website, and views tend to peak around the times we gather with friends and family, which makes sense given how easy this is to make ahead and transport. While the original version calls for freekeh, a dollop of yoghurt and an apple-cider vinegar dressing, I recently started making this with sorghum, pomegranate dressing and whipped feta instead.

Dressing

1 quantity Pomegranate dressing (page 42)

Salad

1 cup (200 g/7 oz) sorghum

½ cup (95 g/3¼ oz) dried French green or beluga lentils

1 red onion, finely chopped

handful of capers, finely chopped

handful of currants

1 bunch flat-leaf parsley, leaves picked and finely chopped

1 bunch coriander (cilantro), leaves picked and finely chopped

1 large handful (30 g/1 oz) pine nuts, lightly toasted

1 large handful (30 g/1 oz) pepitas (pumpkin seeds), lightly toasted

1 large handful (30 g/1 oz) slivered almonds, lightly toasted

1 tablespoon cumin seeds, lightly toasted

a generous sprinkling of pomegranate seeds, to serve

a generous dollop of Whipped feta (page 198)

pomegranate molasses, to garnish

Bring two saucepans of water to a boil. In one, cook the sorghum for 15–20 minutes. In the other, cook the lentils for 15–20 minutes. While you can absolutely cook these in the same pot, I prefer not to in case one takes slightly longer than the other. Once cooked, drain and rinse in cold water, then set aside. See more detailed instructions on page 26.

Place the cooked sorghum and lentils in a large bowl, then add the onion, capers, currants and most of the dressing, and give it a good stir. When ready to serve, add the toasted nuts and seeds and the herbs, reserving some herbs for a garnish.

Transfer to a serving bowl, then top with a generous dollop of whipped feta, drizzle with additional pomegranate molasses and garnish with reserved herbs and lemon.

Epic tip

Pair this with whipped feta topped with dukkah, Pomegranate, eggplant and cabbage (page 115), fried haloumi and pitta for a decadent feast.

Swaps

Add a dollop of Greek yoghurt on top as per the original version, with a dash of sumac for flavour and colour. For a vegan option, top with the whipped tofu on page 198.

Pomegranate, eggplant and cabbage

Serves 3–4

Remember when I said that rules are made to be broken? This here is a perfect example because, despite my harping on about the importance of crunch, this salad contains very little. It just works, though. The star of the show here is the eggplant which, with the help of pomegranate molasses, becomes sweet and caramelised on the outside and tender on the inside. With the added depth of flavour from the roasted cabbage, and the sweet, tart creaminess of the lemon yoghurt tahini dressing, this dish is a showstopper in both looks and flavour.

Dressing

1 quantity Lemon tahini yoghurt dressing (page 42)

Salad

3 tablespoons olive oil
1 teaspoon pomegranate molasses
1 teaspoon ground cumin
½ teaspoon salt
1 large eggplant (aubergine), cut into batons
½ red cabbage, sliced
2 × 400 g (14 oz) tin chickpeas, drained, rinsed and patted dry
60 g (2 oz) baby spinach, chopped
large handful mint leaves, finely chopped, plus extra for garnish
1 tablespoon pine nuts, toasted
handful pomegranate arils, to serve
a few pinches of sumac, to serve

Preheat the oven to 200–220°C (390–430°F).

Put 2 tablespoons of the olive oil, the pomegranate molasses, cumin and salt in a large mixing bowl and mix until well combined. Add the eggplant, toss to coat, then transfer to a baking tray and cook for 30 minutes, turning once during cooking.

Place the cabbage in the same mixing bowl. Toss in any remaining marinade, adding the remaining olive oil if necessary. Spread the cabbage over a separate baking tray and salt generously. Cook for 25 minutes, tossing once during that time.

Combine the chickpeas with two-thirds of the dressing and set aside.

Once the cabbage is cooked, allow it to cool slightly, then toss it with the chickpeas, using your hands to mix it through thoroughly. Add the chopped spinach and mint, and stir to combine.

To serve, transfer half the cabbage and chickpea mixture to a serving dish. Top with half the eggplant. Top with the remaining cabbage and chickpea mix and the remaining eggplant. Drizzle with the rest of the dressing then top with toasted pine nuts, pomegranate arils and sumac. Garnish with reserved mint leaves.

Epic tip
Leftovers are excellent in a warm soft pitta, with haloumi.

Swaps
If you would prefer a bit more crunch, swap out the cabbage for pitta, following the method on page 48 to make flatbread croutons. This will yield a different but outrageously good salad.

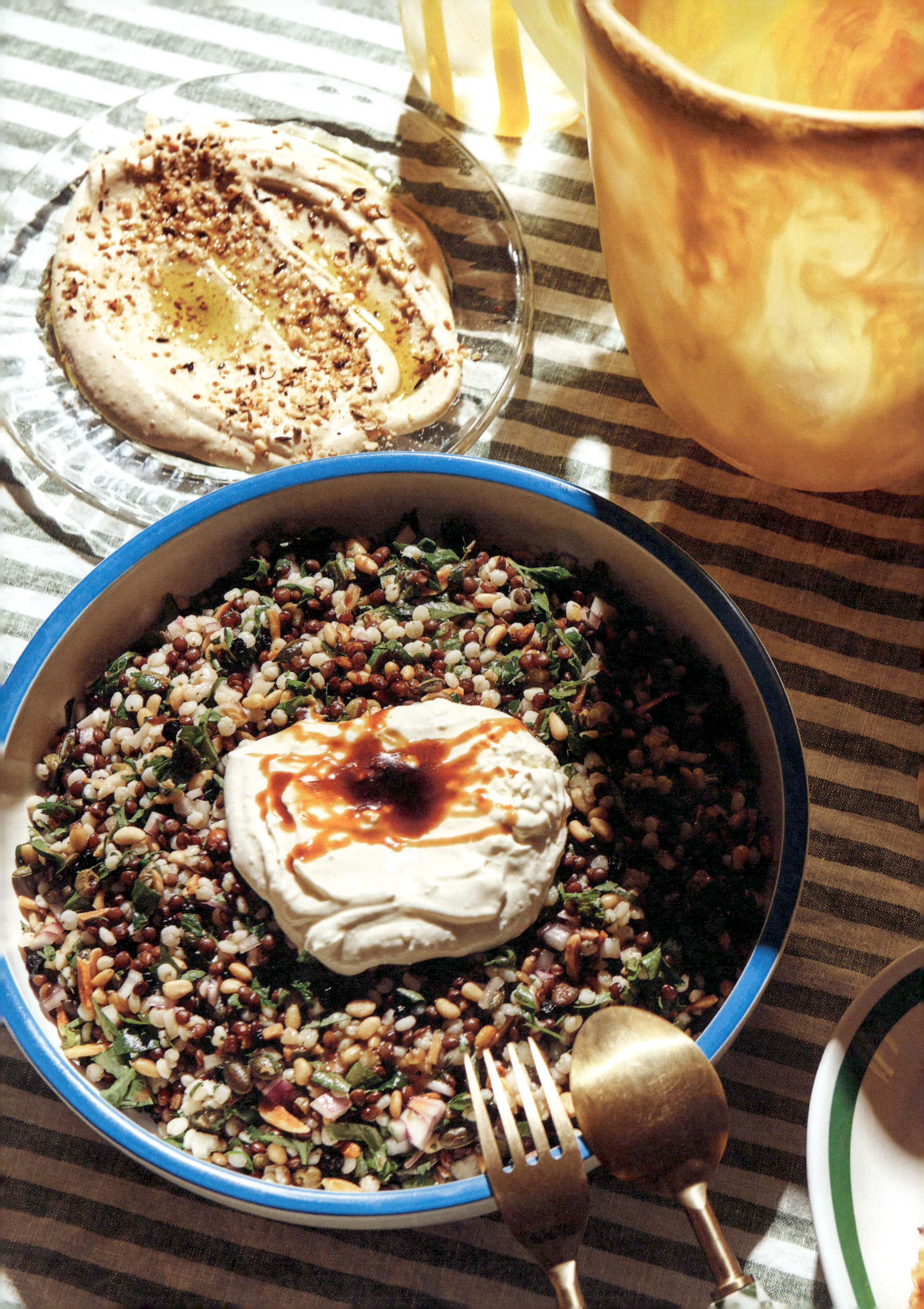

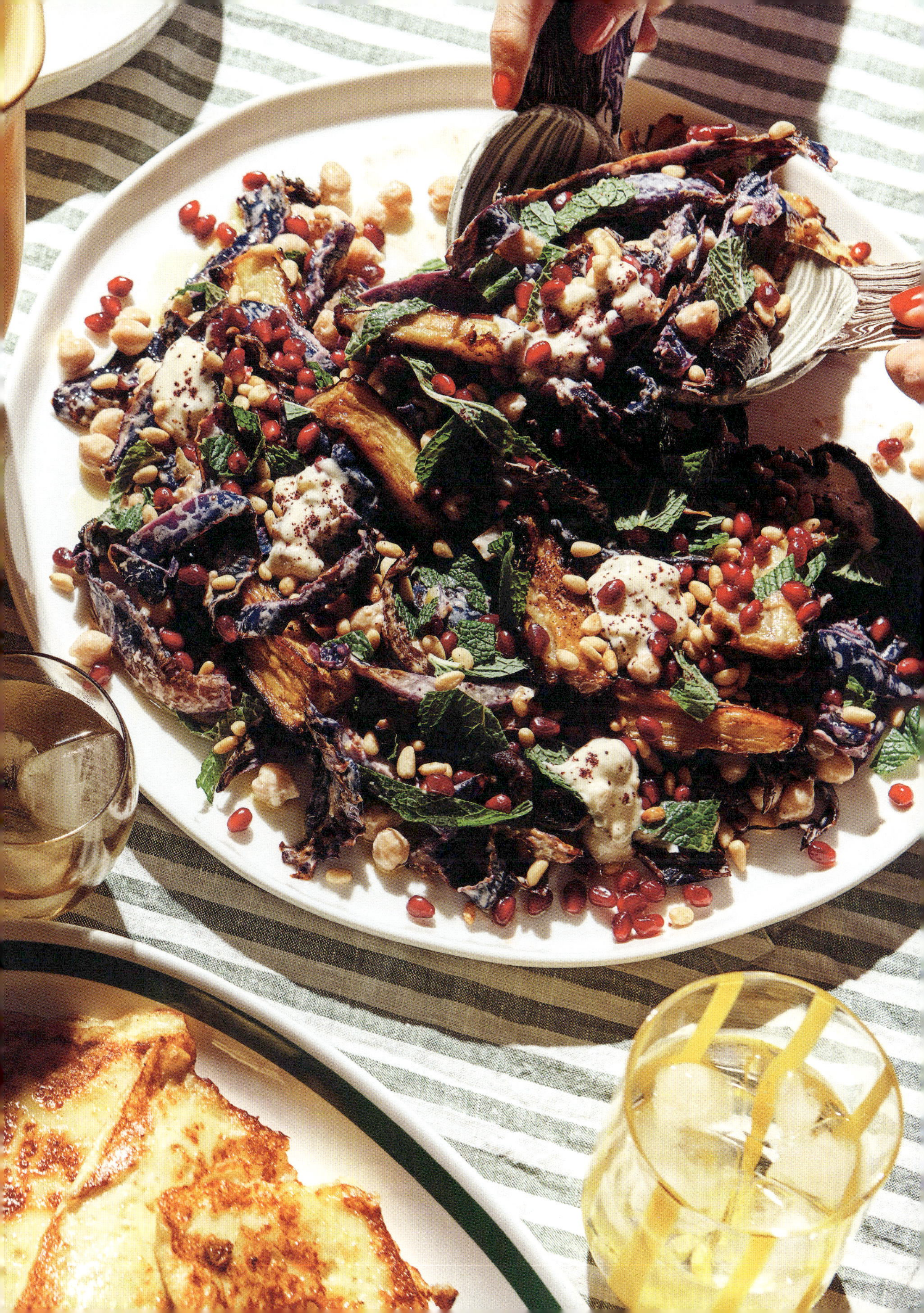

Haloumi chickpea salad

Serves 4

This was my go-to salad at the time of writing this book. It's hearty and filling and so, so moreish, and the leftovers keep well in the fridge for days – so well, in fact, that I made three notes in this recipe draft about how good the leftovers are! That being said, no matter how much salad is left over, there is never any left over haloumi, because no matter how full we are, we always manage to finish it all. If this is you too, be sure to cook extra, especially if feeding a crowd.

Dressing

1 quantity of The GOAT dressing (page 43)

Salad

olive oil, for cooking
½ teaspoon cumin seeds
½ teaspoon coriander seeds, lightly crushed
1 cup (200 g/7 oz) medium-grain rice
1 teaspoon salt
2 cups (70 g/2½ oz) kale, stems removed and finely chopped
200 g (7 oz) haloumi, cut into 5 mm–1 cm (¼–½ in) wide slabs
1 Lebanese (short) cucumber, seeds removed, diced
1 × 400 g (14 oz) tin chickpeas, drained and rinsed
⅓ cup (40 g/1½ oz) flaked or slivered almonds
3–4 tablespoons dried cherries
handful each of flat-leaf parsley and dill
lemon juice, to serve

To cook the rice, place a lick of olive oil in the bottom of a saucepan set over a medium heat. Add the cumin and coriander seeds and cook for a couple of minutes, until fragrant. Add the rice, salt and 2 cups (500 ml/17 fl oz) of water, then cover with a lid. Bring to a boil, then reduce to a low heat and cook for 15 minutes. Remove from the heat and leave to sit, covered, for 5 minutes. Add the kale, stir, and sit for another 5 minutes so the kale can wilt a little before spreading onto a baking tray and allowing to cool. You can also do this ahead of time.

To cook the haloumi, heat a small amount of olive oil in a large, flat-bottomed frying pan over a medium heat. Once the pan is hot, add the haloumi and cook for approximately 3 minutes until golden brown on the underside. Flip, and cook for a further 3 or so minutes, then transfer to a chopping board and allow to sit for a minute before cutting into squares, approximately 1 cm (½ in) in size. (You can go bigger if you like, but the smaller they are, the more mouthfuls of glorious haloumi you get.)

When ready to serve, transfer the cooled rice and kale to a large mixing bowl. Add the cucumber, chickpeas, almonds, cherries, most of the herbs and most of the dressing and stir until well combined. Transfer half the salad to a serving dish and top with half the haloumi. Repeat with remaining salad and haloumi, then drizzle with the remaining dressing. Garnish with remaining herbs and a generous squeeze of lemon.

Swaps

1. If you're not a fan of kale, try rocket (arugula) or spinach, which also work well in this salad. Add these greens at the same time as the chickpeas, cucumber, etc., after the rice has cooled.

2. Olives, capers, pickles and tomatoes all make excellent additions, as does coriander (cilantro) instead of dill, roasted pumpkin (squash) instead of haloumi, or toasted pine nuts instead of almonds.

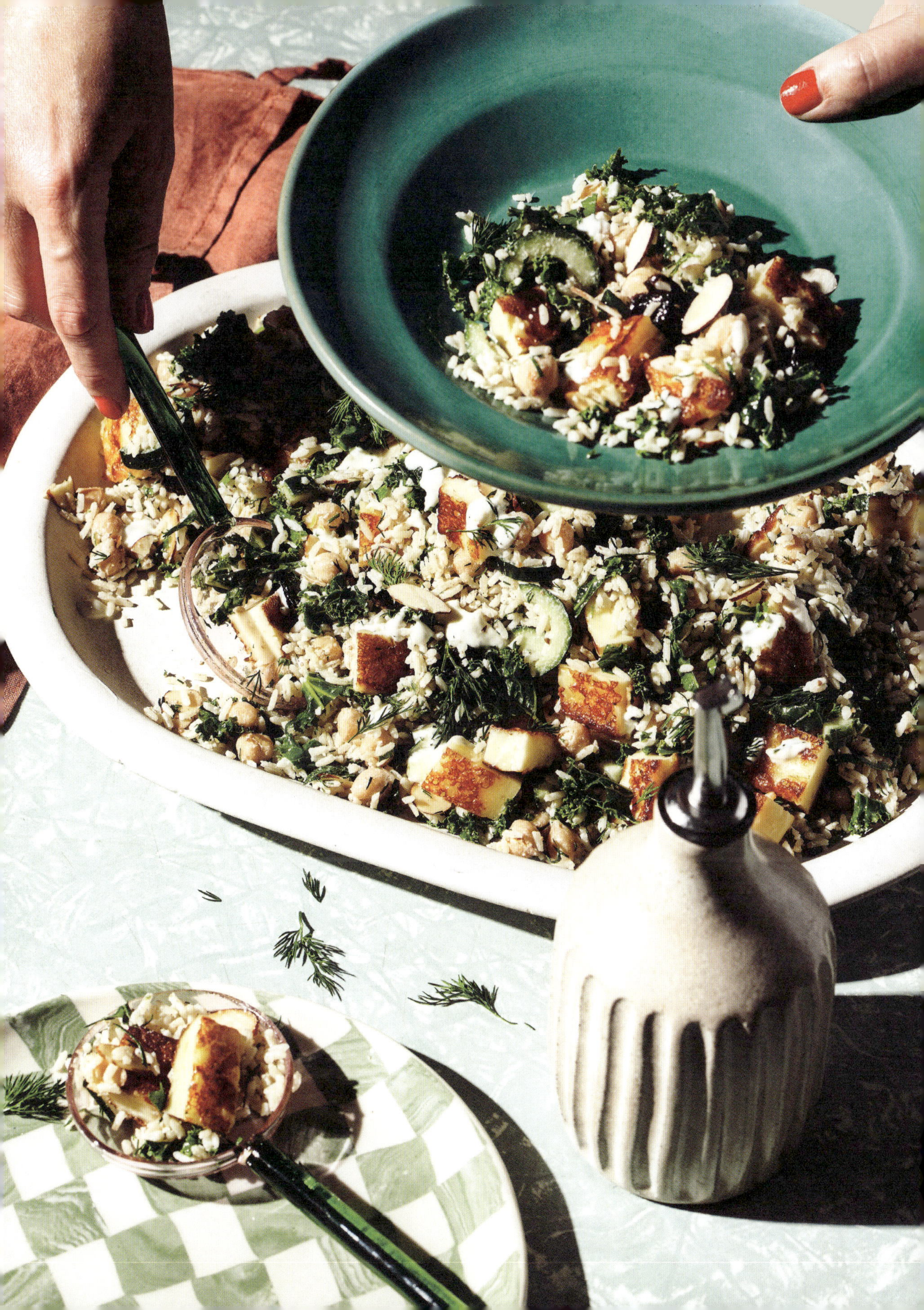

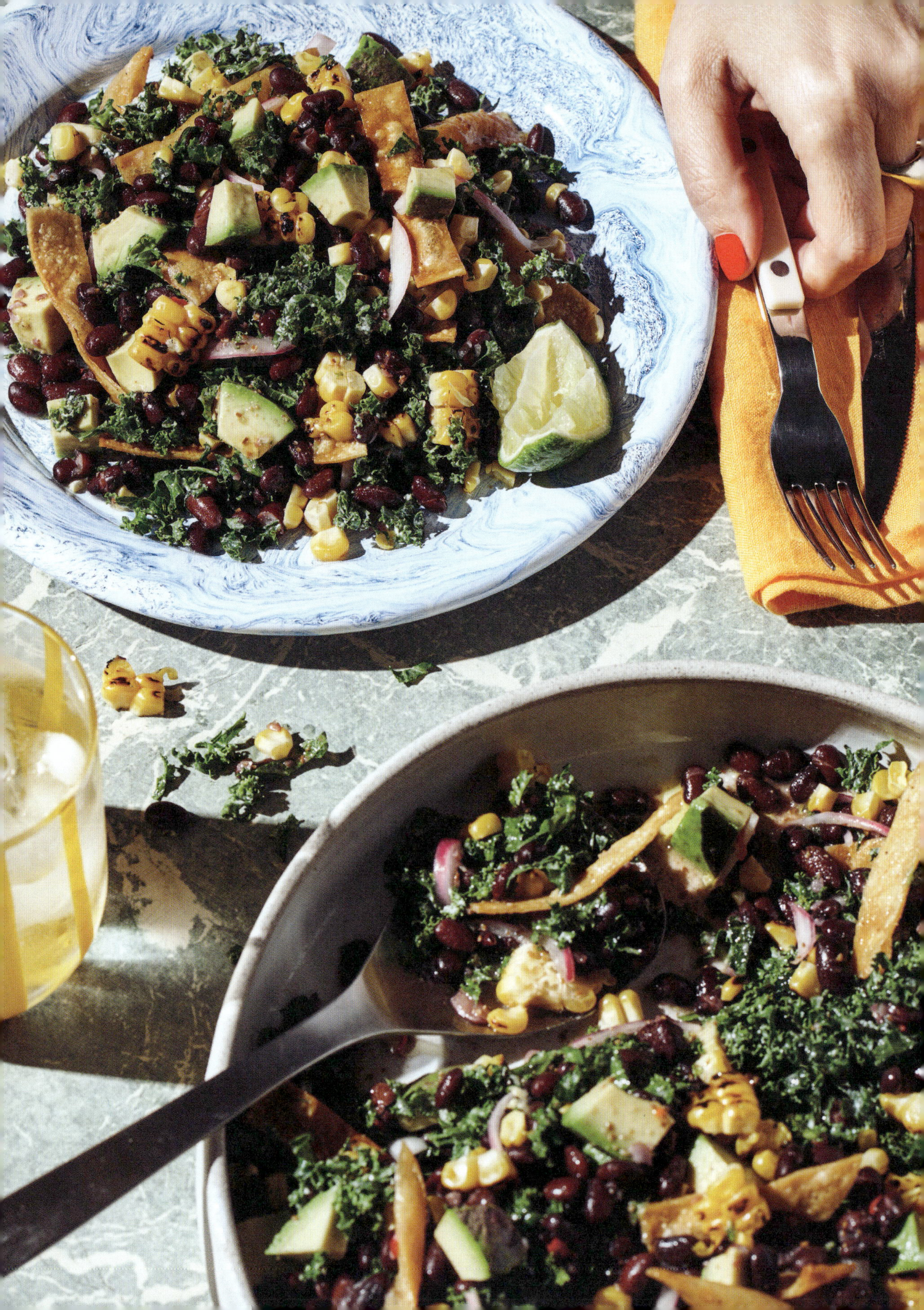

Marinated black beans with crispy tortilla strips

Serves 4

This salad is a labour of love, but it's worth every single step. Marinating the beans overnight imbibes them with the sweet tang of the Chilli lime dressing, which is a match made in heaven for the sweet and salty corn, the creaminess of the avocado, the freshness of the coriander (cilantro) and the playful crunch of crispy tortilla strips.

Dressing
1 quantity Chilli lime dressing (page 39)

Salad
2 × 400 g (14 oz) tins black beans, drained and rinsed
1 small red onion, thinly sliced
1 teaspoon cumin seeds, lightly crushed in a mortar and pestle
1 bunch kale (approx. 8 large leaves), leaves stripped and finely chopped
½ teaspoon salt
1 tablespoon sour cream
2 ears of corn
4–6 corn tortillas, cut into 1 × 5 cm (½ × 2 in) strips
1 avocado, diced
coriander (cilantro) leaves, to garnish

Combine the Chilli lime dressing with the black beans, onion and cumin. Stir to combine then refrigerate in an airtight container overnight, giving it a stir (or simply turning the container upside down) a couple of times when you remember/when you open the fridge.

Massage the kale with the salt, then stir the sour cream through the kale using your hands to really get it all mixed through. Combine with the marinated beans and set aside.

Cook your corn using any of the methods outlined on pages 23 and 24.

To shallow-fry the tortillas, heat a generous glug of oil in a large frying pan over a medium heat. Once the oil is hot (you can test this by placing a piece of tortilla in the pan – it should sizzle), fry the tortilla strips in batches. Place about two tortillas worth of strips into the hot oil (careful not to overcrowd the pan), cook for 2 minutes, or until crispy and a light golden brown, then remove with a slotted spoon and transfer to a paper towel. Repeat with the remaining tortilla strips, topping up the oil in between batches if necessary.

To build the salad, place half the beans, kale and corn on a serving dish and top with half the avocado and fried tortillas. Repeat with the remaining ingredients, then garnish with the coriander leaves and serve. Extra tortilla strips can also be served on the side if you're feeding a crowd.

Swaps
Sour cream can be swapped for a tablespoon of soft goat's cheese or cashew cream.

Roasted zucchini and feta with sorghum

Serves 2–3

This salad is great for that time of year when everyone has more zucchinis (courgettes) than they know what to do with. While the ingredients are simple, it's the herb-rich, flavour-bomb dressing that makes this a salad to remember. Roasting the zucchini gives it an appealing appearance and texture that works perfectly with the softness of the cannellini beans and the chew of the sorghum. With the pop of feta and crunch of pine nuts, this is another simple number that can be doubled for a crowd, upcycled as leftovers and paired with any number of salads in this chapter, either as a feast or to sustain you over a number of days.

Dressing
1 quantity Supergreen dressing (page 43)

Salad
2 zucchini (courgettes) (approx. 350 g/12½ oz), cut into 2 cm (¾ in) cubes
1 red onion, cut into 2 cm (¾ in) cubes
olive oil, for cooking
1 cup (200 g/7 oz) sorghum
1 × 400 g (14 oz) tin cannellini beans, drained and rinsed
2 large handfuls baby spinach or rocket (arugula)
100 g (3½ oz) feta, thinly sliced or crumbled
handful (30 g/1 oz) pine nuts, toasted
chilli flakes, to serve

Preheat the oven to 180–200°C (360–390°F) and bring a saucepan of water to a boil.

In a mixing bowl, combine the zucchini, red onion, olive oil and a generous pinch of salt. Toss to coat the zucchini in the oil, then spread on a baking tray and bake for 20–25 minutes, or until golden brown, giving it a toss about halfway through the cooking time. Once cooked, leave to cool on the tray for 10 minutes.

Once the water is boiling, add the sorghum and cook for 25–30 minutes. Drain, rinse in lots of cold water, and allow to cool. For more detailed cooking instructions see page 24.

When ready to serve, add the zucchini and spinach to the sorghum with half the dressing and toss to combine. Transfer half to a serving dish and top with half the feta and pine nuts. Repeat with the remaining salad, feta and pine nuts, then drizzle over the remaining dressing if desired. Top with chilli flakes and serve.

Swaps
This also works well with asparagus instead of zucchini, and haloumi instead of feta. You can also cook the zucchini in a large frying pan on the stove, as per the recipe on page 165.

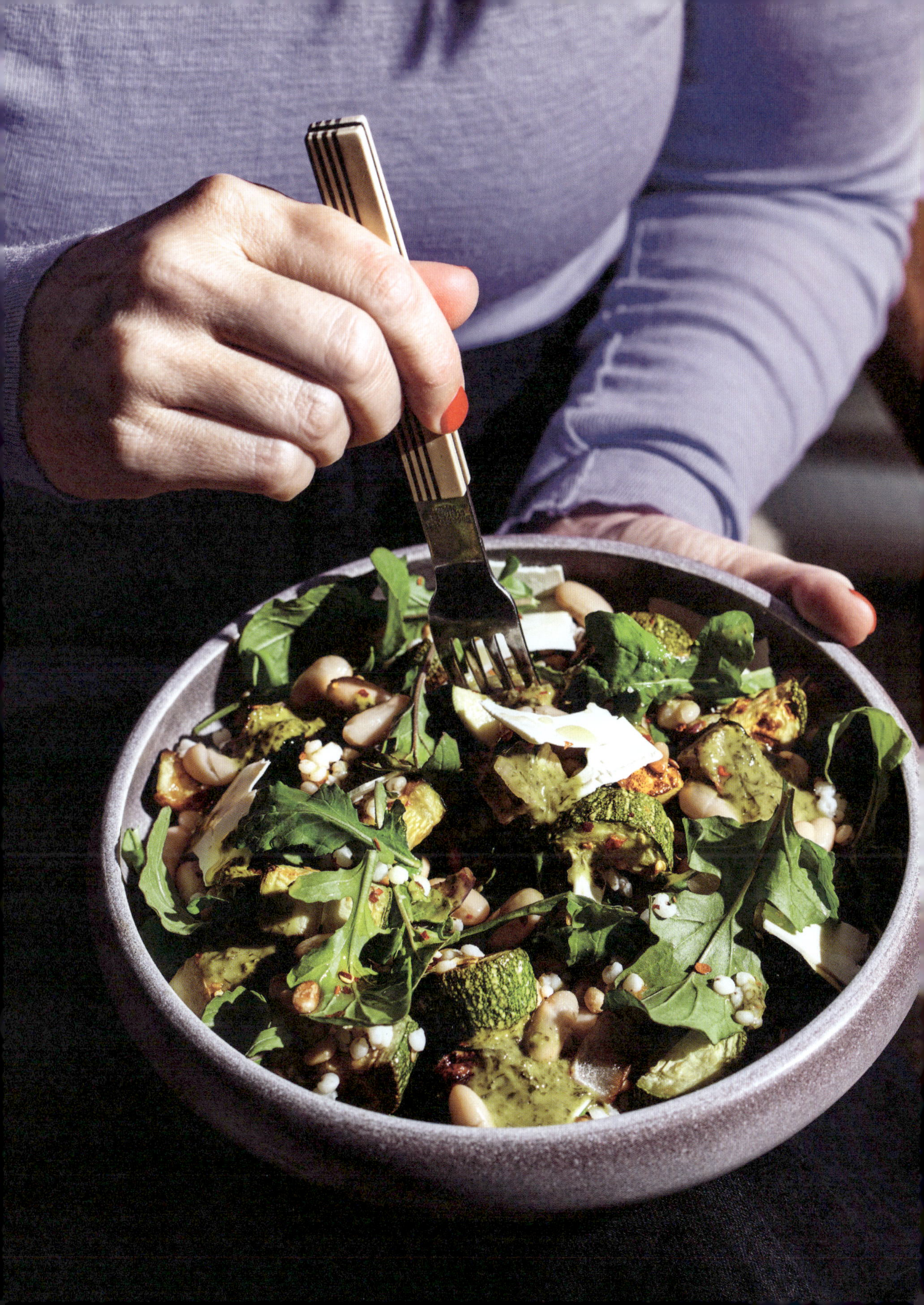

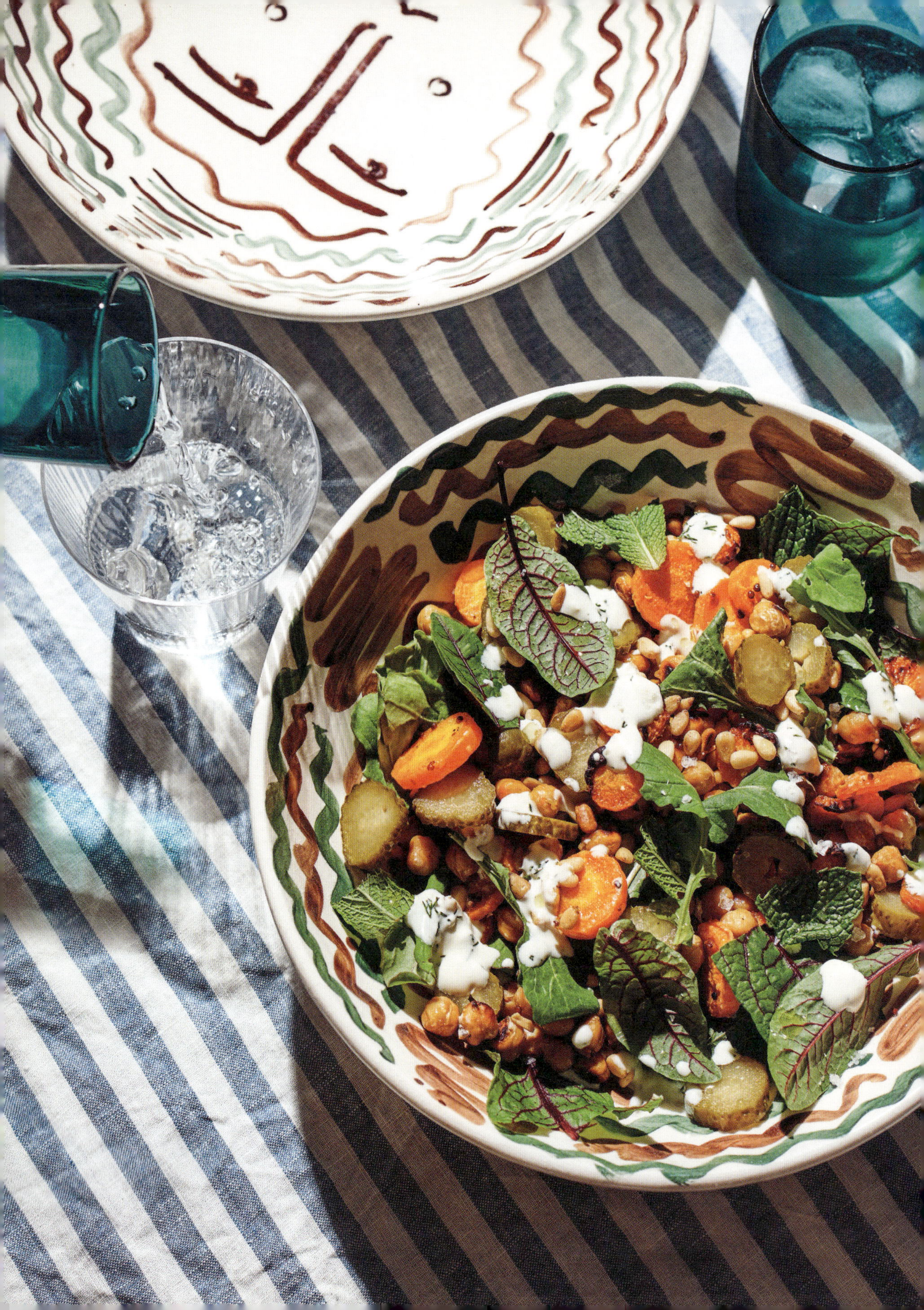

Honey mustard carrot and chickpea salad

Serves 2

This is an easy go-to for a quick lunch or dinner, and the perfect way to transform those forgotten carrots that are going floppy in the bottom of your vegetable drawer. The sweet tang of the honey mustard complements the earthy flavours of the carrots and chickpeas, and the way these two nestle together after they've been roasted and dressed makes this salad a pleasure to eat. With the addition of fresh mint and rocket (arugula), the pop of pickles and the dreamy, creamy, tangy and addictive GOAT dressing, it's also easy to double if feeding a crowd.

Dressing

½ quantity of The GOAT dressing (page 43)

Salad

1 × 400 g (14 oz) tin chickpeas, drained, rinsed and patted dry
2 large carrots, peeled and cut into ½ cm (¼ in) rounds
1 teaspoon wholegrain mustard
1 teaspoon runny honey
½ teaspoon salt
1 tablespoon olive oil
1 tablespoon pine nuts, toasted
large handful (30 g/1 oz) rocket (arugula), washed and dried
a few sprigs of mint
¼ cup cornichons or pickles, diced

Preheat the oven to 200–220°C (390–430°F).

Put the chickpeas and carrots in a large mixing bowl. Add the mustard, honey, salt and olive oil, and toss until the chickpeas and carrots are evenly coated. Transfer to a baking tray and bake for 20 minutes. Give the mixture a careful toss, add the pine nuts and return to the oven for another 5 minutes.

When ready to eat, place a couple of tablespoons of dressing in the bottom of each serving bowl. Add the rocket, some of the mint, top with the chickpeas and carrots, then add another 2 tablespoons of the dressing. Top with diced pickles and additional mint, and devour.

Epic tips

1. This recipe is easy to double if feeding a crowd. You can also bulk it out by serving it with haloumi in pitta pockets, or by serving it alongside any of the other salads in this chapter.
2. Use the other half of The GOAT on the Egg salad (page 64) or the Chickpea, celery and walnut salad (page 64).

Swaps

Use maple syrup in place of honey. Use 2 teaspoons of honey mustard instead of wholegrain if you have access to a good one.

Grains and legumes

Roasted pumpkin, maple walnut and blue cheese

Serves 3–4

Blue cheese lovers, this one's for you! I developed this recipe for my husband Andy, who is quite possibly the greatest blue cheese lover of them all. He declares it to be the best salad in this book.

The sweet, nutty, soft and creamy roasted pumpkin (squash) pairs beautifully with the earthy lentils and pungent blue cheese, with the maple walnuts elevating it all to make an absolute showstopper of a dish.

Dressing
1 quantity Basic balsamic dressing (page 39)

Salad
¼ kent pumpkin (winter squash) (approx. 750 g/1 lb 11 oz), skin scrubbed, seeds removed
1 cup (250 g/9 oz) beluga lentils
2 large handfuls (60 g/2 oz) rocket (arugula), chopped
large handful flat-leaf parsley, chopped
100 g (3½ oz) creamy blue cheese, torn into bite-sized pieces
1 cup (100 g/3½ oz) Maple walnuts (page 51)

Preheat the oven to 180–200°C (360–390°F) and bring a saucepan of water to a boil.

Cut the pumpkin in half and then into wedges, approximately 2 cm (¾ in) wide at the widest point. Brush a roasting tin with oil. Place the pumpkin wedges on the tray, flat-side down, and brush the other cut side with oil. Sprinkle with salt and bake for 25–30 minutes, or until golden brown, flipping the pumpkin wedges about halfway through the cooking time. Cool on the tray for 10 minutes.

When the water is boiling, add the lentils and cook for 15–20 minutes. Drain and rinse under cool water. Shake off any excess water, then place the lentils in a mixing bowl along with half the dressing.

Add the rocket and parsley to the lentils and toss to combine. Transfer half the lentil mixture to a serving platter and top with half the roasted pumpkin, blue cheese and the maple walnuts. Repeat with the remaining lentils, pumpkin, blue cheese and maple walnuts.. Drizzle with the remaining dressing and serve.

This is best served warm or at room temperature.

Epic tip
The maple walnuts make this a showstopper of a dish, but you can absolutely go for raw or roasted walnuts if you're making a simple weeknight dinner and don't want the extra sugar. Roughly chop the walnuts and place them on baking tray for the final 5 minutes while cooking the pumpkin.

Swaps
Don't like blue cheese? Use a soft goat's cheese instead.

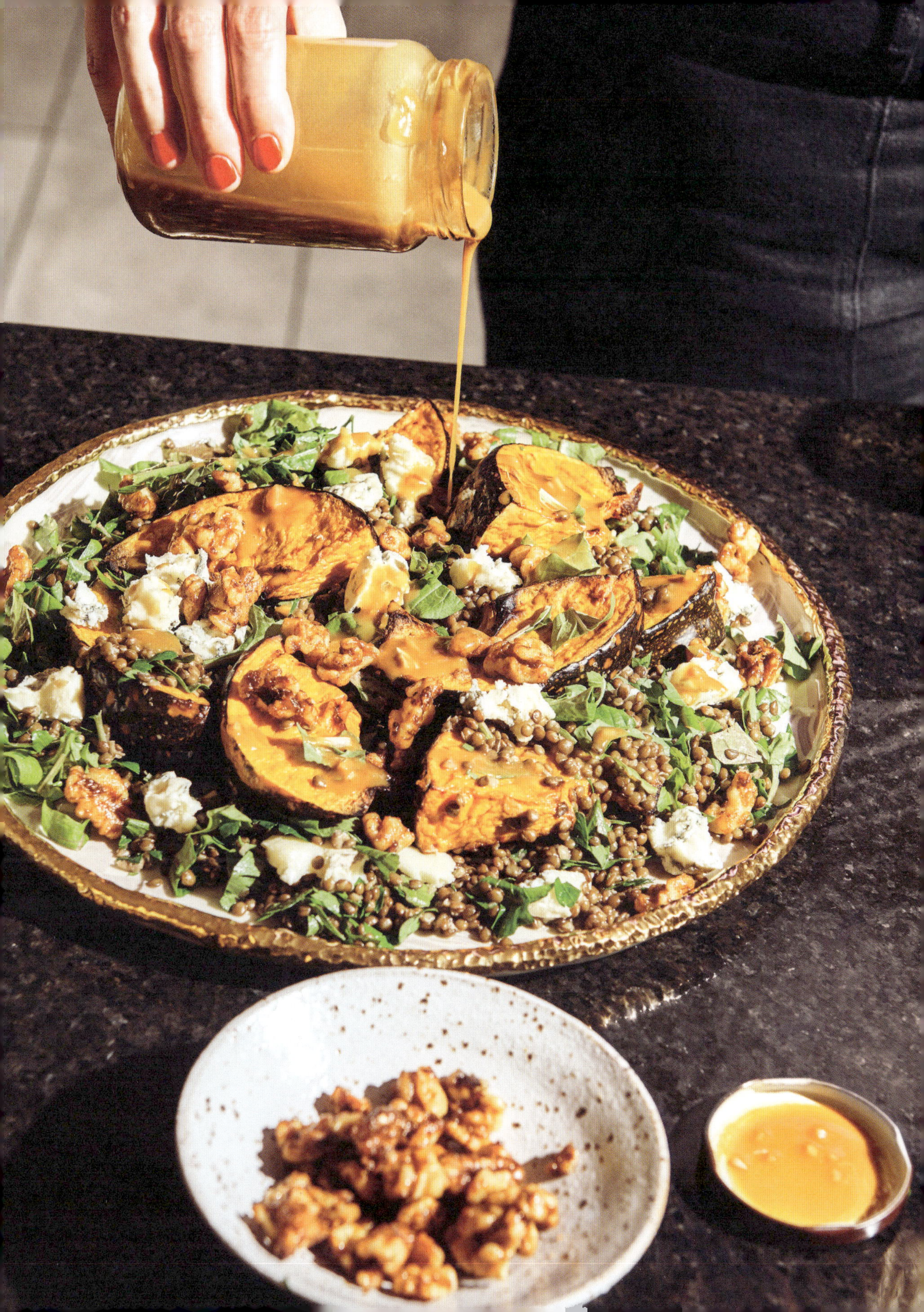

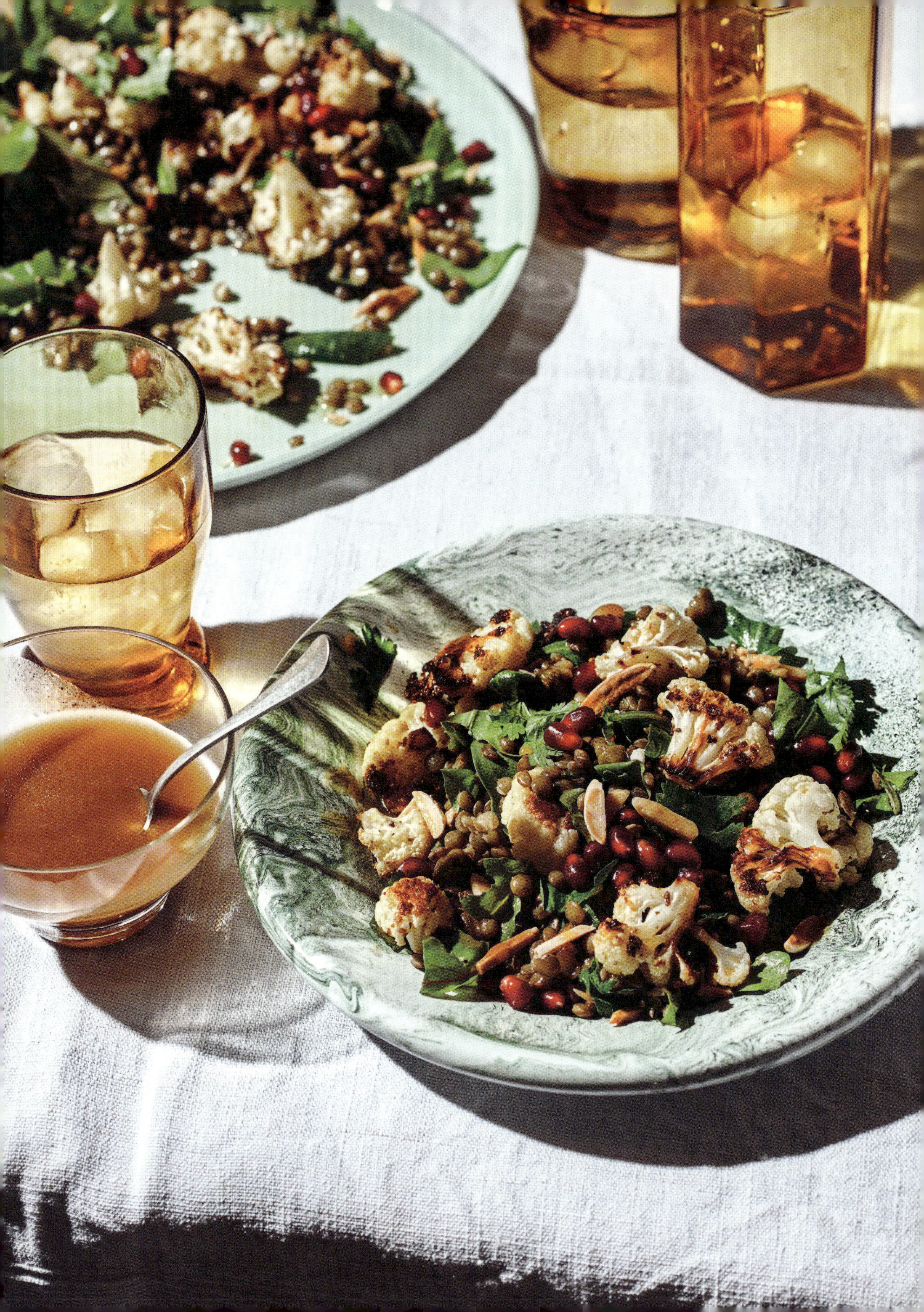

Roasted cauliflower salad

Serves 4

After sharing a version of this in my *Vegan One-Pot Wonders* cookbook, it has become a mainstay in many homes, including my own. Cumin and cauliflower are a match made in heaven, and when combined with earthy beluga lentils, zingy capers, crunchy almonds and a sweet pop of fruit, you've got a salad that is a perfect and moreish contrast of tastes and textures.

Dressing
- 1 quantity Pomegranate dressing (page 42)

Salad
- 1 whole cauliflower, cut into florets, stalks trimmed and cut into bite-sized pieces
- olive oil, for drizzling
- 1 teaspoon salt
- 1 teaspoon ground cumin
- ½ cup (95 g/3¼ oz) beluga lentils
- a few handfuls of baby spinach or rocket (arugula)
- handful (30 g/1 oz) pomegranate seeds or currants
- handful (30 g/1 oz) baby capers
- handful (30 g/1 oz) toasted slivered almonds
- fresh coriander (cilantro) leaves, to garnish

Preheat the oven to 190°C (375°F) and bring a pot of water to the boil.

Place the cauliflower in a mixing bowl and drizzle with oil. Toss to coat the cauliflower in oil, then add the salt and cumin and toss again. Spread the cauliflower evenly across a baking tray and bake for 25 minutes, or until the edges of the florets are slightly blackened. Remove from the oven and allow to cool for 10 minutes. (If your slivered almonds aren't already toasted, add them for the final 3 minutes of cooking time.)

When the water is boiling, add the lentils and cook for 15–20 minutes. Drain and rinse under cool water. Shake off any excess water, then place the lentils in a mixing bowl along with half of the dressing.

Combine the lentils with the spinach or rocket, pomegranate seeds or currants and capers. Place half of this mixture on a platter with half the roasted cauliflower and almonds. Repeat, then drizzle with the remaining dressing and fresh coriander.

Swaps

This salad is also amazing with the Honey mustard dressing on page 78.

Roasted zucchini, crispy pitta and beans

Serves 4

Drawing inspiration from the beloved Middle Eastern fatteh, this salad combines silky roasted zucchini (courgette) and soft cannellini beans with crispy pitta croutons, pine nuts and salty feta. The sweet, creamy and tangy dressing pulls everything together, while the pop of colour from the parsley and pomegranate seeds elevates the entire dish.

Dressing

1 quantity Lemon tahini yoghurt dressing (page 42)

Salad

2 zucchini (courgettes) (approx. 350 g/12½ oz), sliced into ½ cm (¼ in) rounds

⅓ cup (80 ml/2½ fl oz) olive oil

1 garlic clove, ½ minced

4 × pitta breads (approx. 300 g/10½ oz)

3 cups cooked cannellini beans (from 1 cup/200 g/7 oz dry beans or 2 × 400 g/14 oz tins)

2 handfuls rocket (arugula), roughly chopped

1 handful flat-leaf parsley, finely chopped

100 g (3½ oz) feta

30 g (1 oz) pine nuts, toasted

handful pomegranate seeds (optional)

Preheat the oven to 200–220°C (390–430°F).

Combine the zucchini with 2 teaspoons of the olive oil, the minced garlic and a generous pinch of salt. Spread on a baking tray in an even layer and bake for 20 minutes, turning halfway through cooking. Once cooked, leave on the tray to cool for 10 minutes. Leave the oven on to cook the pitta breads.

Rub the pittas with the unminced garlic and cut into 2 cm (¾ in) squares. Toss with the remaining olive oil and a generous pinch of salt, and spread on a baking tray. Bake for 5–10 minutes, keeping an eye on them and giving them a toss when the edges of the squares start to turn brown.

Combine the beans with two-thirds of the dressing and set aside.

To build the salad, place most of the rocket in the bottom of a serving dish. Add the pitta squares, then top with most of the beans. Add the zucchini, remaining beans and remaining rocket, then drizzle with the rest of the dressing. Top with feta, pine nuts and pomegranate seeds, if using.

Epic tip

1. This recipe calls for roasted zucchini, but you can absolutely cook it on the stove or barbecue, too. You can cook your pittas in a pan too, as per the recipe on page 49.

2. Got leftovers? This salad is delicious even 2 days later, when the pitta is soggy. There is a strange magic about soggy pitta, it just works.

Grains and legumes

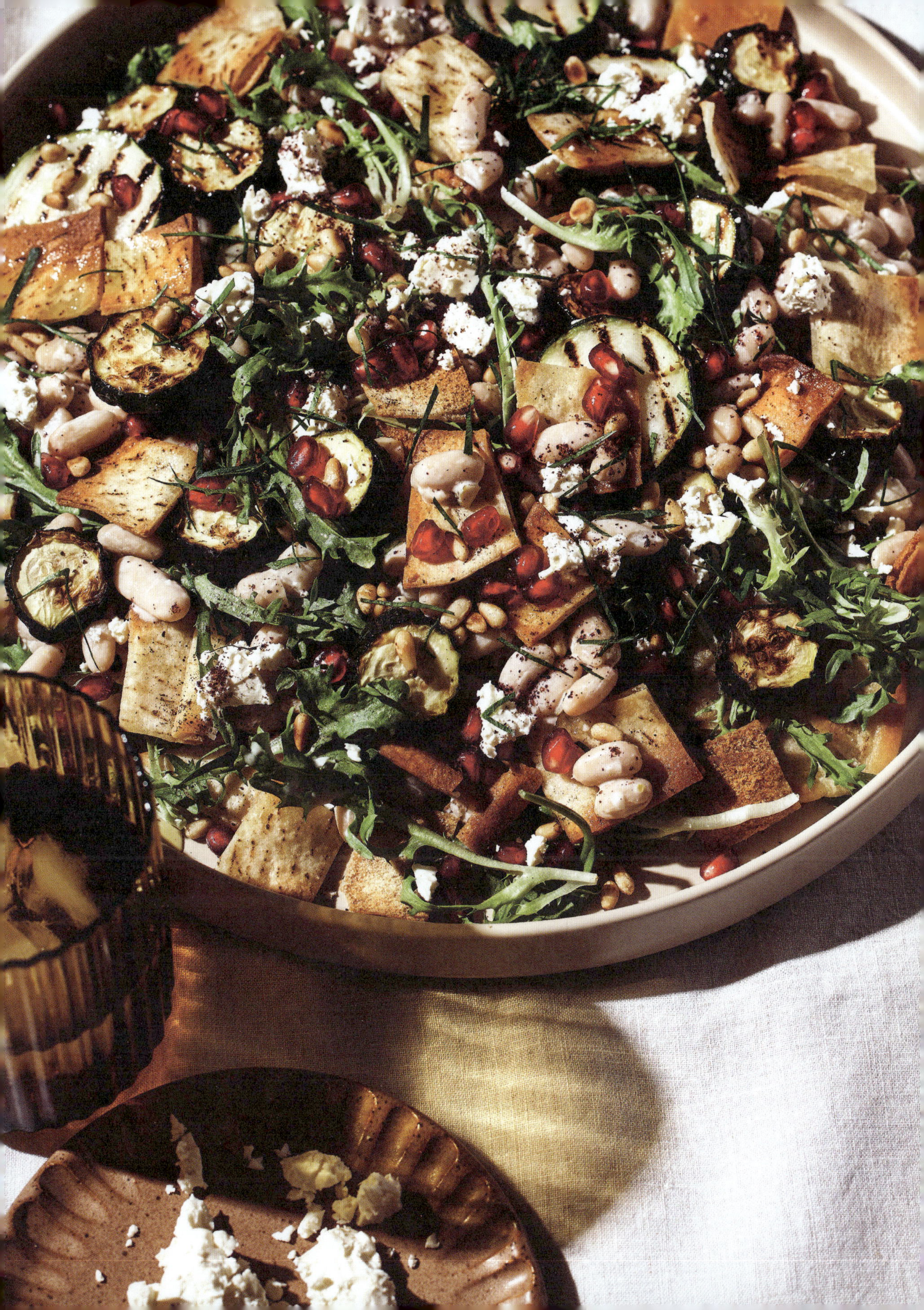

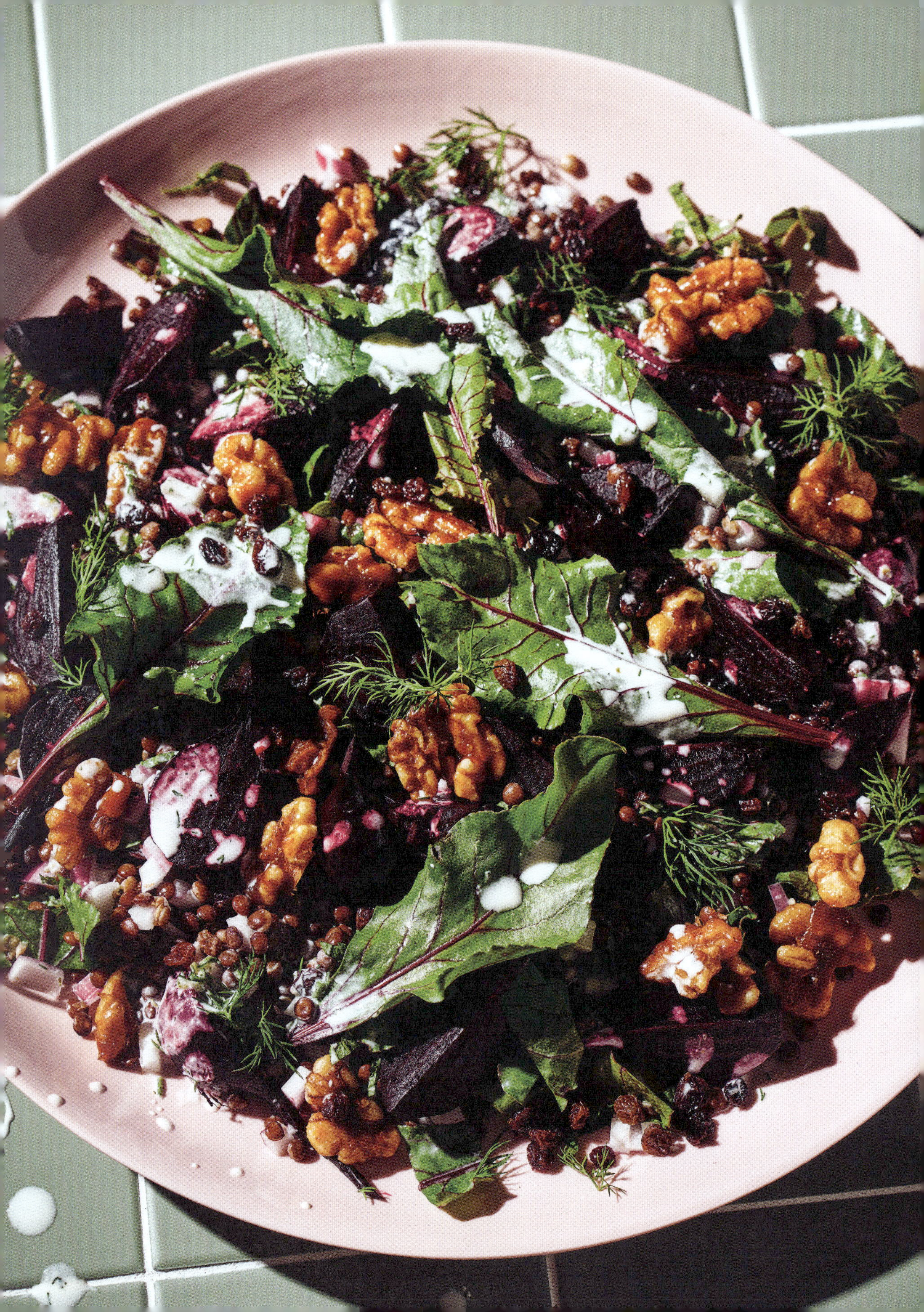

Root-to-leaf beet salad

Serves 3–4

The beauty of this salad is that it uses (almost) the entire vegetable. Rather than throwing them away, the glossy green leaves of the beet act as the leaf in this salad – cool, right? Beetroot (beet) leaves are delicious, good for you, and hold up for a few days in the fridge, even when coated with dressing. The earthy beetroot, hefty lentils and sweet currants pair beautifully with The GOAT dressing, with the maple walnuts bringing a welcome crunch.

Dressing

1 quantity The GOAT dressing (page 43)

Salad

1 bunch beetroots (beets), leaves intact and in good condition
½ cup (95 g/3¼ oz) dried beluga lentils
½ red onion, very finely chopped
handful (30 g/1 oz) currants
large handful mint leaves
dill fronds, to garnish
1 cup (100 g/3½ oz) Maple walnuts (page 51)

Preheat the oven to 200–220°C (390–430°F) and bring a small saucepan of water to a boil.

Trim off the beetroot leaves and set aside. Scrub the beetroots clean and wrap each beetroot individually in aluminium foil, then cook on a baking sheet for 50–60 minutes, or until they can be easily pierced with a fork. Allow to cool before rubbing the skins off with your hands (you can use gloves for this if you want to avoid pink hands), then cut into bite-sized wedges.

When the water is boiling, add the lentils and cook for 15–20 minutes. Drain and rinse under cool water. Shake off any excess water, and set aside.

Cut the stems off the beetroot leaves and discard. Stack around ten leaves on top of each other then cut into strips, approximately 2 cm (¾ in) wide. Wash twice, then spin dry.

To serve, combine the cooked lentils, red onion, currants and greens in a large mixing bowl and stir through half the dressing. Place half the salad on a serving platter. Top with half the cooked beetroot wedges and maple walnuts. Repeat with remaining salad, beetroot and walnuts, then drizzle with the rest of the dressing and top with mint leaves and dill fronds.

Serve as is, or with an array of other delicious salads.

Swaps

If you can't find beetroots (beets) with their leaves attached, worry not. Baby spinach, rocket (arugula), sorrel or kale can all be used in their place – kale will hold up best if you're planning to eat this over a couple of days.

Chipotle corn and chickpea salad

Serves 2–4

It's a running joke that whenever I hand in a book manuscript, I come up with another recipe that works perfectly in that book a couple of weeks after submission. This is that recipe.

The marriage of charred corn with the natural sweetness of roasted sweet potatoes, hearty chickpeas, smoked almonds and salty cheese creates a satisfying dish that's perfectly tied together by the creamy kick of the chipotle mayo. If you can't get your hands on salted ricotta – fret not! Danish feta works just as well.

Dressing
- 3 tablespoons mayo
- 1 teaspoon chipotle sauce

Salad
- 1 sweet potato (approx. 500 g/ 1 lb 2 oz), peeled and diced
- olive oil, for drizzling
- 3 ears of corn, husks removed
- 1 small red onion, very finely chopped
- 30 g (1 oz) smoked almonds, roughly chopped
- handful (30 g/1 oz) baby spinach, sliced
- large handful (15 g/½ oz) coriander (cilantro) leaves, very finely chopped
- 1 × 400 g (14 oz) tin chickpeas, drained and rinsed
- 100 g (3½ oz) salted ricotta, crumbled
- juice of 1 lime, to serve (optional)

Preheat oven to 180–200°C (360–390°F).

Place the sweet potato in a mixing bowl with a drizzle of olive oil and a pinch of salt. Toss to evenly coat, then spread on a baking tray and roast in the hot oven for 20–25 minutes, tossing once during cooking time.

Cook the corn, following any of the methods outlined on page 23, then remove the kernels from the husks and set aside.

Put the mayo and chipotle sauce in a mixing bowl. Stir to combine, then add the roasted sweet potato, cooked corn, red onion, almonds, spinach, coriander and chickpeas. Stir to combine, season to taste, then add the salted ricotta and lightly toss. Squeeze over the lime juice just before serving, if desired. Devour.

Epic tip
Got leftovers? This is SO good in a quesadilla. Also amazing with cheese or in a wrap with hummus.

Swaps
Swap the coriander for mint or parsley. You could also add tomatoes – slow-roasted baby roma tomatoes like the ones on page 201 would be amazing. Use any kind of onion you like, and maybe add pickled jalapeños. You could also use roasted almonds instead of smoked if you aren't a fan of smoked things.

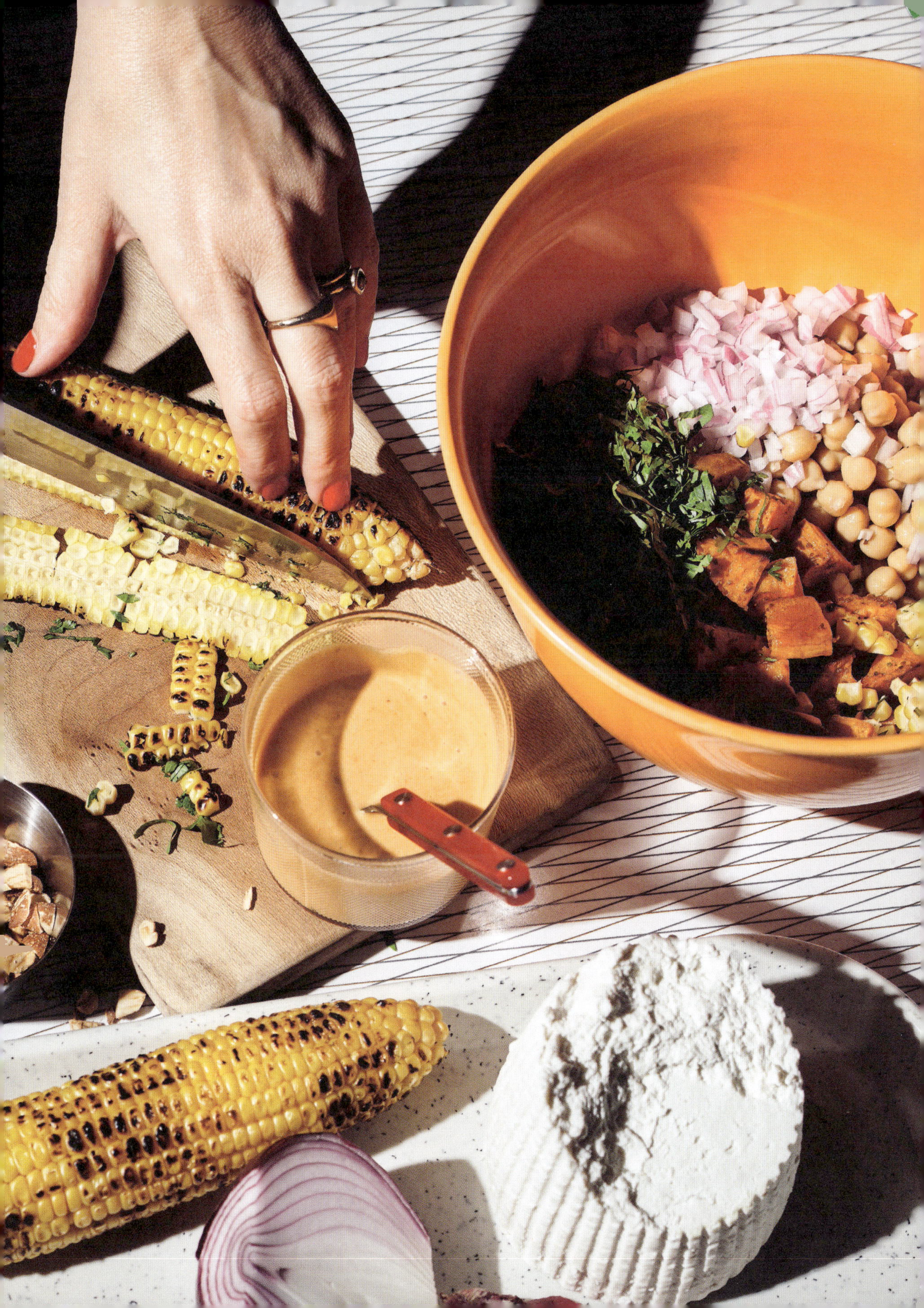

PASTA AND

NOODLES

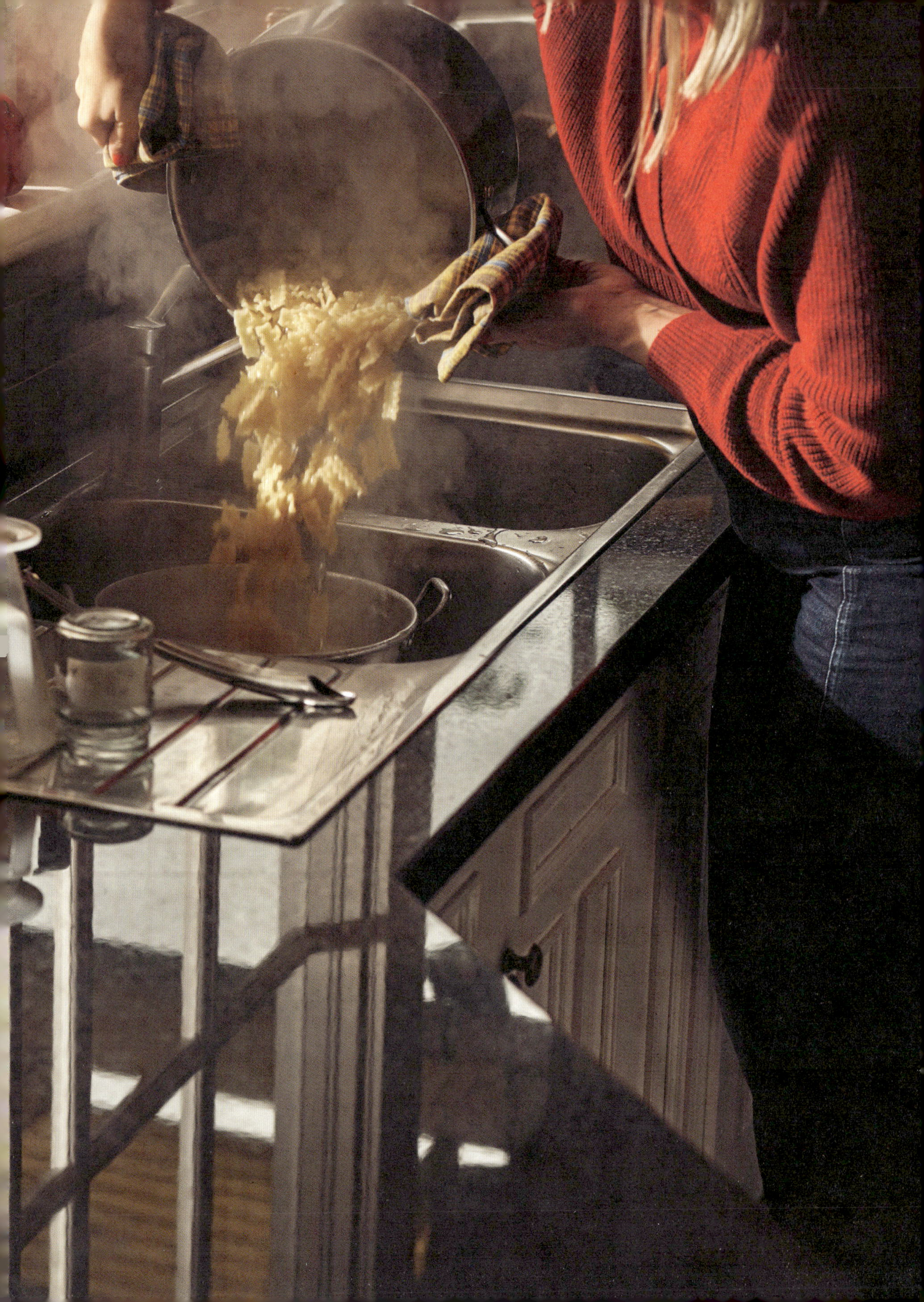

Ah, the joy of pasta!

In this chapter you'll find salads that are comforting and moreish. In an ode to pasta's versatility, these recipes reimagine everyone's favourite comfort food and transform it into vibrant salads that satisfy those carb cravings while enjoying the contrast of crisp, colourful produce.

Many of these salads not only hold up to the fork but also to the fridge, meaning they can be prepared ahead of time and enjoyed over a number of days. Most of them also travel well, making them great for picnics and potlucks.

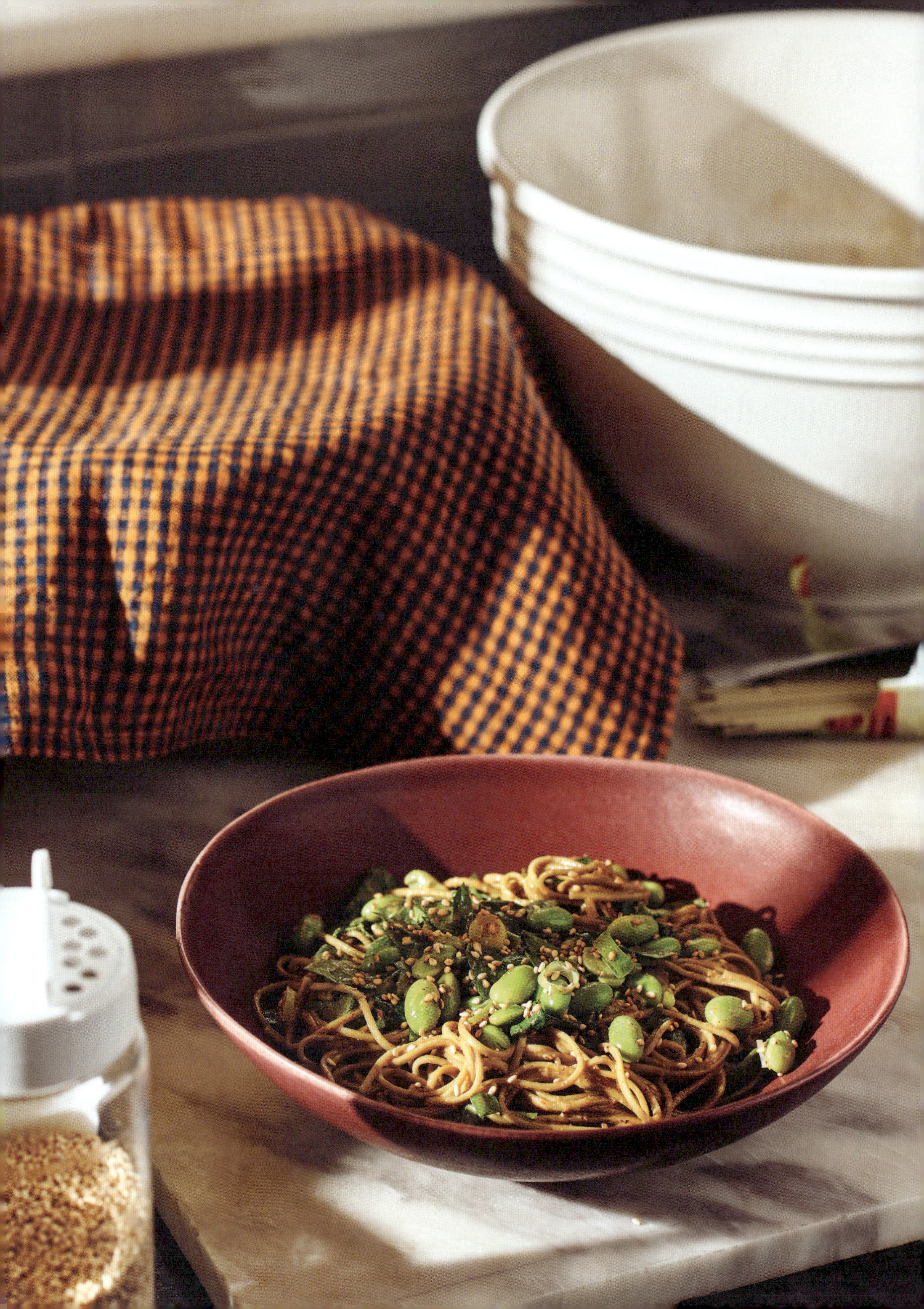

Simple soba for one

Serves 1

I adore this salad for its simplicity. It is so quick and easy to make – the longest step is waiting for the water to boil! I use this time to make the dressing (unless I've made it ahead of time) and prep the rest of my ingredients, and this salad comes together in moments.

You can, of course, scale it to feed more people, which you may wish to do because the flavours are so good! However, when feeding a crowd I prefer the Soba salad with edamame and corn (page 161).

Dressing

- 1 tablespoon peanut butter
- 2 teaspoons soy sauce
- 1 teaspoon toasted sesame oil
- 1 teaspoon maple syrup
- ¼ garlic clove, microplaned (optional)
- ¼ teaspoon grated fresh ginger, microplaned

Salad

- 50 g (1¾ oz) shelled edamame beans
- 75 g (2¾ oz) soba noodles
- small handful baby spinach, cut into approx. 1 cm (½ in) strips
- 1 teaspoon toasted sesame seeds
- 1 spring onion (scallion), sliced

Place all dressing ingredients in a serving bowl and stir to combine.

If your edamame beans aren't already defrosted, place them in a heatproof bowl, cover with boiling water and allow to sit for 2 minutes. Drain, refresh with cold water, then drain again and set aside.

Bring a large pot of water to a boil. Add the noodles and cook according to the directions on the packet, then drain and run under cool water. Shake the noodles to remove as much excess water as possible, then put them in the bowl with the dressing. Stir to combine.

Add the spinach, edamame, sesame seeds and spring onion, toss and devour immediately.

Epic tips

1. Got leftovers? They're delish, but the cold noodles get a bit sticky – I prefer to eat them warm. Add a teaspoon of water before reheating.
2. Double the edamame beans or add an egg if you are looking for an extra protein hit.
3. If your edamame beans are still fully or partially frozen, throw them in with the noodles, or pop them in a colander and pour the noodle water over them.

Swaps

Use tahini instead of peanut butter if you can't do nuts.

Pasta and noodles

Antipasti pasta salad

Serves 4–6

This salad is a flavour bomb of everyone's favourite antipasti ingredients, and is a great recipe to have up your sleeve if you don't love to cook. If you can boil a pot of pasta, you can make this salad. The rest of the work is done through the mastery of pickling and preserving – *other people's* pickling and preserving. With the added freshness of rocket (arugula) and basil, the tang of parmesan and the crunch of pine nuts, this pasta salad is a crowd pleaser that never fails to hit the spot.

Dressing

2 tablespoons olive tapenade (store bought or see method), plus extra if needed

Salad

300 g (10½ oz) dried pasta (I like penne for this one)
2 tablespoons olive oil, plus extra if needed
2 tablespoons (30 g/1 oz) capers
100 g (3½ oz) semi-dried (sun-blushed) or slow-roasted tomatoes, halved
100 g (3½ oz) roasted red capsicum (bell pepper), sliced
100 g (3½ oz) artichoke hearts, preferably the kind that are pickled in vinegar, quartered
handful rocket (arugula), sliced if stems are long
handful basil leaves, larger ones roughly chopped or sliced
handful (30 g/1 oz) pine nuts, toasted
100 g (3½ oz) shaved parmesan cheese
chilli flakes or black pepper, to serve

Bring a large pot of salted water to a boil. Add the pasta and cook according to the directions on the packet. Drain, then run under lots of running cold water until cool. Shake off any excess water, then stir the tapenade through the pasta, ensuring it is evenly coated.

Add the capers, semi-dried tomatoes, roasted capsicum and artichokes, and stir so everything is well combined. Depending on whether your deli delights were pickled in brine or marinated in oil, the pasta should be coated in a thin layer of oil, but not dripping. Add olive oil, 1 teaspoon at a time, or tapenade if you think it needs it.

When ready to eat, add the rocket, basil, most of the pine nuts and most of the parmesan. Toss to combine, then top with the remaining pine nuts and parmesan, and chilli flakes or freshly cracked black pepper, to taste.

To make your own olive tapenade: Place 100 g (3½ oz) pitted kalamata olives in a food processor or blender with a small chamber attachment. Blitz until the olives are in small chunks, then slowly pour approx. 2 tablespoons of olive oil in with the blender running and continue to run until the tapenade is as smooth as you would like (I like to leave mine on the chunky side).

Epic tips

1. If time allows, slow roast your own tomatoes following the directions on page 201.
2. Most of these ingredients will keep in the fridge for a while, so you can buy up big and have this recipe up your sleeve for multiple events in a row.

Swaps

1. Don't like olives? Use basil pesto instead of olive tapenade. Don't like pine nuts? Try Pangratatto (page 48) for crunch.
2. You can also make a hand-chopped version of the olive tapenade à la the method used in the Raw zucchini, pea and straciatella salad (page 158).

Coriander pesto and roasted pumpkin pasta salad

Serves 4

This is one of those salads that really gets the crowd going. The combination of vibrant coriander (cilantro) pesto and sweet roasted pumpkin (squash) pair beautifully with the creaminess of the avocado and feta, but it's the unexpected zing of the pickled jalapeños that really take things up a notch. With spinach for freshness and pepitas (pumpkin seeds) for crunch, this is a refreshing twist on a traditional pasta salad that gets rave reviews and recipe requests every time I make it.

Dressing

1 quantity Coriander pesto (page 39)

Salad

½ small red onion, sliced
1 tablespoon apple-cider vinegar
500 g (1 lb 2 oz/approx. ¼) kent pumpkin (winter squash)
olive oil, for cooking
300 g (10½ oz) dried pasta
2 tablespoons pickled jalapeños, finely chopped
2 handfuls baby spinach (60 g/2 oz) washed, dried and chopped
60 g (2 oz) salted ricotta, crumbled
1 ripe avocado, sliced
2 handfuls pepitas (pumpkin seeds) (60 g/2 oz), toasted

Preheat the oven to 200–220°C (390–430°F), and bring a large saucepan of water to a boil.

Place the red onion in a small bowl and cover with the vinegar, then set aside.

Cut the pumpkin into wedges, approx. 1 cm (½ in) wide at the widest (skin side) point. Brush a large baking tray with olive oil and top with pumpkin slices, flat side down. Collect any excess oil from around the tray and brush onto the tops of the pumpkin slices. Sprinkle everything with salt, then roast for 25–30 minutes, turning halfway through.

Cook the pasta in the boiling water according to the directions on the packet. Drain, then rinse in cold water. Allow to sit for a couple of minutes, then shake off any excess water and transfer to a bowl. Add two-thirds of the pesto and all the onion and jalapeños and stir to combine, then set aside while you prepare the remaining ingredients.

Once the pumpkin is cooked, allow to cool for a few minutes until cool enough to handle. Toss the cooled pasta with the spinach and transfer half to a serving dish. Top with half the roasted pumpkin (tearing any large chunks into smaller pieces through the skin), half the salted ricotta, avocado and pepitas. Top with the remaining pasta, pumpkin, salted ricotta, avocado, pesto and pepitas. Season to taste, then devour.

Epic tips

Got leftovers? This is outrageously good the next day — the flavours just get better with time. You may need to add some more oil, as the pasta can soak up all the pesto. If making for work lunches, you may wish to reserve some of the pesto and dress the salad right before eating.

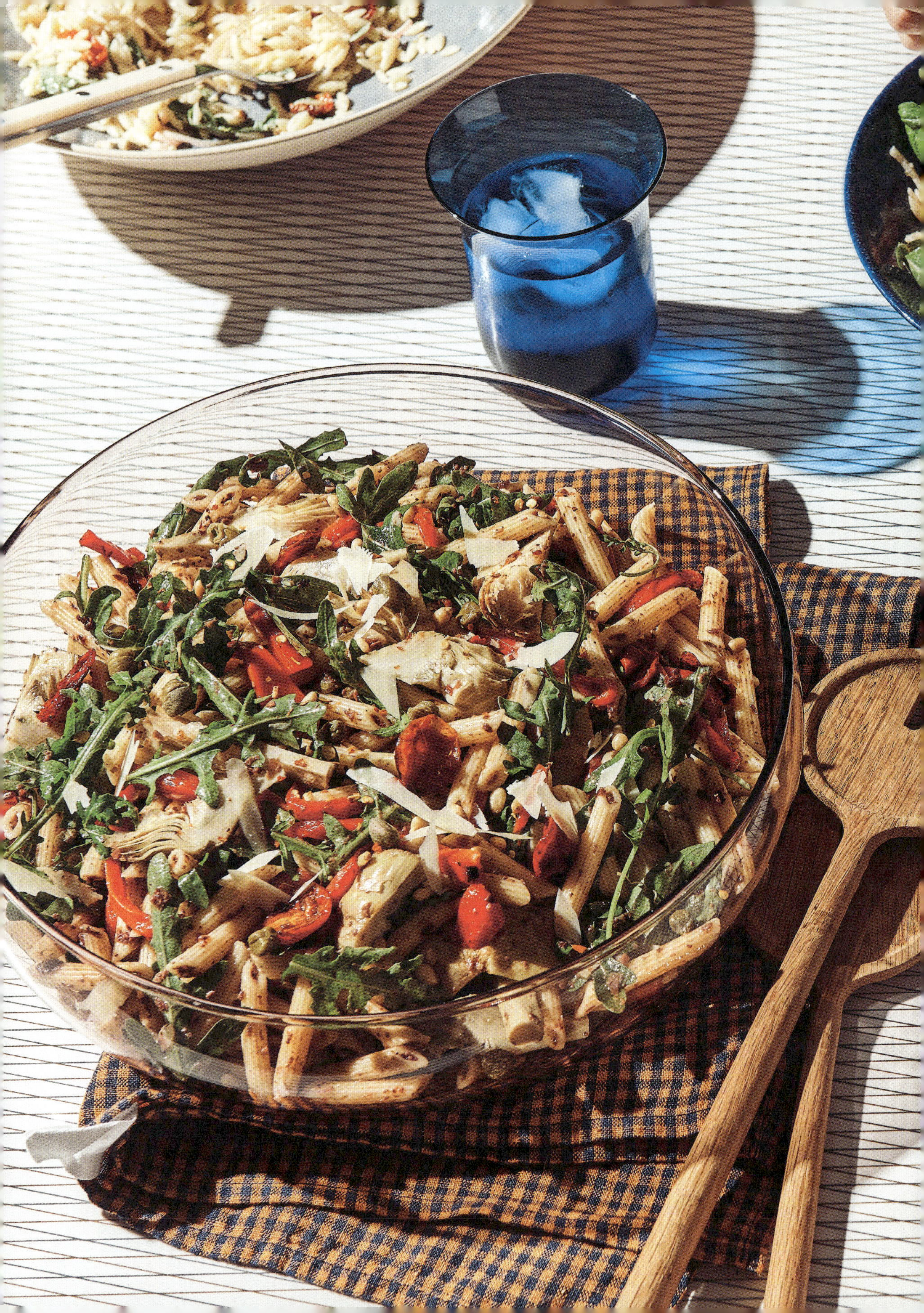

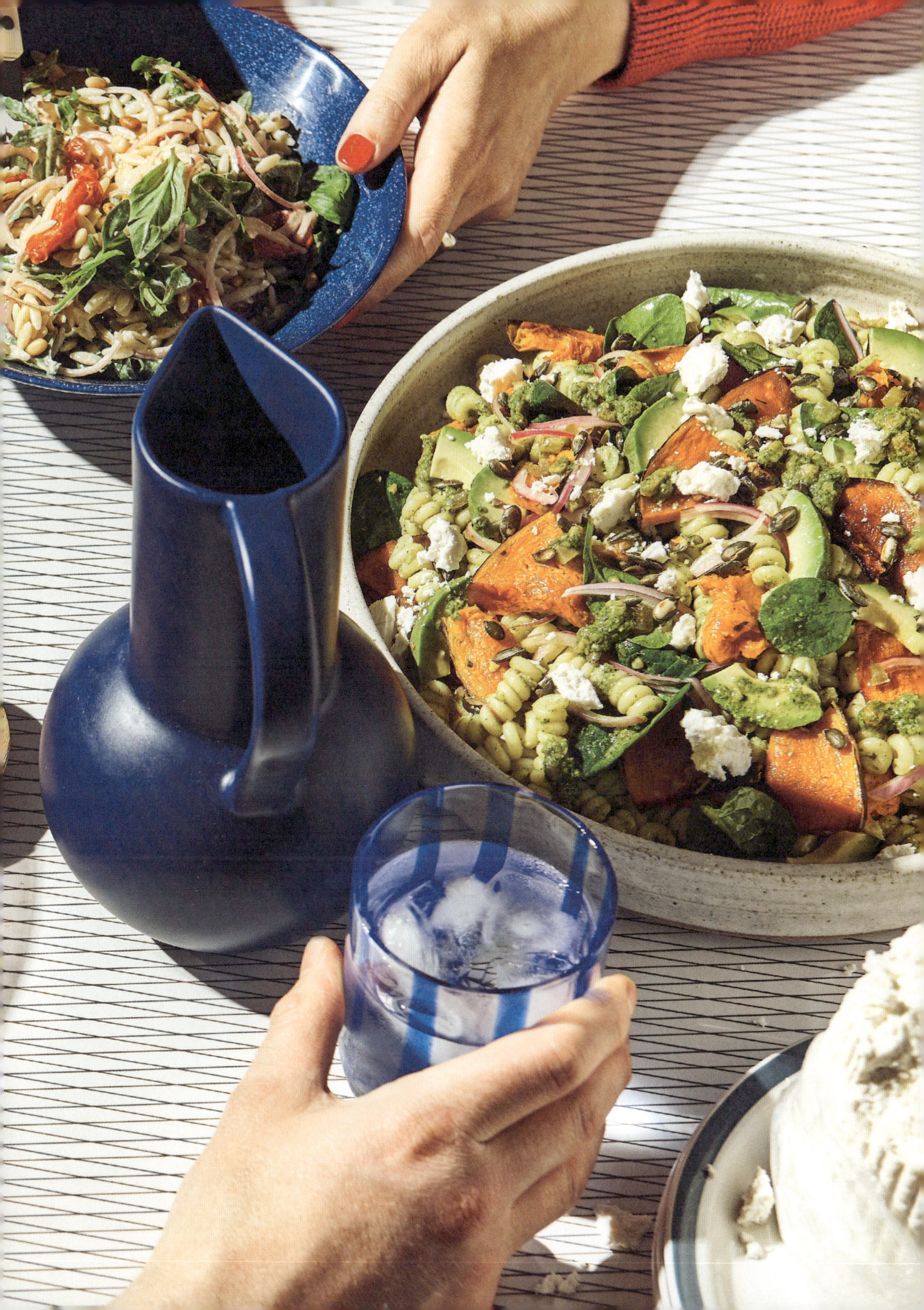

Roasted tomato orzo salad

Serves 4

An anytime wonder, this dependable salad roasts baby roma tomatoes to ensure they are at their flavourful best, no matter what time of year you are eating them. Paired with aromatic basil, peppery rocket (arugula) and comforting orzo, the creamy and tangy GOAT dressing ties everything together and leaves you wanting more with every mouthful. This is one of those salads that can be served hot, cold, or at room temperature.

Dressing

1 quantity The GOAT dressing (page 43)

Salad

1 French shallot, very finely sliced
2 tablespoons sherry vinegar
3 cups (400 g/14 oz) baby roma tomatoes
⅓ cup (80 ml/2½ fl oz) olive oil
½ teaspoon sugar
½ teaspoon salt
1 cup (200 g/7 oz) orzo or risoni
2 handfuls (60 g/2 oz) basil leaves, plus extra for garnish
60 g (2 oz) rocket (arugula), roughly chopped
¼ cup (40 g/1½ oz) pine nuts, toasted
freshly cracked black pepper, to serve

Preheat the oven to 160°C (320°F).

Put the shallot and sherry vinegar in a small bowl, toss to combine, and set aside.

Cut the tomatoes in half lengthwise, placing them in a bowl as you go. Add 1 tablespoon of the olive oil with the sugar and salt. Stir to combine, then place the tomatoes on a baking sheet, cut side up, and season with greshly ground black pepper. Roast for 40 minutes, or until tomatoes are shrivelled and starting to blacken, then set aside to cool.

Bring a large saucepan of salted water to a boil. Add the orzo and cook for 10 minutes. Once cooked, drain and rinse in lots of cold water until cool. Allow to drain, then combine with two-thirds of the dressing, the shallots (hold the vinegar), basil leaves and rocket.

When ready to serve, transfer half the pasta to a serving dish and top with half the tomatoes and half the pine nuts. Repeat with the remaining pasta, tomatoes, pine nuts and dressing. Garnish with more black pepper and a few extra basil leaves.

Epic tip

Got leftovers? They'll be great, however the pasta does absorb a lot of the dressing, so you may want to loosen the salad with a little bit of olive oil before serving.

Swaps

Capers, olives, parsley, baby spinach, kale, feta, pistachios all work wonderfully in this salad.

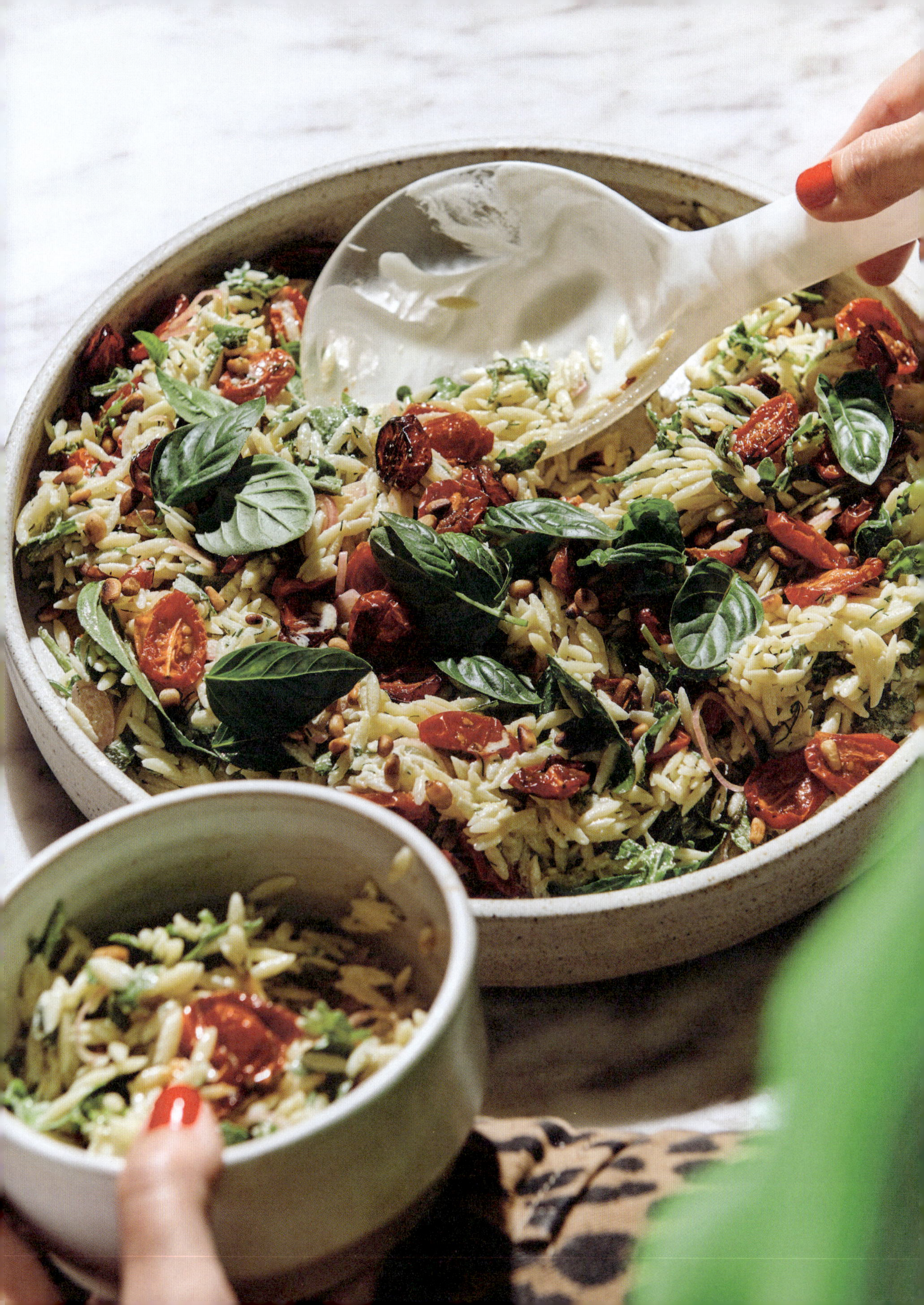

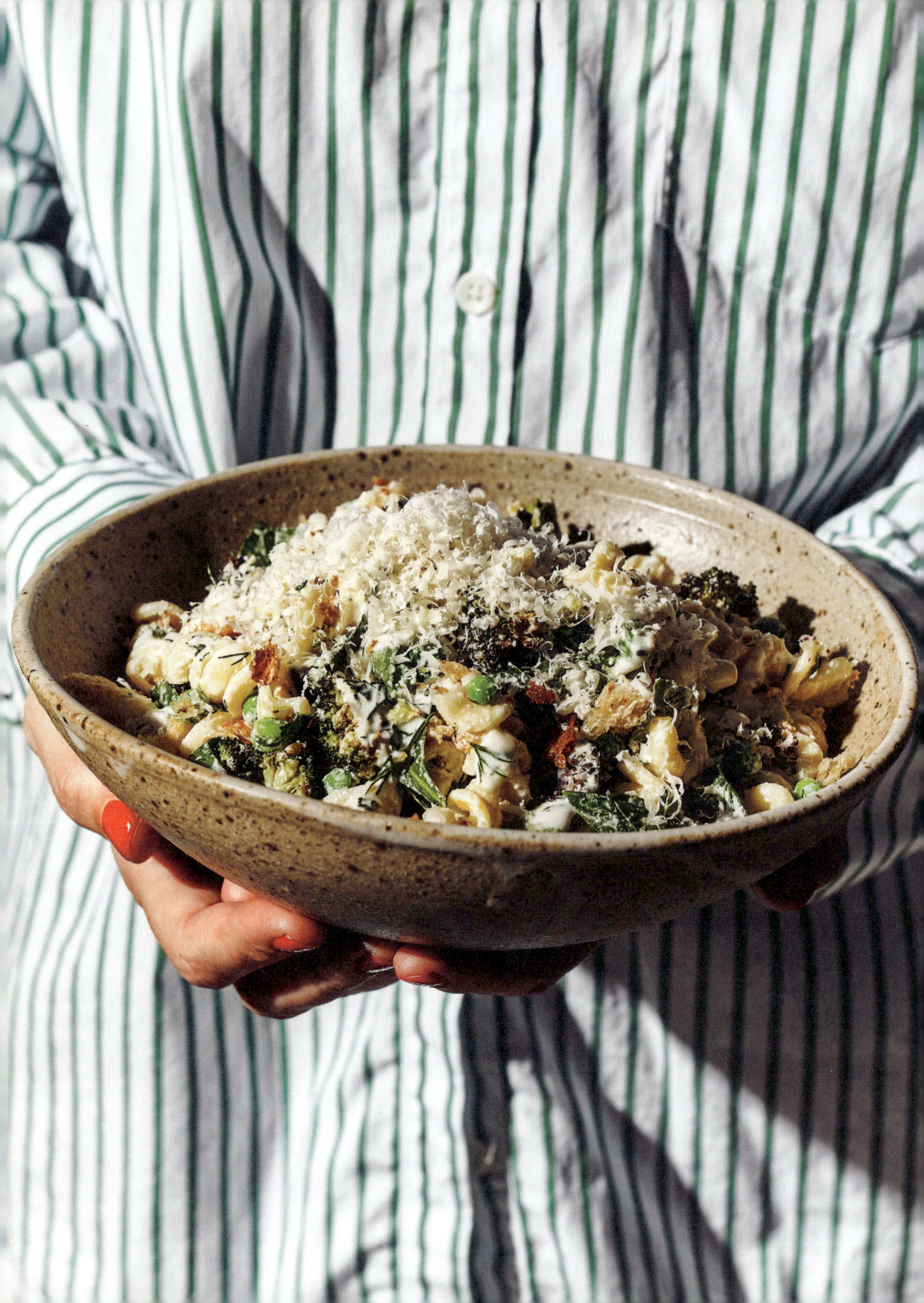

Charred broccoli and pea pasta salad

Serves 3–4

Charring broccoli gives it a rich and smoky flavour and transforms the florets to tender morsels with crispy edges. This pairs perfectly with the contrasting textures of orecchiette, peas and crispy pangratatto, and the creamy, tangy, flavour-bomb that is The GOAT dressing which elevates it all, bringing you a pasta salad that is far greater than the sum of its parts.

Dressing
1 quantity The GOAT dressing (page 43)

Salad
300 g (10½ oz) dried pasta
1 cup (150 g/5½ oz) frozen peas
1 head broccoli
olive oil, for cooking
2 handfuls of baby spinach or rocket (arugula), chopped
Pangratatto (page 48), to serve
freshly grated parmesan cheese, to serve

Preheat the oven to 180–200°C (360–390°F), and bring a large saucepan of water to a boil.

Once the water is boiling, add the pasta and cook according to the directions on the packet, adding the peas for the final 2 minutes of cooking. Once cooked, drain, allow to sit for a couple of minutes, then shake off any excess water and transfer to a bowl. Add two-thirds of the dressing, stir to combine, then set aside while you prepare the remaining ingredients.

Cut the broccoli into *truly* bite-sized florets. Take your time with this – the smaller they are, the more enjoyable the salad will be. Put the florets in a large mixing bowl along with enough olive oil to coat and a pinch of salt and freshly cracked black pepper and toss to combine. Spread onto a large baking tray, making sure not to overcrowd it (use two trays if necessary), then bake for 15–20 minutes, or until lightly blackened, tossing once during the cooking time. Allow to cool on the tray for 10 minutes.

When ready to serve, place half the pasta on a platter and top with half the baby spinach or rocket, half the cooked broccoli and half the pangratatto. Repeat with the remaining pasta, spinach/rocket, broccoli and dressing, then top with a cloud of parmesan and the remaining pangratatto.

Epic tip
Got leftovers? They'll be delish, excellent, but potentially dry as the pasta has a tendency to soak up its dressing. If this is the case, just add a little extra olive oil or, if making for work lunches, reserve some dressing until ready to serve.

Lemon ricotta pasta salad

Serves 3–4

For a recipe with so few ingredients, this pasta salad packs a punch. The bright, lemony ricotta and the sweetness and crunch of maple walnuts pair perfectly with the bitter radicchio and the freshness of parsley and spinach, creating a simple yet flavourful affair that's lifted by a classic and dependable balsamic dressing. It's a minimalist's dream.

Dressing
1 quantity Basic balsamic dressing (page 39)

Salad
300 g (10½ oz) dry pasta
125 g (4½ oz) ricotta
juice and zest of 1 lemon
1 garlic clove, microplaned
50 g (1¾ oz) parmesan cheese
½ fennel bulb, sliced paper thin, some fronds reserved
2 large handfuls (60 g/2 oz) radicchio, leaves torn
2 large handfuls (60 g/2 oz) flat-leaf parsley, chiffonade
1 cup (100 g/3½ oz) Maple walnuts (page 51)
chilli flakes, to serve

Bring a large saucepan of water to a boil. Add the pasta and cook according to the directions on the packet. Drain and shake dry, then toss in 3 tablespoons of the balsamic dressing. Set aside to cool.

Combine the ricotta with the lemon juice and zest, and the garlic. Set aside.

Add the parmesan to the cooled, dressed pasta and stir to combine. Add the fennel, radicchio and most of the parsley and the maple walnuts to the pasta and stir to combine.

Place half the pasta in a serving dish. Dot with teaspoons of ricotta and then top with the remaining pasta and ricotta. Top with remaining herbs and walnuts, add chilli flakes to taste, then drizzle with additional balsamic vinaigrette.

Swaps
This also works well with halved grape tomatoes, olives, capers.

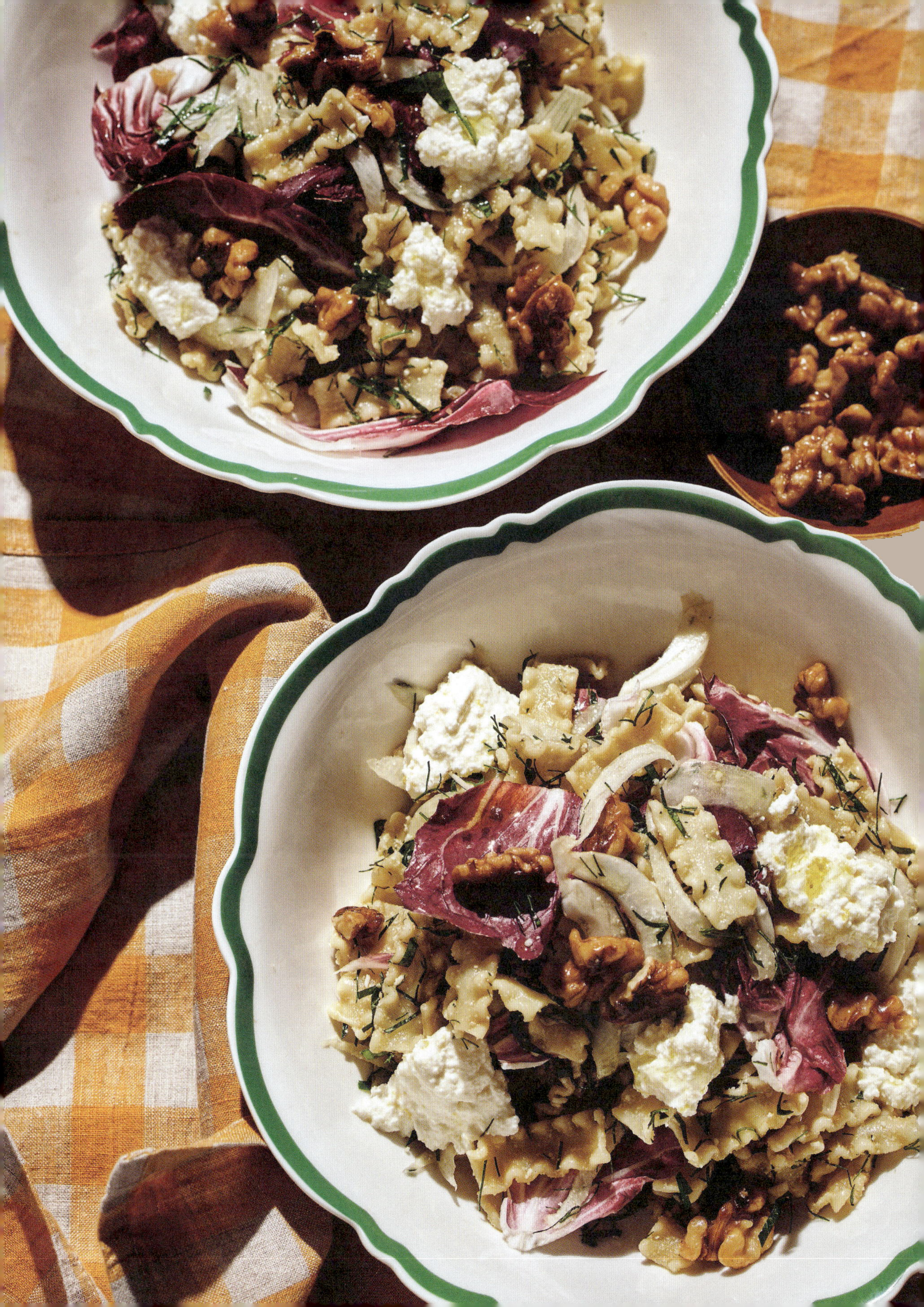

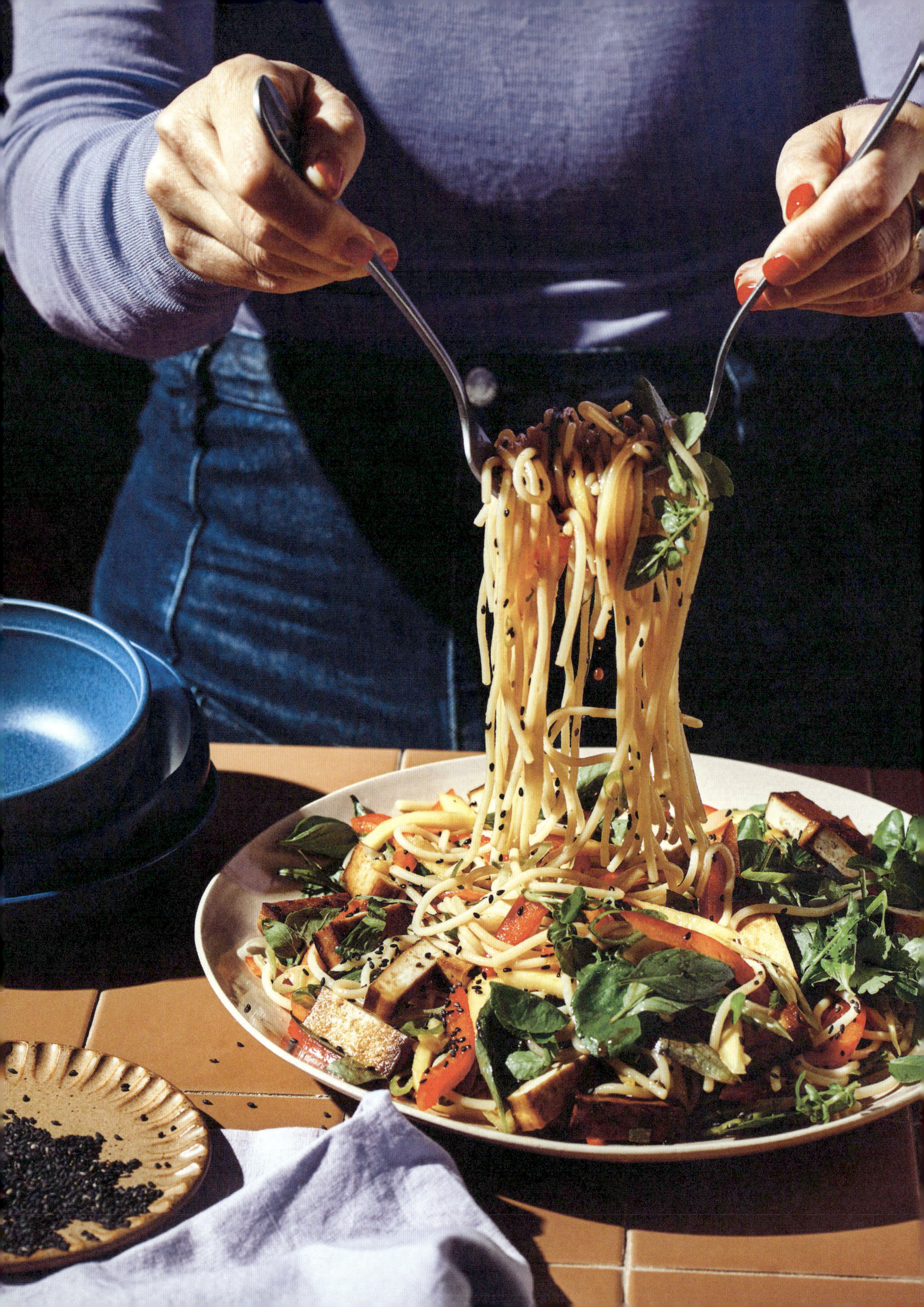

Rice noodle salad with marinated tofu

Serves 4

Perfect for a hot day, this light but filling noodle salad pairs marinated tofu with the juicy sweetness of mango, then uses the tofu marinade as the salad dressing – genius, no? Fresh herbs, colourful capsicum (bell pepper) and sweet, soothing mango tie together to create a refreshing summer salad that can be eaten for lunch or dinner.

Tofu/Dressing

2 tablespoons soy sauce
1 tablespoon lemon juice
1 tablespoon sesame oil
1 tablespoon maple syrup
1 teaspoon tamarind paste
400 g (14 oz) block firm tofu, drained, pressed and cut into 1 cm (½ in) thick slabs

Salad

300 g (10½ oz) rice noodles
1 red capsicum (bell pepper), julienned
1 mango, julienned
large handful watercress, leaves picked
1–2 large handfuls coriander (cilantro), Vietnamese mint or Thai basil, plus extra to garnish
2–5 spring onions (scallions), sliced
2 tablespoons black sesame seeds

Combine the soy sauce, lemon juice, sesame oil, maple syrup and tamarind in a dish that will comfortably fit your cut tofu. Whisk to combine, then add the tofu slabs, turning and moving around until both sides are completely covered in marinade. Set aside for at least 30 minutes, or overnight if possible.

Bring a large saucepan of water to a boil and place a large frying pan over a medium–high heat.

Once the pan is hot, add a tablespoon of neutral cooking oil to the bottom of the pan. Add the tofu and cook for 3–5 minutes until starting to brown on the underside. Keep the marinade as you will use this for dressing the salad. Gently flip and cook the other side for another 3–5 minutes, or until golden brown. Once cooked, transfer to a paper towel and allow to cool for 5 minutes, then slice into 1 cm (½ in) wide strips.

Once the water has boiled, cook the noodles according to the directions on the packet, then drain and rinse under lots of cold running water until cool. Drain well, then transfer to a large mixing bowl. Add the remaining tofu marinade and toss to combine. Taste, and add more soy if needed.

Add the capsicum, mango, watercress, herbs, spring onions and sesame seeds to the noodles, and use your hands to combine everything together. Transfer to serving dishes and top with cooked tofu and additional herbs.

Swaps

1. This is great with a drizzle of Japanese mayo, too.
2. While the mango is incredible, it's not a dealbreaker if you want to make this when they're out of season.

Pasta and noodles

Spicy peanut udon salad

Serves 2–4

This dependable noodle salad combines spicy peanut noodles with flavoursome marinated tofu, along with fresh veggies and roasted peanuts for crunch. The addition of zesty lime brings depth and vibrancy to every bite, making for a moreish and satisfying balance of flavours and textures.

Dressing

1 quantity Spicy peanut dressing (page 42)

Tofu

2 tablespoons soy sauce
1 tablespoon rice vinegar
1 tablespoon sesame oil
1 teaspoon freshly grated garlic
1 teaspoon freshly grated ginger
1 × 400 g (14 oz) block tofu, drained and pressed, cut into 1 cm (½ in) thick slabs

Salad

200 g (7 oz) rice or udon noodles
1 head of cos (romaine) lettuce, very thinly sliced
1 carrot, peeled and julienned
1 Lebanese (short) cucumber, seeds removed and julienned
3 spring onions (scallions), thinly sliced
large handful roasted peanuts
large handful coriander (cilantro) leaves, finely chopped
juice of 1 lime, to serve

For the tofu, combine all the marinade ingredients in a small dish that will fit your tofu once cut. Whisk to combine, then add the tofu slabs, turning and moving around until both sides are completely covered in marinade. Set aside for at least 30 minutes, or overnight if possible.

Bring a large pot of water to a boil. Once the water has boiled, cook the noodles according to the directions on the packet, then drain and rinse under lots of cold running water until cool. Drain well, then transfer to a large mixing bowl. Add half the dressing and toss to combine.

Place a large frying pan over a medium–high heat. Once the frying pan is hot, add a tablespoon of neutral cooking oil to the bottom of the hot frying pan. Add tofu – marinade and all – and cook for 3–5 minutes, until the tofu starts to brown on the underside. Gently flip and cook the other side for another 3–5 minutes, or until golden brown. Once cooked, transfer to a paper towel and allow to cool for 5 minutes, then slice into 1 cm (½ in) wide strips.

Combine the noodles with the lettuce, carrot, cucumber, spring onions, most of the peanuts and most of the coriander. Stir to combine, then place half on a serving dish and top with half of the tofu. Repeat with the remaining noodles and tofu, then drizzle with the remaining dressing. Top with the remaining peanuts and coriander, and squeeze with lime right before serving.

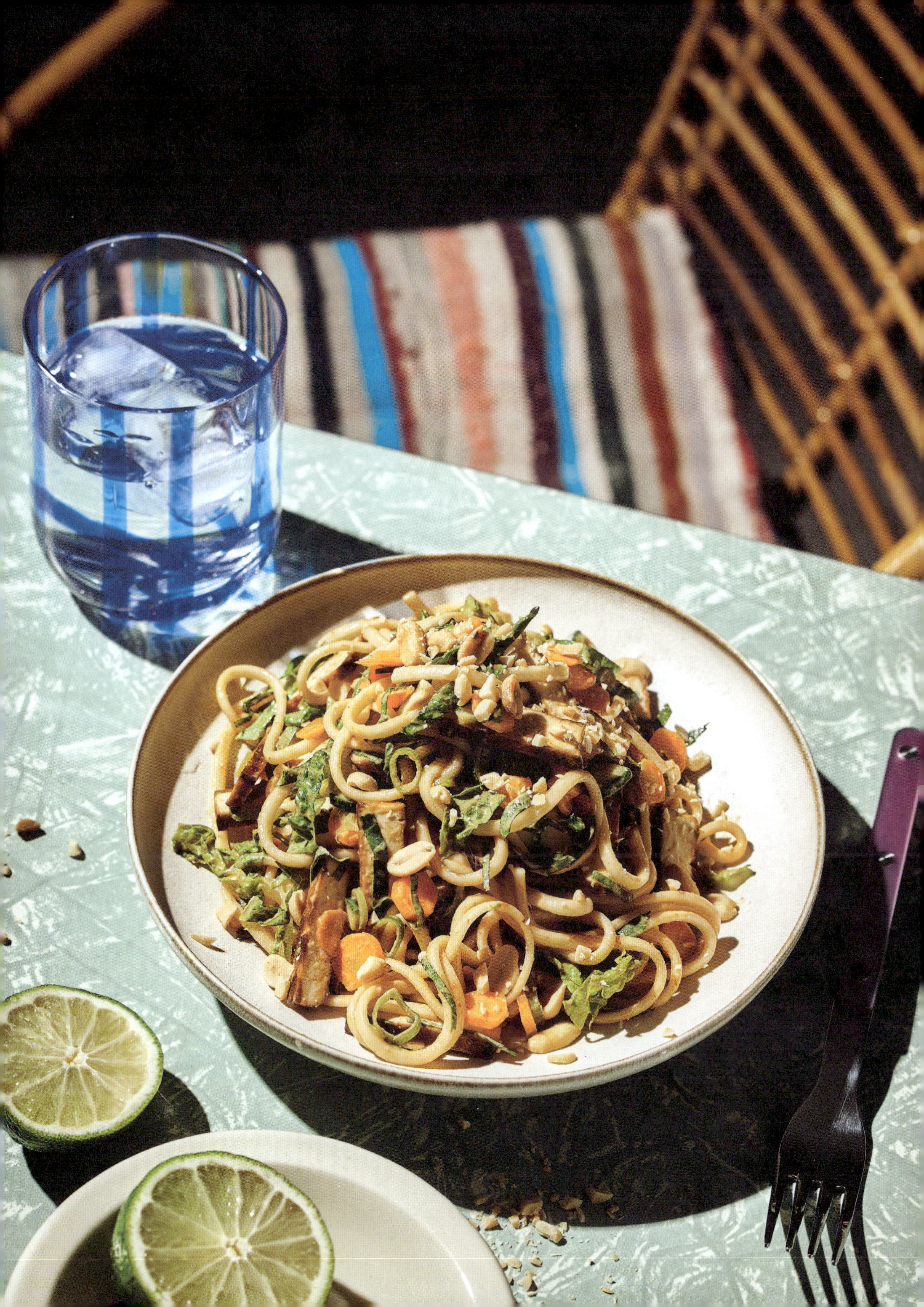

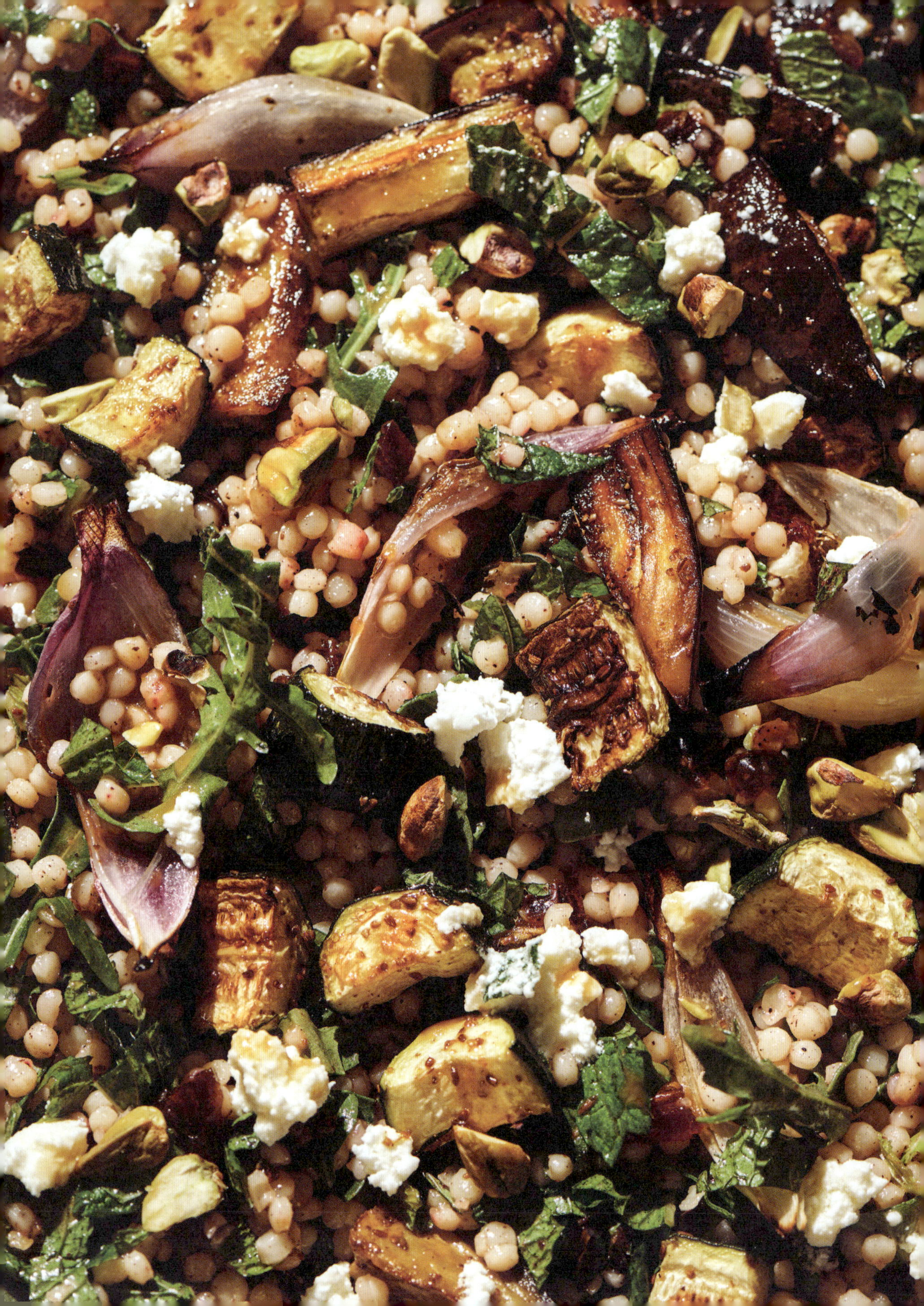

Roasted eggplant and zucchini with pearl couscous

Serves 3–4

This salad is perfect for when the weather is cool but you need a veggie hit. The hint of cumin, the sweetness of medjool dates and the soft tang of goat's cheese come together under a pomegranate dressing, making a dish that's comforting, moreish and rich in both flavour and texture.

Dressing

1 quantity Pomegranate dressing (page 42)

Salad

1 large eggplant (aubergine) (approx. 450 g/1 lb), cut into 2 cm (¾ in) dice
2 zucchinis (courgettes) (approx. 350 g/12½ oz) cut into 1 cm (½ in) semi-circles
1 red onion, peeled, roots intact, cut into eighths
3 tablespoons olive oil
1 teaspoon ground cumin
1 cup (180 g/6½ oz) pearl couscous
5 medjool dates, stones removed, finely chopped
2 large handfuls (60 g/2 oz) rocket (arugula), washed, spun dry, roughly chopped
handful mint or flat-leaf parsley, or both
120 g (4½ oz) soft goat's cheese
small handful pistachios, shells removed

Preheat the oven to 180–200°C (360–390°F) and bring a large saucepan of water to the boil.

Toss the eggplant, zucchini and red onion with the olive oil (eggplant is thirsty, so you'll be surprised at how much oil it absorbs), cumin and a generous pinch of salt, then spread on a baking tray and bake for 25–30 minutes, or until golden brown, giving them a toss about halfway through the cooking time. Once cooked, leave to cool on the tray for 10 minutes.

Once the water is boiling, add the couscous and a generous pinch of salt and cook for approximately 8 minutes, or until al dente. Once cooked, drain and rinse in cold water, then shake off any excess water and place in a large mixing bowl along with half the dressing and the chopped dates.

When ready to serve, add the rocket and herbs to the couscous and toss to combine. Transfer half the couscous to a serving platter and top with half the roasted veggies, goat's cheese and pistachios. Repeat with the remaining ingredients, drizzle with the rest of the dressing and serve. Leftovers keep well for between 2 to 4 days in the fridge and are best served at room temperature.

Pasta and noodles

Raw zucchini, pea and stracciatella

Serves 4–6

Paper-thin raw zucchini (courgette) has a crisp yet delicate texture that contrasts beautifully against tender peas and creamy stracciatella in this surprising and moreish salad. The addition of a salty tapenade brings a welcome pop of flavour that is both refreshing and filling.

Salad

200 g (7 oz) dried pasta
1 cup (150 g/5½ oz) frozen peas
1 tablespoon olive oil
2 zucchini (courgettes), julienned
juice of 1 lemon
large handful (60 g/2 oz) spinach
large handful (30 g/1 oz) flat-leaf parsley
100 g (3½ oz) stracciatella
handful (30 g/1 oz) flaked almonds, toasted

Chopped tapenade

1 tablespoon olive oil
60 g/2 oz pitted kalamata olives, roughly chopped
handful (30 g/1 oz) flat-leaf parsley, very finely chopped
zest of 1 lemon
1 teaspoon microplaned garlic

Bring a large saucepan of water to a boil. Add the pasta and a generous pinch of salt, and cook according to the directions on the packet, adding the peas for the final 2 minutes of cooking time.

Toss the zucchini in the lemon juice, and set aside until ready to use.

Once the pasta is cooked, drain and rinse in cold water, then shake off any excess water and place in a large mixing bowl along with the olive oil, zucchini, spinach and parsley. Stir to combine, and season generously with salt and pepper.

To make the chopped tapenade, combine all ingredients in a small bowl and set aside.

Place two-thirds of the pasta on a serving dish. Top with dollops of stracciatella and almonds, then follow with the remaining pasta, stracciatella and almonds. Spoon the tapenade over the top and serve immediately.

Epic tip

Got leftovers? They'll be yum as is, however in a surprise twist, I have also found that this dish makes for an excellent pasta bake if you wish to reheat leftovers in the oven – perfect for that time of year where it's hot one day and cold the next.

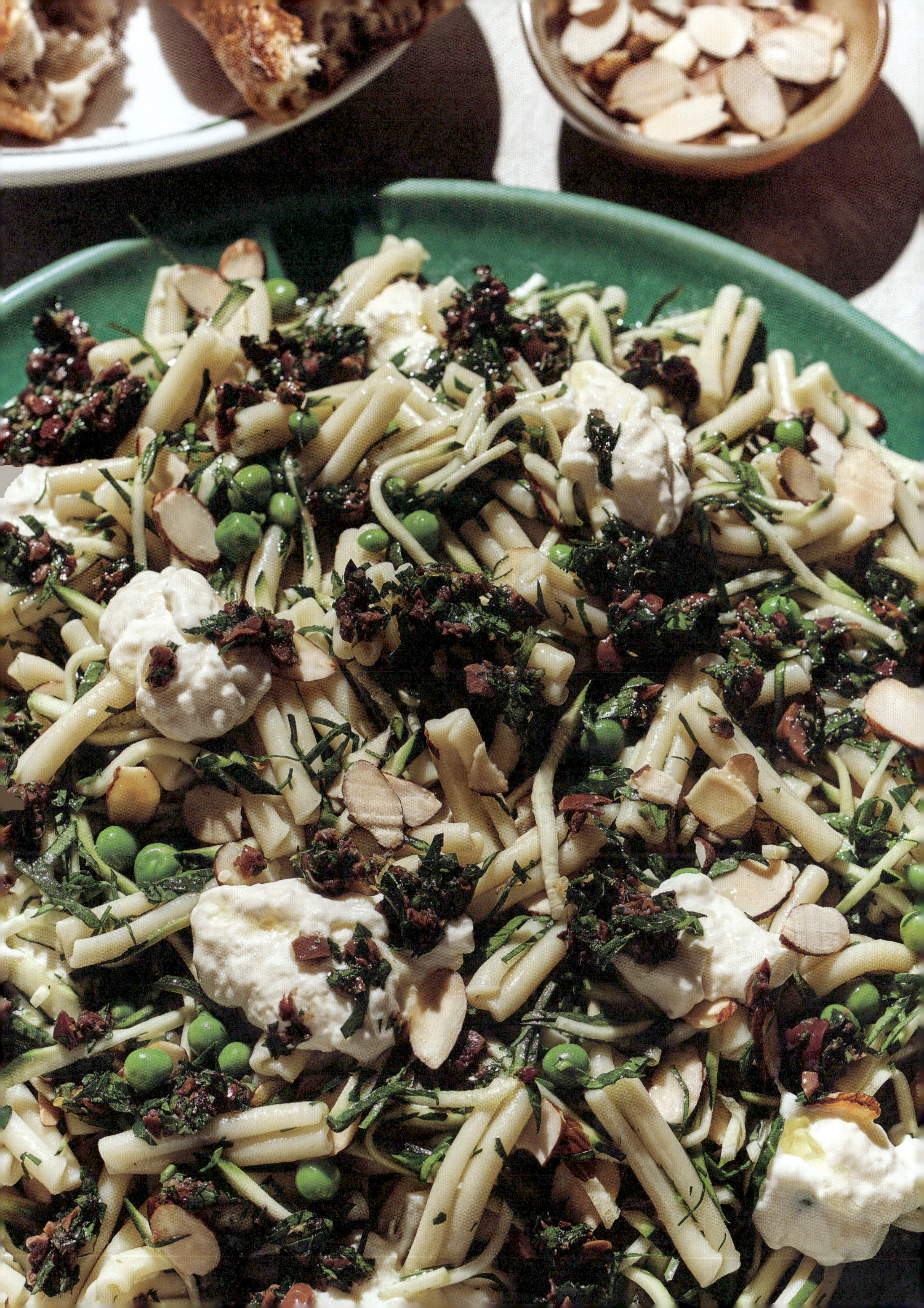

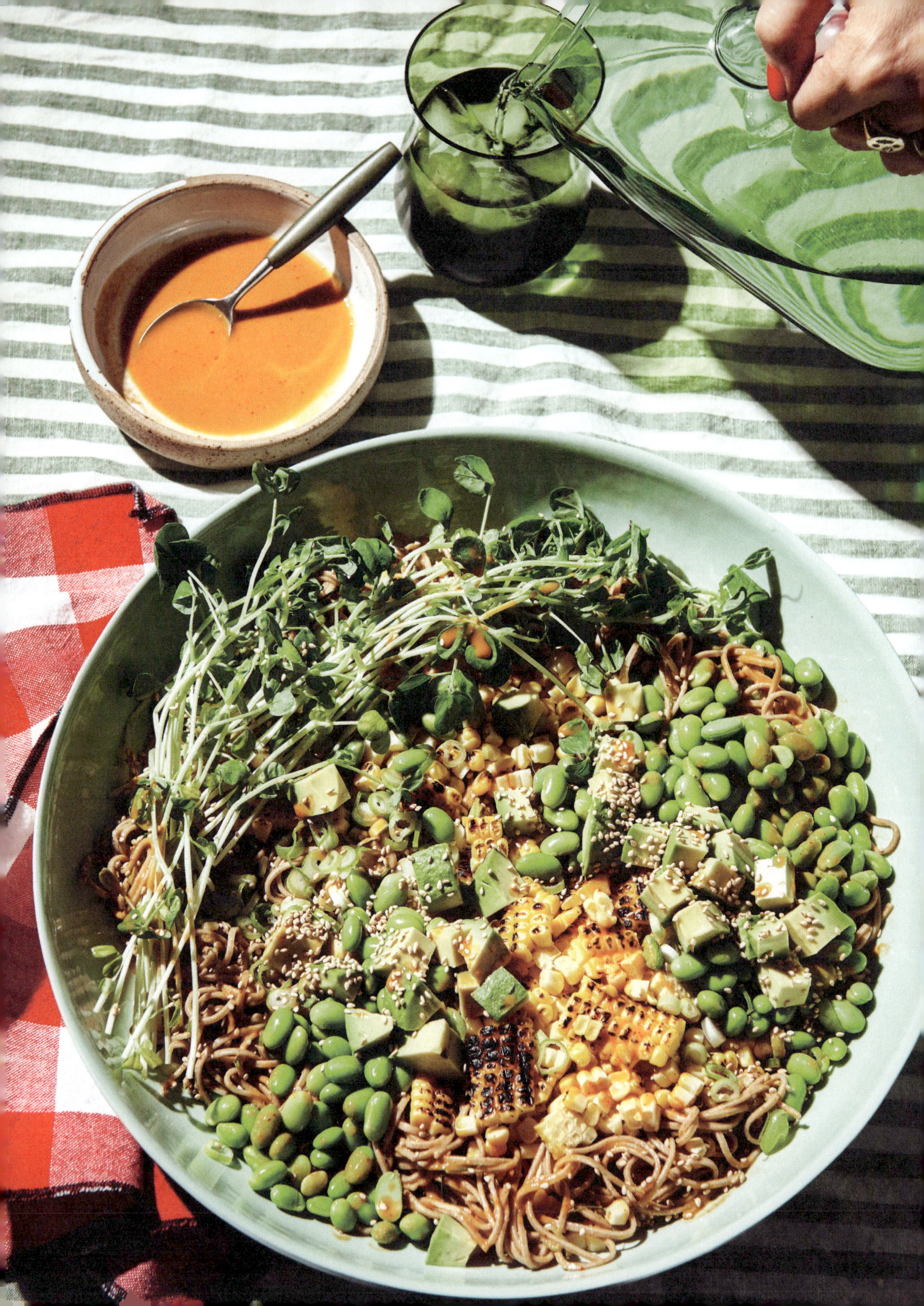

Soba salad with edamame and corn

Serves 4–6

Vibrant and delicious, here the spicy peanut dressing works its magic once again to render a simple collection of ingredients a showstopper. The mix of soba noodles paired with the sweetness of corn, the crunch of edamame and the creaminess of avocado is foolproof, but it's the unique flavour of makrut leaves that really elevates this dish.

Dressing
1 quantity Spicy peanut dressing (page 42)

Salad
200 g (7 oz) shelled edamame beans
300 g (10½ oz) soba noodles
2 large handfuls sprouts
4 makrut leaves, very thinly sliced
2 ears of corn, husks removed and kernels cut from cob
4 spring onions (scallions), sliced
1 ripe avocado, diced
1 tablespoon toasted sesame seeds

If your edamame aren't already defrosted, place them in a heatproof bowl, cover with boiling water and allow to sit for 2 minutes. Drain, refresh with cold water, then drain again and set aside.

Bring a large saucepan of water to a boil. Add the noodles and cook according to the directions on the packet, then drain and run under cool water. Shake to remove as much excess water as possible, then transfer to a mixing bowl and add the makrut leaves and most of the dressing. Stir to combine, then transfer to a serving dish.

Cook the corn kernels in a frying pan over a medium heat until slightly blackened. Add to the noodles, along with the edamame, spring onions, avocado, sprouts and sesame seeds. Lightly toss to combine and serve.

Epic tip
Got leftovers? They're best eaten on the day of cooking. Leftovers are yummy, but depending on the brand, the noodles may stick together. They can be loosened with a little water.

Swaps
Use spinach or watercress in place of sprouts, if you prefer. These can be chopped and stirred in with the noodles before topping with the other goodies.

Spicy soy noodle salad with warm tofu puffs

Serves 2

We return to this salad time and time again because it is so quick and easy, and because my kids love the tofu puffs.

As lifelong vegetarians, tofu nuggets are to my kids what chicken nuggets are to many others. For that reason, while this recipe calls for ten tofu puffs, I almost always cook the entire packet, as I know they will be eaten.

Dressing
- 1 tablespoon soy sauce
- 1 tablespoon lemon juice
- 1 tablespoon olive oil
- 1 tablespoon toasted sesame oil
- 1 teaspoon sambal oelek
- 1 teaspoon maple syrup

Salad
- 150 g (5½ oz) soba noodles
- 10 tofu puffs (or just cook the whole packet because, yum)
- 2 handfuls baby spinach, sliced
- 1 tablespoon hemp seeds, toasted
- 10 baby roma tomatoes, halved lengthwise
- 2 spring onions (scallions), sliced
- small handful coriander (cilantro), Vietnamese mint or Thai basil
- ½ avocado, diced (optional)

Preheat the oven to 180–200°C (360–390°F) and bring a large saucepan of water to a boil. Once the water is boiling, cook the noodles according to the directions on the packet, then drain, rinse in lots of cold water, and soak in a bowl of cold water until you are ready to use them.

Once the oven is hot, place the tofu puffs on a baking tray and cook for 5–10 minutes. (I find they are fine after 5 minutes if you are too hungry to wait, but are better after 10 minutes.) Remove from the oven and set aside. These are best warm, so if you're not making the salad now, hold off on heating them until you are ready to serve. They can also be cooked in an air fryer for 5 minutes.

When ready to use, drain the noodles, shake off excess water, then transfer to a mixing bowl along with the spinach, hemp seeds and half the dressing. Toss to combine, then split the noodles between two serving bowls. Toss the baby roma tomatoes and avocado in the remaining dressing (use the same bowl the noodles were in) then add to the salad bowls along with the spring onions and herbs. Once the tofu is cool enough to touch, slice into thin squares and place on top of the salad.

Devour.

Swaps

1. This is also good with the Spicy soy dressing (page 43), but it's best to make the dressing ahead of time to let the flavours mingle.

2. Try using marinated tofu – marinate it in this salad dressing like the recipes on page 153 and 154. Add literally any veggie – even if it's weird, it will be great. Roasted pumpkin (squash) – yes. Grilled asparagus – also yes. Miso eggplant (aubergine) – absof*ckinglutely yes!

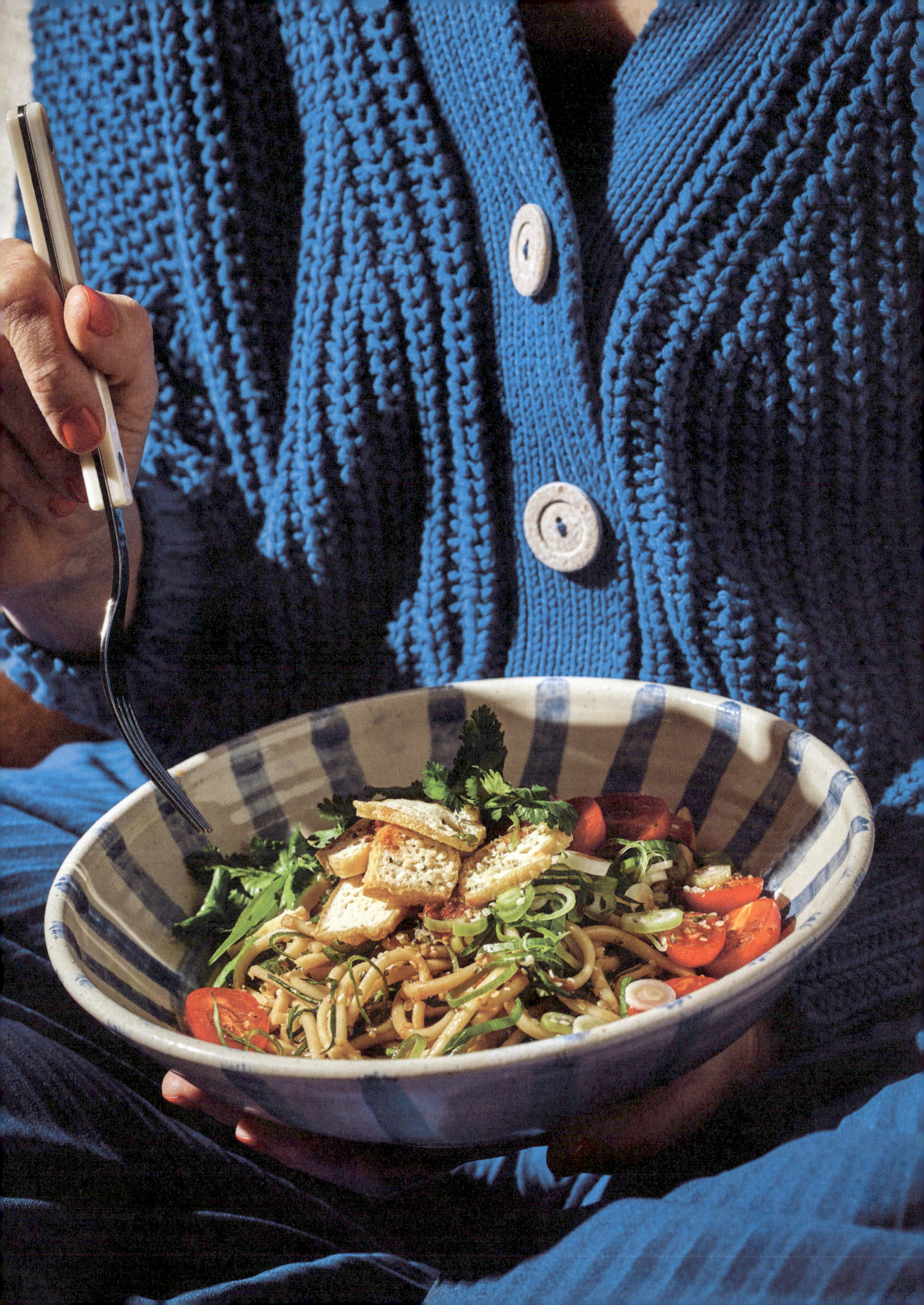

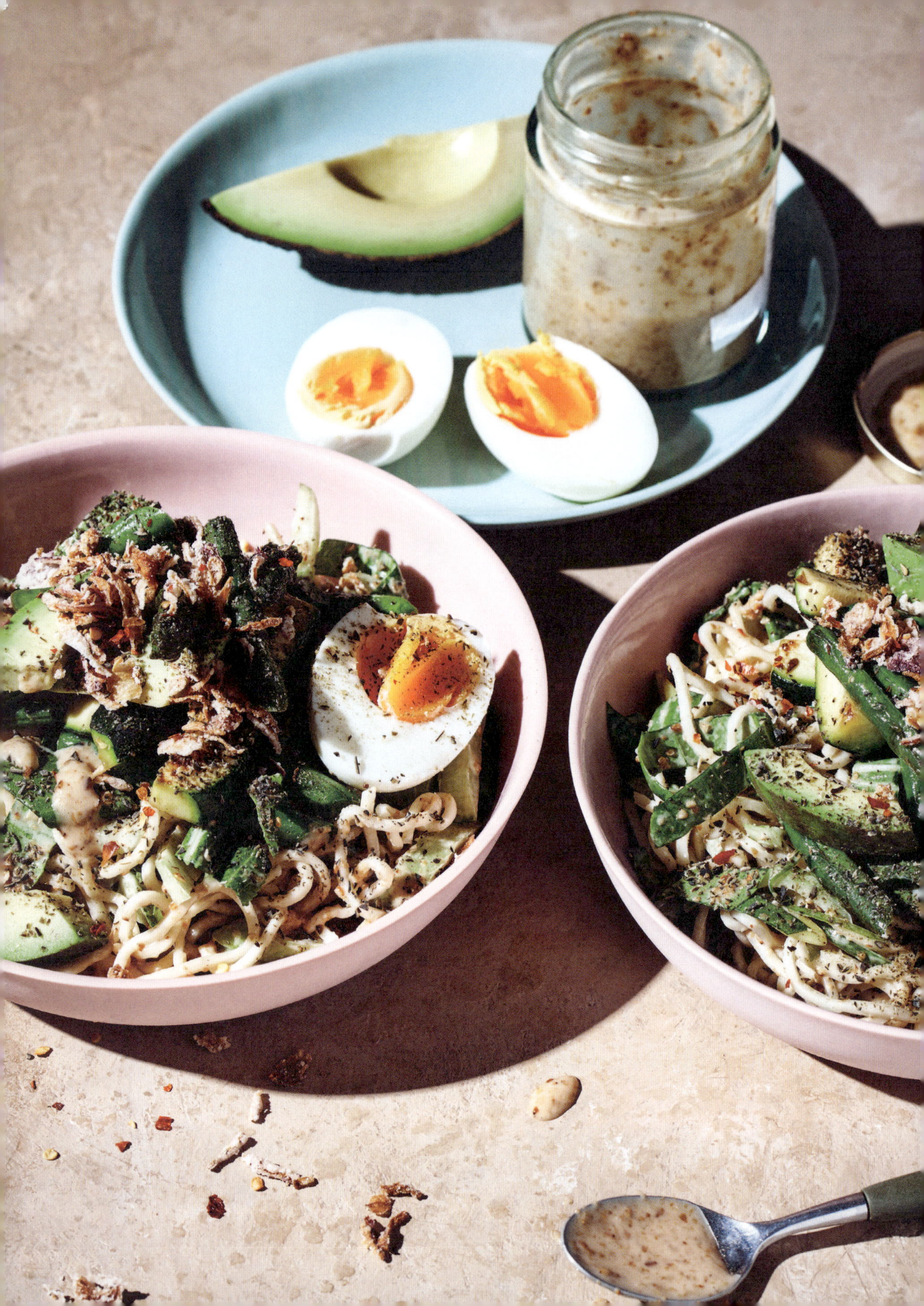

Warm greens noodle salad

Serves 2–3

This is one of those salads that toes the line between salad and not-salad territory. Is it a salad? Or is it a noodle dish parading as a salad? Either way, it's DELICIOUS, and an excellent way to get a green fix when it's too cold for a classic salad.

Dressing

1 quantity Sesame mayo (page 42)

Salad

3 eggs
150 g (5½ oz) noodles (soba are great, but wheat noodles are wonderful here too)
1 bunch asparagus (approx. 6 spears)
1 zucchini (courgette)
100 g (3½ oz) green beans
2 spring onions (scallions)
1 tablespoon olive oil
1 bunch bok choi
½ ripe avocado, quartered
crispy shallots or chilli flakes, to garnish (optional)

Bring a small saucepan of water and a large saucepan of water to a boil. Prepare an ice bath for the boiled eggs. Boil the eggs in the small saucepan according to the method on page 34 and then drain, cool and peel. Once peeled, cut the eggs into quarters.

Once the large saucepan of water is boiling, cook the noodles according to the directions on the packet. Drain and rinse in cold water, then set aside.

Cut the woody ends from the asparagus, then cut into 4 cm (1½ in) pieces, on a diagonal. Cut the zucchini into batons about the same length, then top and tail the beans and cut the roots and greens off the spring onions.

Toss the veg in a mixing bowl with the olive oil and a pinch of salt, then sauté in a frying pan over a medium heat, turning often until brown all over. You may need to do this in batches to prevent overcrowding.

Slice the spring onions, then add to the noodles along with the spinach and half the sesame mayo. Use your hands or a fork to combine, then transfer to serving bowls. Top with warm veg, drizzle with the remaining dressing, then top with avocado and eggs, and crispy shallots or chilli flakes – or both.

Epic tips

1. To pump up the protein, serve this with any of the tofu recipes from pages 30 to 32 or throw some tofu puffs in a hot oven for 10 minutes. Add 50–100 g (1¾–3½ oz) shelled edamame beans.

2. If it's a cold day and you want to roast the veg, preheat the oven to 200–220°C (390–430°F). Toss the broccoli and zucchini in a mixing bowl with a lick of olive oil and a pinch of salt. Spread on a baking tray and roast for 20 minutes, tossing once during the cooking time.

SHOWSTOPPING

SIDES

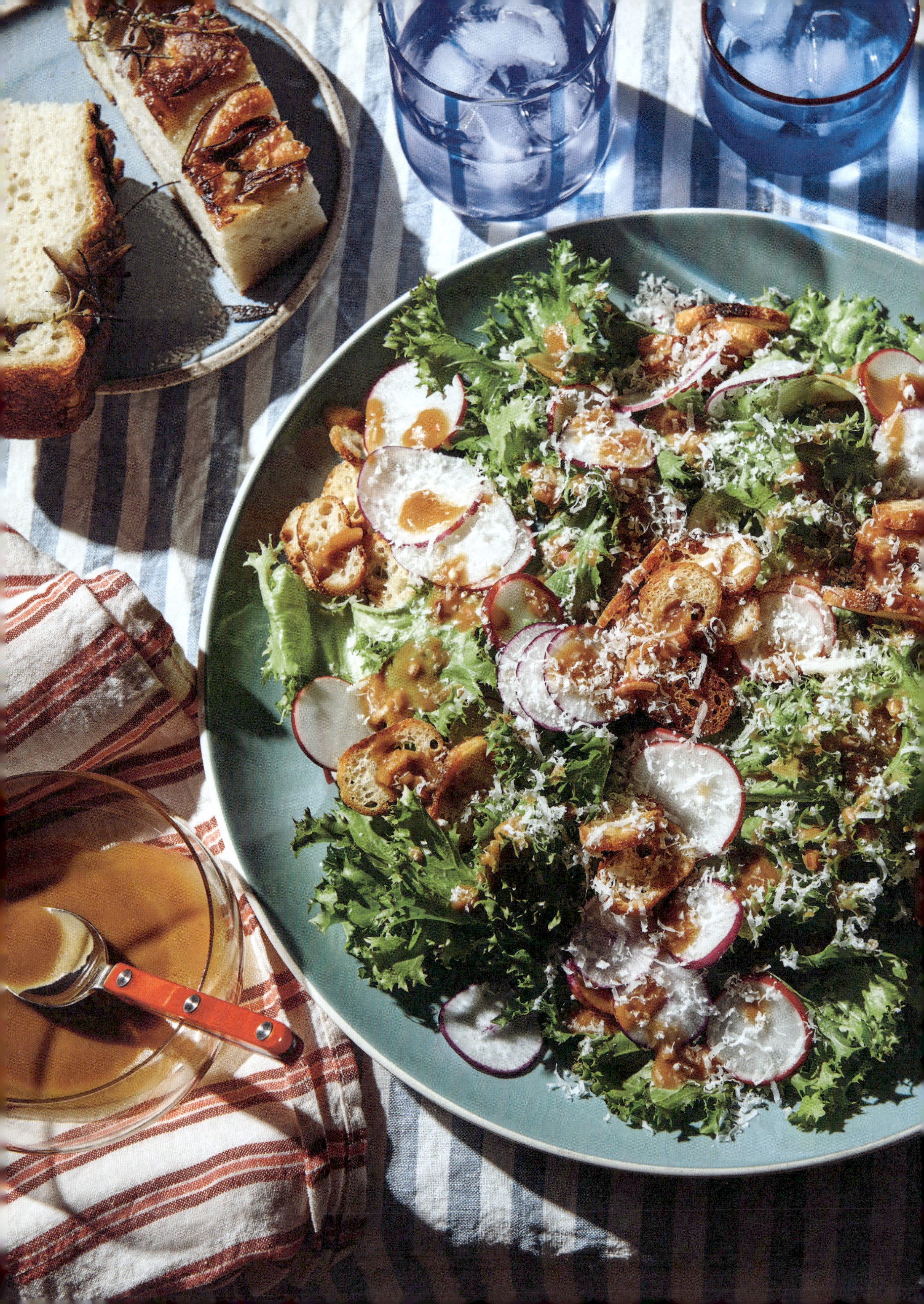

While the majority of the salads in this book can be eaten as standalone meals, this chapter is for when you need something to complement the main affair.

For that reason, this chapter is about breaking all the rules. Many of these recipes don't contain protein *or* body. One of them doesn't even contain a leaf – *gasp*! Instead, they celebrate simple combinations of the freshest ingredients and share ideas to make them sing.

Make these dishes to accompany your own favourite recipes at home, or take them to a barbecue or gathering where a side salad (or three!) is in order.

Alternatively, when you're in the mood for a low-fuss, delicious and feel-good dinner with friends, throw a couple of these sides together and order pizzas when everyone arrives.

Greens with avocado, pepitas and sesame seeds

Serves 4–6 as a side

Dressing
1 quantity Basic balsamic dressing (page 39)

Salad
1 head butter lettuce, frisee or any other lettuce of your liking
1 ripe avocado, sliced
large handful (30 g/1 oz) pepitas (pumpkin seeds), toasted
large handful (30 g/1 oz) sesame seeds, toasted

Wash, dry and spin the lettuce, then tear into bite-sized pieces. Toss in the dressing and place in a serving dish. Top with avocado and a sprinkle of salt, then scatter the seeds over the top, and serve.

Pictured overleaf →

Cos, parmesan, fried pasta, basil

Serves 4–6 as a side

Dressing
1 quantity The GOAT dressing (page 43)

Salad
1 tablespoon olive oil
1–2 handfuls leftover cooked pasta – a smaller, chewier variety works best here
1 head of baby cos (romaine) lettuce
½ head radicchio
2 tablespoons grated/crumbled parmesan cheese
large handful basil leaves

Heat the olive oil in a large frying pan over a medium–high heat. Add the pasta and jiggle the pan so that it is evenly spread out. You want each piece of pasta to be touching the bottom of the pan, rather than stacked on top of each other.

Allow to sit, untouched, for 2–3 minutes, or until the underside starts to turn golden and crispy. Toss, jiggle and flip so the other sides of the pasta can get a little golden and crispy too, then sprinkle with a generous pinch of salt, toss to combine, then set aside while you prepare the rest of the ingredients.

Wash, dry and spin the leaves, then tear into bite-sized pieces. Toss the leaves in the dressing and place in a serving dish. Top with half the parmesan and basil, then follow with the fried pasta. Add the remaining parmesan and basil over the top, then serve.

Epic tips
1. If you've never fried leftover cooked pasta, you are in for a treat. It takes on a whole new flavour and texture: crispy crunchy chewy. Frying is THE best way to upcycle leftover pasta IMO!
2. I prefer a smaller, chewier pasta. Use good quality if you can – cheap, thin pasta may stick and tear.

Pictured overleaf →

Kale and crouton side salad

Serves 4–6 as a side

Dressing
½ quantity The GOAT dressing (page 43)

Salad
1 bunch curly kale (approx. 8 large leaves)
salt
olive oil, for drizzling
Croutons (page 48), to serve

Remove the kale leaves from the tough stems, then tear into truly bite-sized pieces. This might feel like a bit of work, but it's worth it for all that extra surface area you'll have to soak up the garlicky, salty goodness of the dressing. Rinse thoroughly, spin dry, then place in a large bowl with a pinch of salt and a drizzle of olive oil. Massage and scrunch the leaves between your fingers for 2–3 minutes, until the kale starts to soften and wilt. Stir in the dressing and set aside.

To build your salad, place the massaged, dressed kale in a serving bowl and top with croutons. Drizzle with remaining dressing and garnish with dill, or any other herbs you have to hand.

Epic tips

1. This pairs well with the Tomato salad with fried capers and pine nuts (page 185). Also good with shaved parmesan. All over it. Pop it on before adding the croutons, and *voila*.
2. Massaging the kale helps to break down its tough cellulose structure and gives the kale a softer texture and a milder flavour.
3. Add a boiled egg, a tin of chickpeas or some grilled haloumi to pump up the protein.

Pictured overleaf →

Greens with radish, parmesan and garlic croutons

Serves 4–6 as a side

Dressing
1 quantity Basic balsamic dressing (page 39)

Salad
1 head of butter lettuce or frisee
1 bunch radishes, thinly sliced, leaves removed
2 tablespoons grated parmesan
100 g (3½ oz) Ficelle croutons (page 48)

Remove the leaves from the roots of the lettuce, wash and either pat or spin dry, then tear the leaves into bite-sized pieces.

Put the lettuce leaves in a large mixing bowl. Add most of the dressing and toss to coat the leaves, then add parmesan and toss again, ensuring the leaves are evenly coated.

Transfer to a serving dish, add the radish and croutons, and drizzle with the remaining dressing. Serve.

← Pictured on p. 168

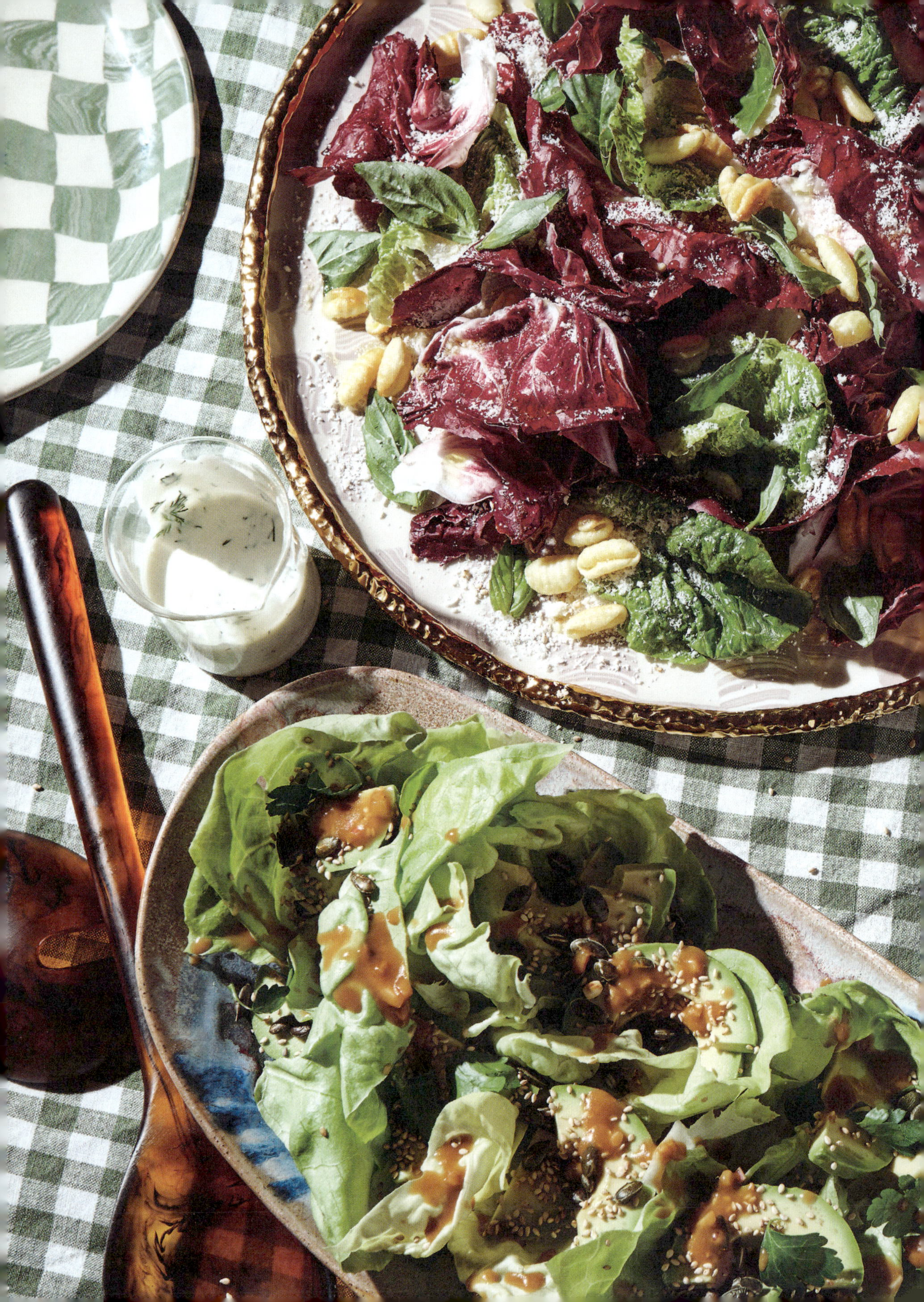

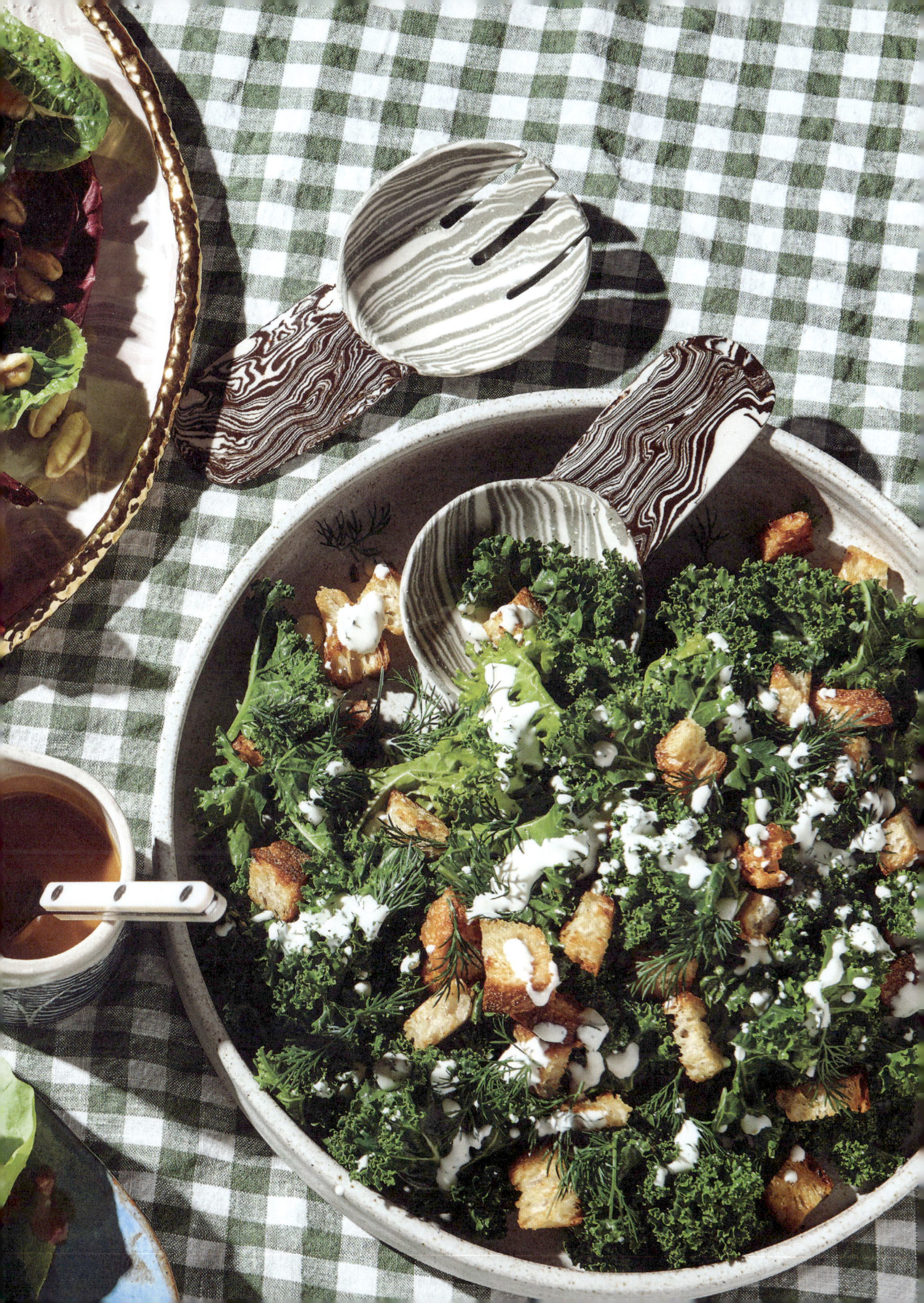

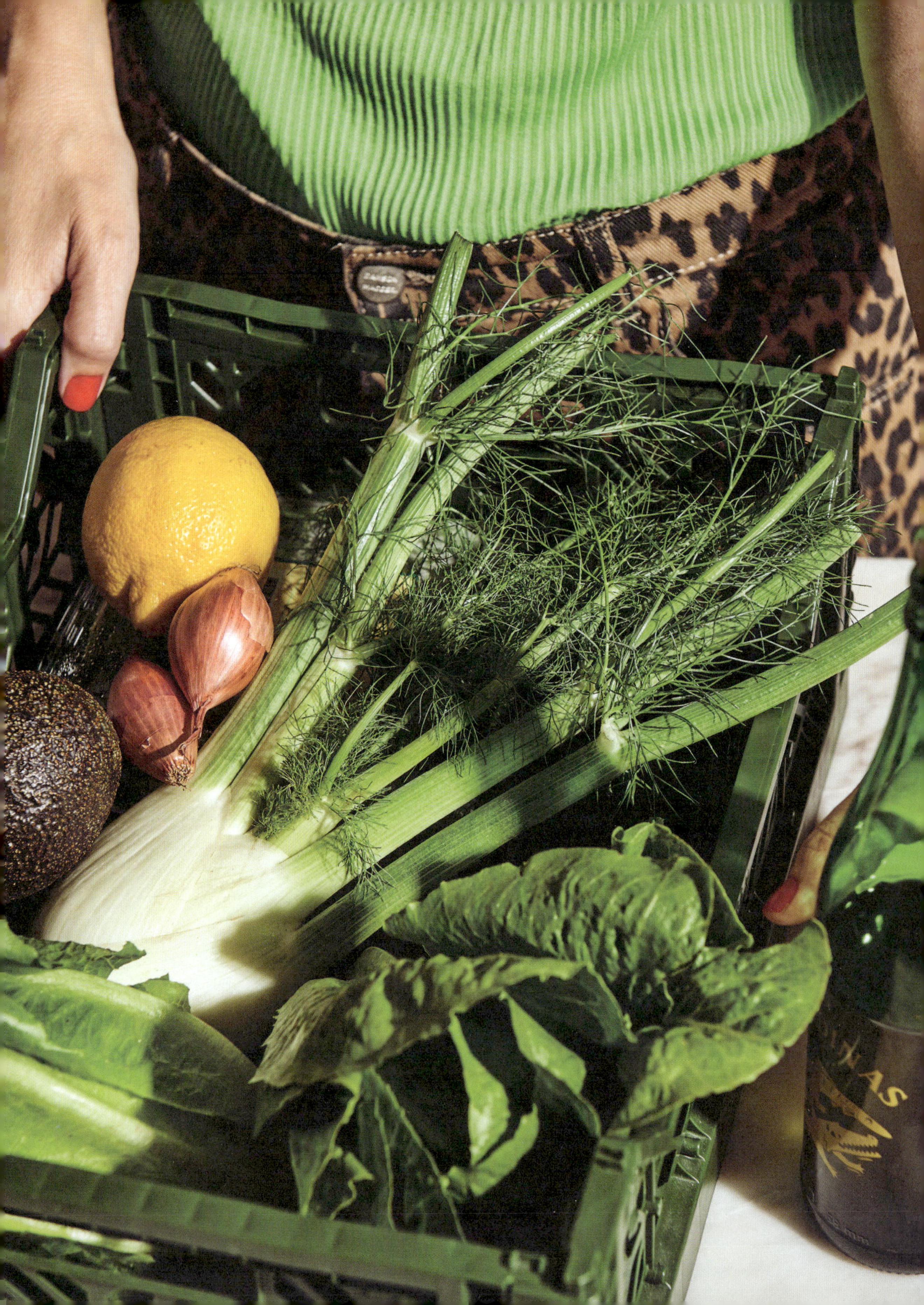

Leafy-side-salad map

Using the previous salads as inspiration, allow this map to guide you in creating your own leafy green masterpieces. The key here is to keep things simple.

Pick your leaf

Cos (romaine)
Baby cos (romaine)
Butter lettuce
Kale
Mixed leaves
Frisee
Radicchio

Pick your crunch

Pepitas (pumpkin seeds)
Pine nuts
Sunflower seeds
Sesame seeds
Pangratatto (page 48)
Croutons (page 48)

Add herbs (optional)

The idea of a leafy green salad is to keep it simple, so while fresh herbs are wonderful to use if you have them to hand, they aren't a dealbreaker.

Pick one extra ingredient

Avocado
Baby roma tomatoes
Capers
Cucumber
Fennel
Olives
Parmesan
Pickles
Radish
Red onion

Pick your dressing

The GOAT (page 43)
Basic balsamic (page 39)
Honey mustard (page 78)
Supergreen (page 43)
Lemon juice, olive oil and salt

Method

Wash and dry the greens, and chop or tear into bite-sized pieces. Toss in half the dressing. Add most of your extra ingredients and crunchy elements toss again, then transfer to a serving dish. Top with the remaining extra ingredients and crunchy bits, and either drizzle the remaining dressing over the top, or serve it on the side.

Cabbage and pea slaw

Serves 4–6 as a side

This salad was inspired by the cabbage and pea slaw that I first tried at Karen Martini's restaurant Mr Wolf in my early twenties. It's slowly morphed into a beast of its own, with kale instead of cabbage and the addition of fennel, but it's the combination of lemon, chilli, peas and parmesan that really makes this salad stand out. I love it so!

Dressing

juice and zest of 1 lemon

Slaw

2 cups (260 g/9 oz) frozen peas

1 head Tuscan kale, tough stems removed, leaves sliced into paper-thin ribbons

3 radishes, julienned

½ head fennel, thinly sliced

1 green chilli, seeds removed and finely sliced

¼ cup (7 g/¼ oz) flat-leaf parsley, finely chopped

50 g (1¾ oz) parmesan cheese, crumbled

50 g (1¾ oz) Pangratatto (page 48)

Prepare an ice bath and boil the kettle.

Place the peas in heatproof bowl. Cover with boiling water, allow to sit for a couple of minutes and then drain and shake away any excess water. Transfer to the ice bath for a couple of minutes to fix their colour.

Massage the kale with a pinch of salt. Add the lemon juice and zest, and toss to combine, then add the peas, radish, chilli, parsley and parmesan. Toss to combine, then place in a serving dish and top with the pangratatto.

Epic tip

1. You can make this a meal by adding beans or an egg.
2. Leftovers are wonderful with a boiled egg the following day.

Swaps

I usually reach for parsley because I have it in abundance, but mint and coriander (cilantro) also work wonderfully.

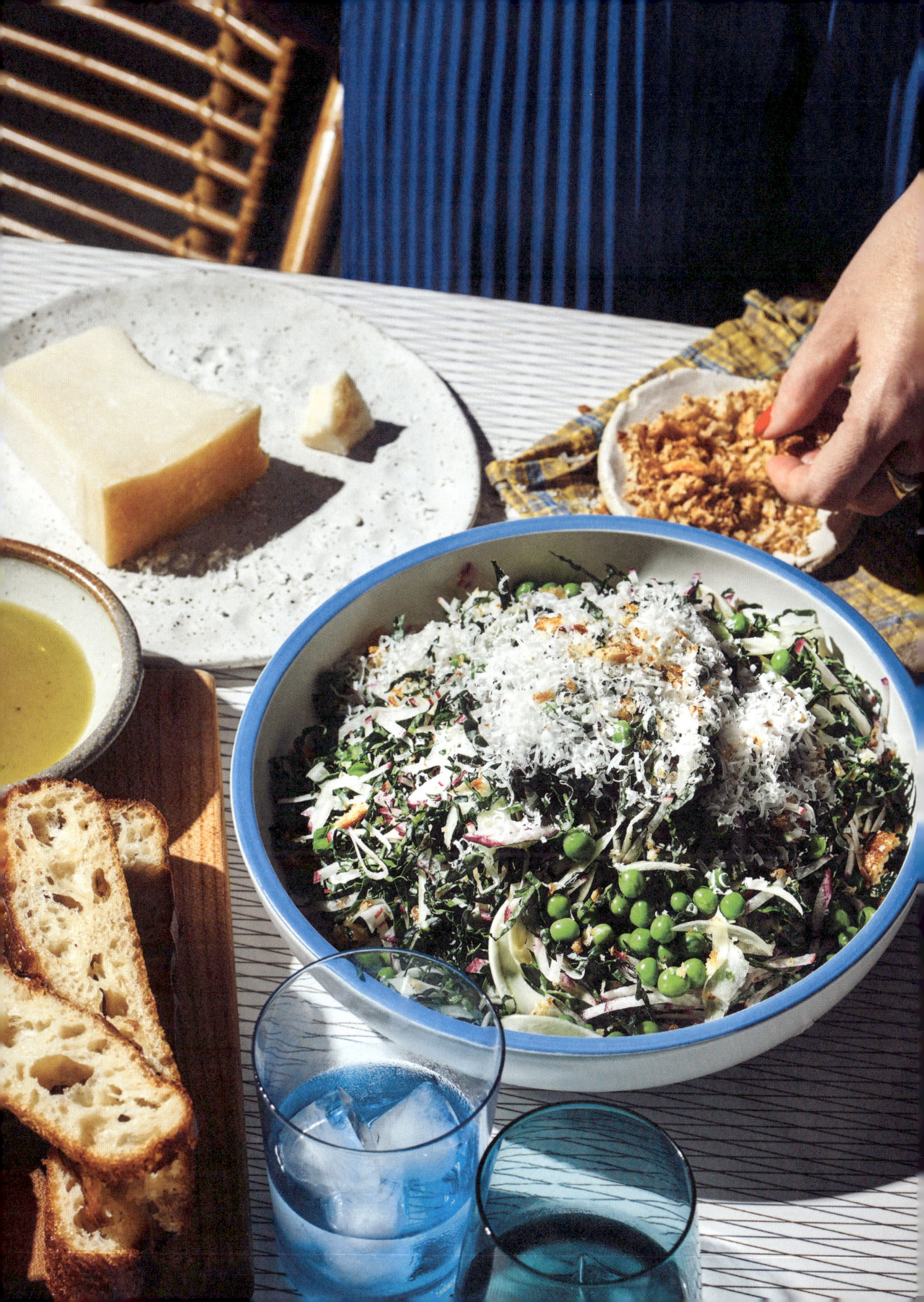

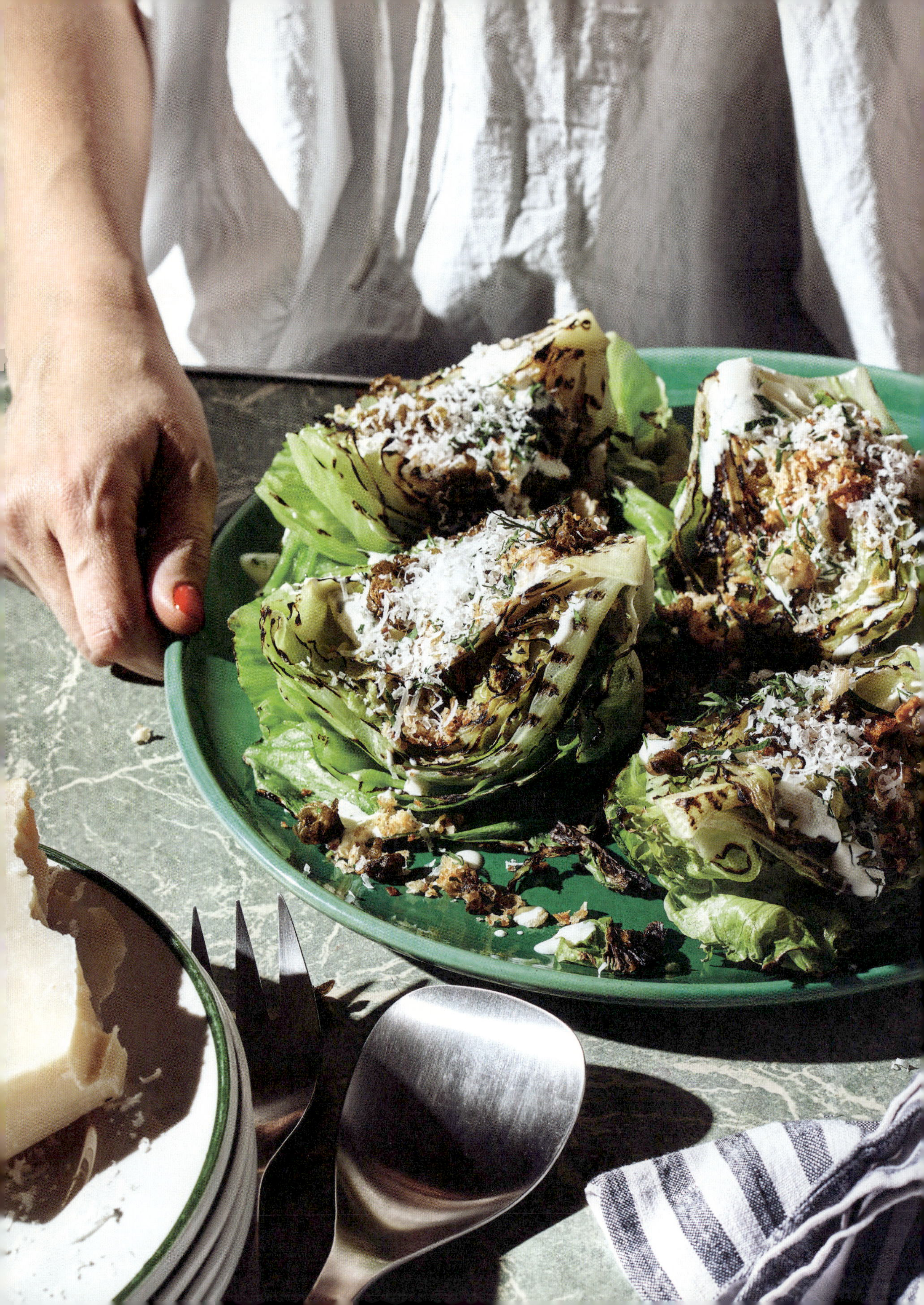

Grilled iceberg lettuce with capers

Serves 4–8

This recipe takes the humble iceberg lettuce and puts it over an open flame, creating a smoky flavour that pairs so well with the fresh crunch of the lettuce, the creamy tang of the dressing and the zesty crunch of the capers. This is most definitely a showstopper and is the perfect thing to make when having friends over for a barbecue, or to fancy up a Friday night pizza party.

Dressing
1 quantity The GOAT dressing (page 43)

Salad
2 tablespoons capers
olive oil, for cooking
1 iceberg lettuce
50 g (1¾ oz) parmesan cheese, grated
50 g (1¾ oz) Pangratatto (page 48)
fresh flat-leaf parsley or dill, to garnish

To fry your capers, heat a good inch of olive oil in a small saucepan over a medium heat. Pat the capers dry using a paper towel or tea towel (dish towel), then carefully add them to the hot oil and step back – they will release water at first, which can cause the oil to splatter. Cook in the hot oil, shaking the pan regularly, for approximately 2–3 minutes, until they bloom and turn golden brown. Remove from the hot oil with a slotted spoon and lay in a single layer on a paper towel to absorb excess oil. Set aside until ready to use.

Remove any limp, outer leaves from the lettuce, then cut into eight wedges, leaving the core intact so the leaves stay together.

Char your lettuce using one of the following methods:

Hot pan or barbecue: Heat a barbecue, chargrilll pan or stainless-steel frying pan over the hottest heat. Brush the cut sides of the lettuce wedges with a lick of oil and then put them on the hot surface, cut-side down. Keeping an eye on it (you want it to lightly char but not overcook), use tongs to turn each wedge as the underside starts to blacken.

Open flame: Using tongs, hold each wedge over the open flame on your gas stove, turning until the cut sides are slightly charred.

Arrange the lettuce wedges on a plate. Drizzle with the dressing then top with capers, parmesan and pangratatto. Garnish with herbs.

Epic tip
Serve this with the Roasted zucchini, crispy pitta and beans salad (page 130), also cooked on the grill.

Swaps
Can't get your head around the idea of grilled lettuce? No worries! Serve this with raw lettuce.

Showstopping sides

Ever-versatile tomato and cucumber salad

Serves 2–4

This refreshing side salad complements so many dishes and cuisines, and forms one part of one of my fave dinners of all time – the other two parts being jasmine rice and Two-minute tofu (page 32). The key to this recipe is to chop everything into evenly sized pieces, à la my beloved chopped salads.

1 small red onion, cut into 1 cm (½ in) dice
2 tomatoes, cut into 1 cm (½ in) dice
1 Lebanese (short) cucumber, seeds removed, cut into 1 cm (½ in) dice
1 cup (155 g/5½ oz) roasted cashews
1 red chilli, seeds removed, very finely chopped
juice of 1 lime

Combine all ingredients in a bowl, stir to combine, season with salt and pepper then serve. It's that simple!

Swaps
I've kept this simple, using lime juice for the dressing, but you could also use the Chilli lime dressing (page 39) if you have some of this in excess. Alternatively, use lemon juice, yoghurt and sumac for a Middle Eastern twist.

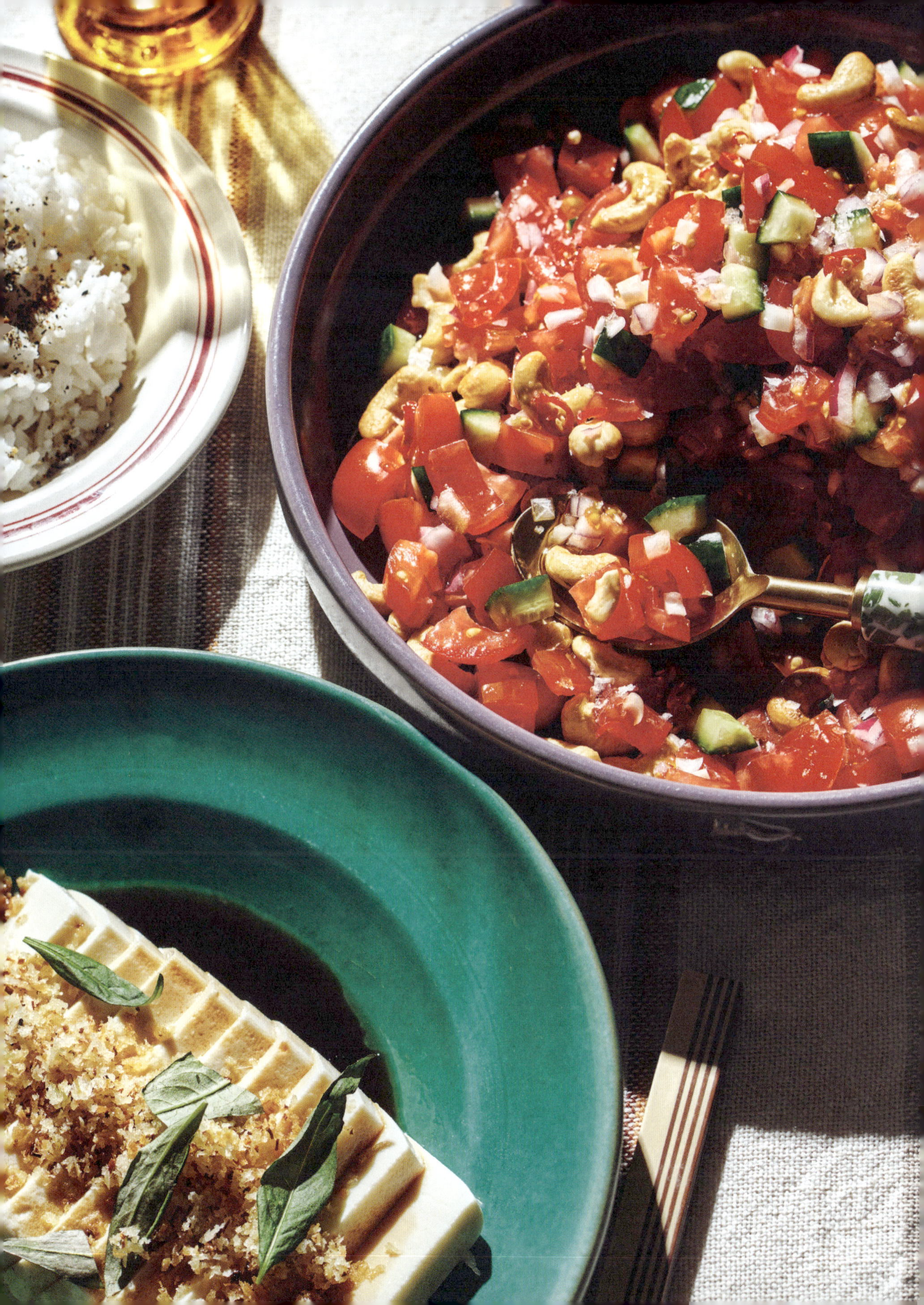

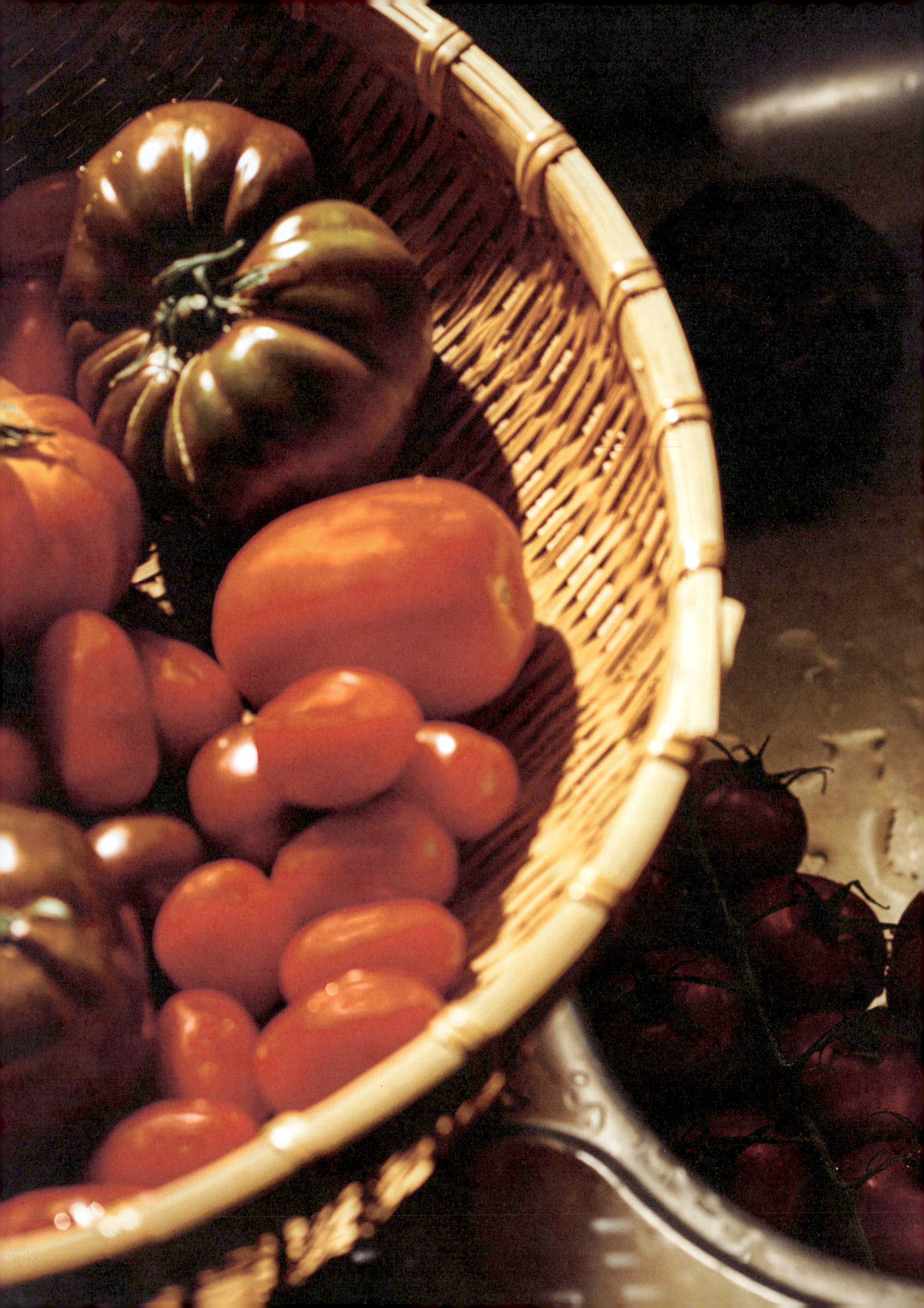

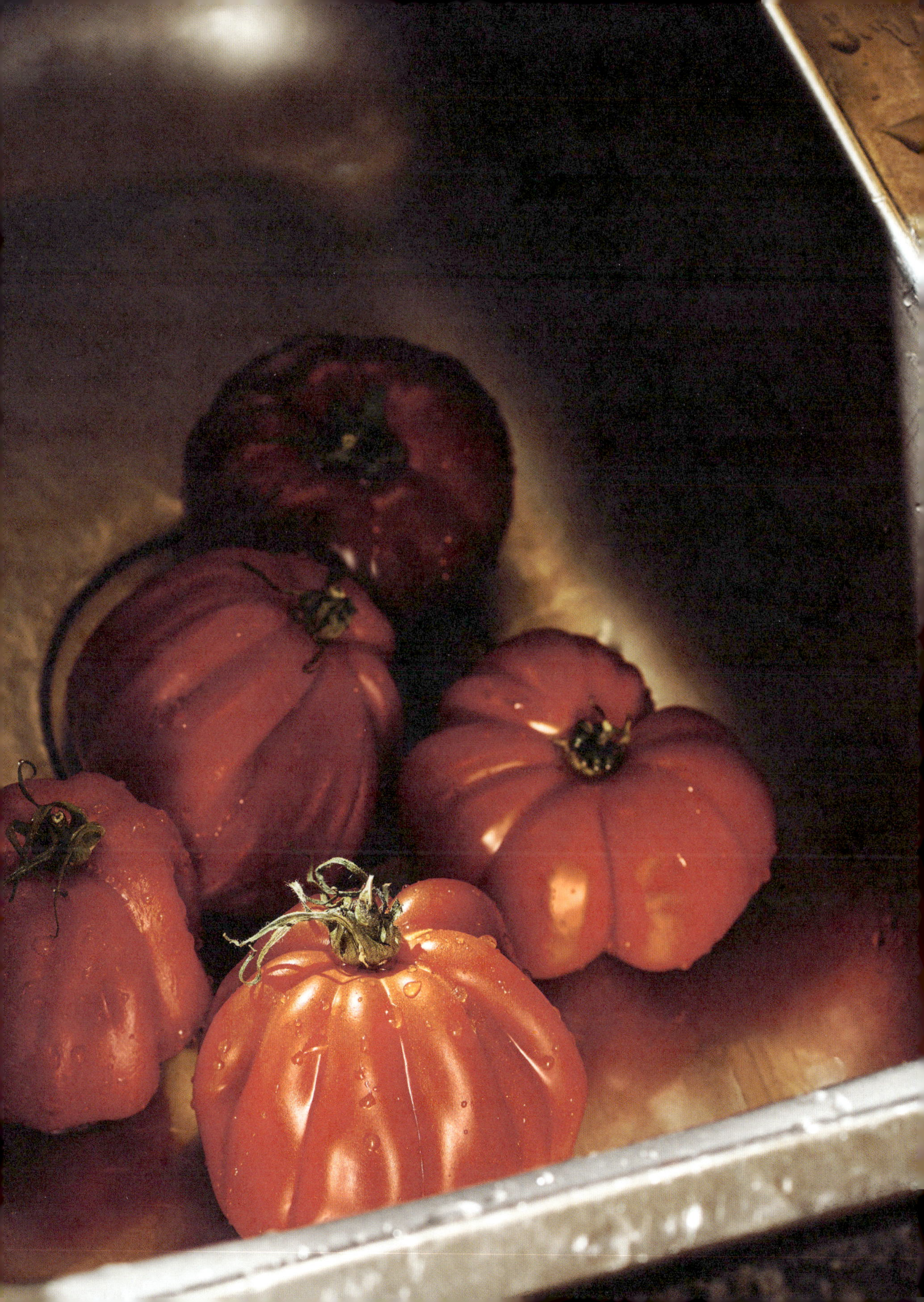

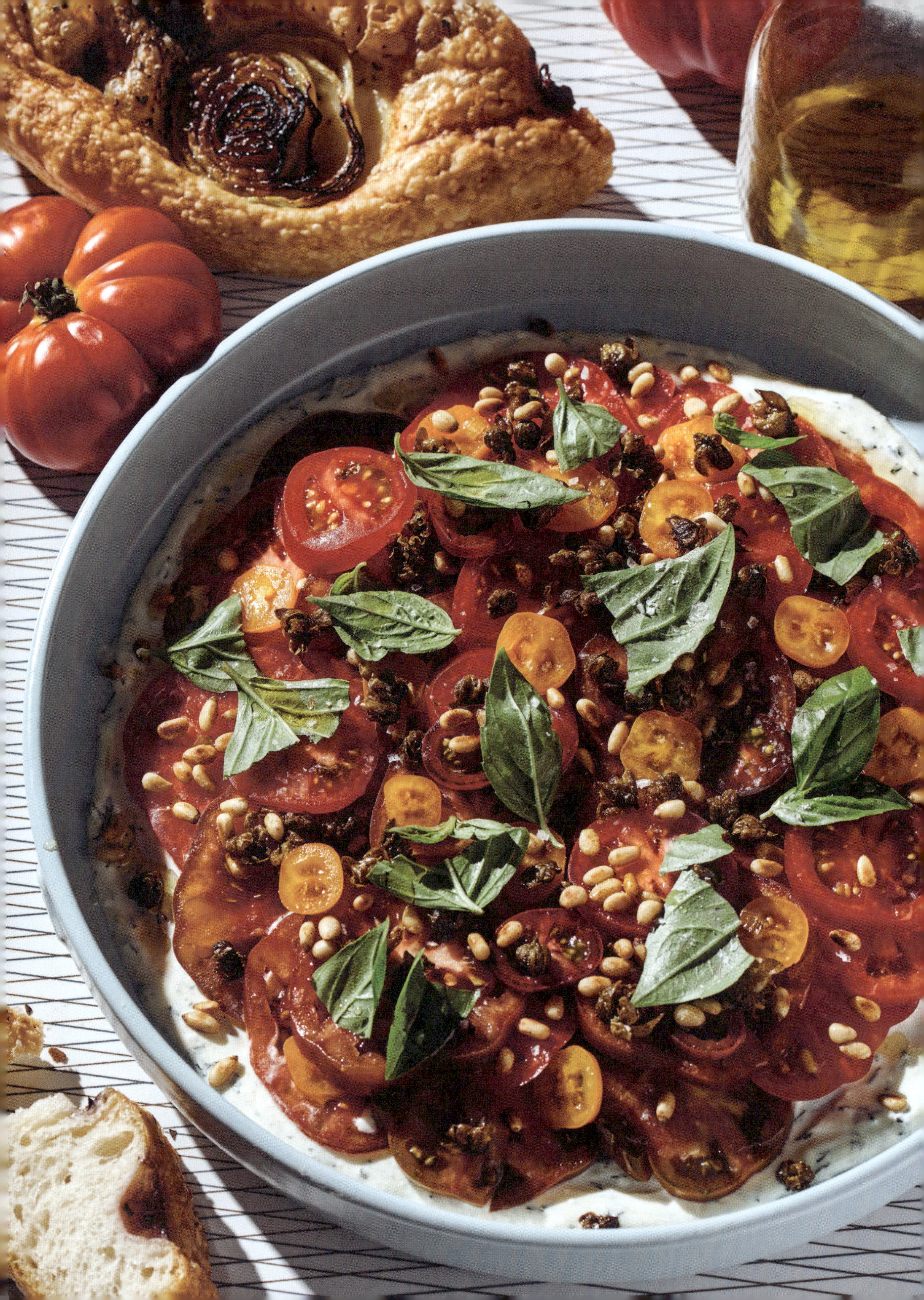

Tomato salad with fried capers and pine nuts

Serves 4 as a side

This is the perfect salad to make with fresh, ripe, juicy, end-of-summer tomatoes – the ones that are bursting with flavour and can be enjoyed with a pinch of salt and nothing else.

Tomatoes shouldn't be stored in the fridge, and this is especially true for the tomatoes in this recipe. Ideally, you want to enjoy this salad on a hot, hot day when the tomatoes are either fresh off the vine, or warm from being on your kitchen bench all day. The contrast of the warm, sweet tomatoes against the chilled, creamy, tangy dressing really is something, and the addition of fried capers and pine nuts takes this dish to the next level.

Dressing

1 quantity The GOAT dressing (page 43)

Salad

olive oil, for cooking
2 tablespoons capers
6 ripe tomatoes
2 tablespoons pine nuts, toasted
basil leaves, to garnish

To fry your capers, heat a good inch of olive oil in a small saucepan over a medium heat. Pat the capers dry using a paper towel or tea towel (dish towel), then carefully add them to the hot oil and step back – they will release water at first, which can cause the oil to splatter. Cook in the hot oil, shaking the pan regularly, for approximately 2–3 minutes, until they bloom and turn golden brown. Remove from the oil with a slotted spoon and lay in a single layer on a paper towel to absorb the excess oil. Set aside until ready to use.

Spread most of the dressing over the bottom of a serving dish and smooth it with the back of a spoon.

Cut the tomatoes into slices approx. ½ cm (¼ in) thick and arrange the slices over the dressing. Season with a little salt and pepper, then drizzle with the remaining dressing. Top with the fried capers, pine nuts and basil leaves.

Serve with focaccia, bruschetta or any kind of bread so you can soak up the delicious juices and creamy dressing – a truly otherworldly flavour. Enjoy alongside any assortment of salads and proteins; you can't go wrong.

Epic tip

If making a meal for two, halve this recipe and use the other half of the dressing on the Kale and crouton side salad (page 171). Add a soft-boiled egg and voila, you have a perfect meal.

Raw cauliflower and broccoli salad

Serves 4–6 as a side

This salad is one of the many dishes in this book that is inspired by a salad I ate at La Pinta – my favourite restaurant in Melbourne – many moons ago. They told me the recipe at the time (they are very generous like that), and the only part I remember is the yoghurt. In my determination to recreate it, I came up with The GOAT dressing that dominated an entire season of my life.

The raw cauliflower and broccoli are the perfect vehicle for the creamy and tangy dressing, which is complemented by the sweetness of dried cherries and the satisfying crunch of the flaked almonds.

This is intended as a side salad, but I sometimes make it and inhale it as a meal, it's that good.

Dressing
1 quantity The GOAT dressing (page 43)

Salad
1 head broccoli, washed and dried
1 head cauliflower, washed and dried
60 g (2 oz) baby spinach, roughly chopped
large handful dried cherries
large handful slivered almonds, toasted
flat-leaf parsley, to garnish

Cut the broccoli and cauliflower into florets. Take your time with this, cutting around each large floret to get lots of tiny florets, rather than hacking at it with a knife and making a big mess, or rushing and leaving the florets too big. The smaller they are, the better the dressing-to-veg ratio, which is what makes this salad so damn good.

Put the florets in a mixing bowl with the dressing and stir to combine. Add the spinach, cherries and two-thirds of the almonds and stir again. Spoon into a serving bowl and garnish with the parsley and remaining almonds, then serve.

Epic tip
To pump up the protein, add an egg – boiled, fried or an omelette; you choose!

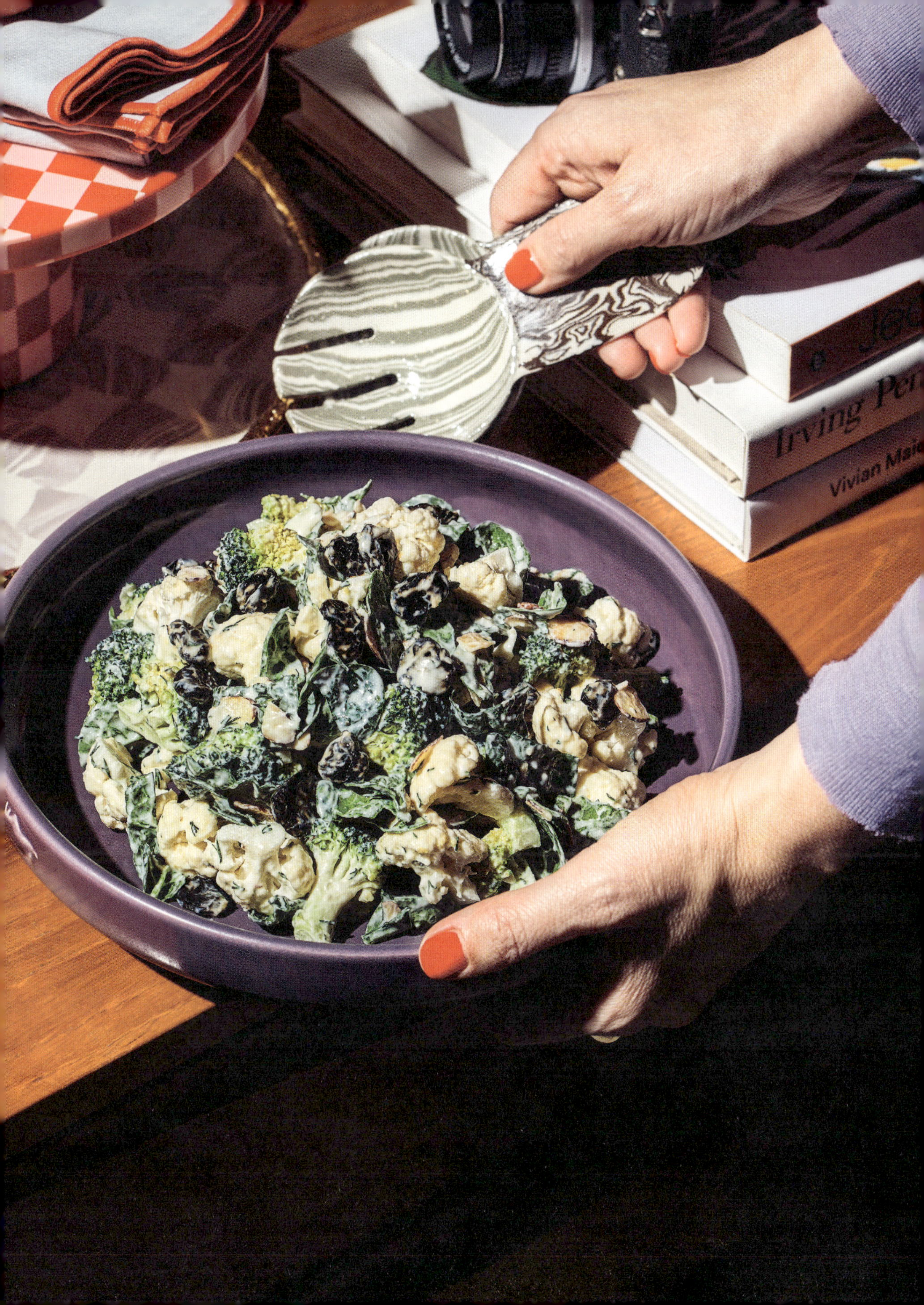

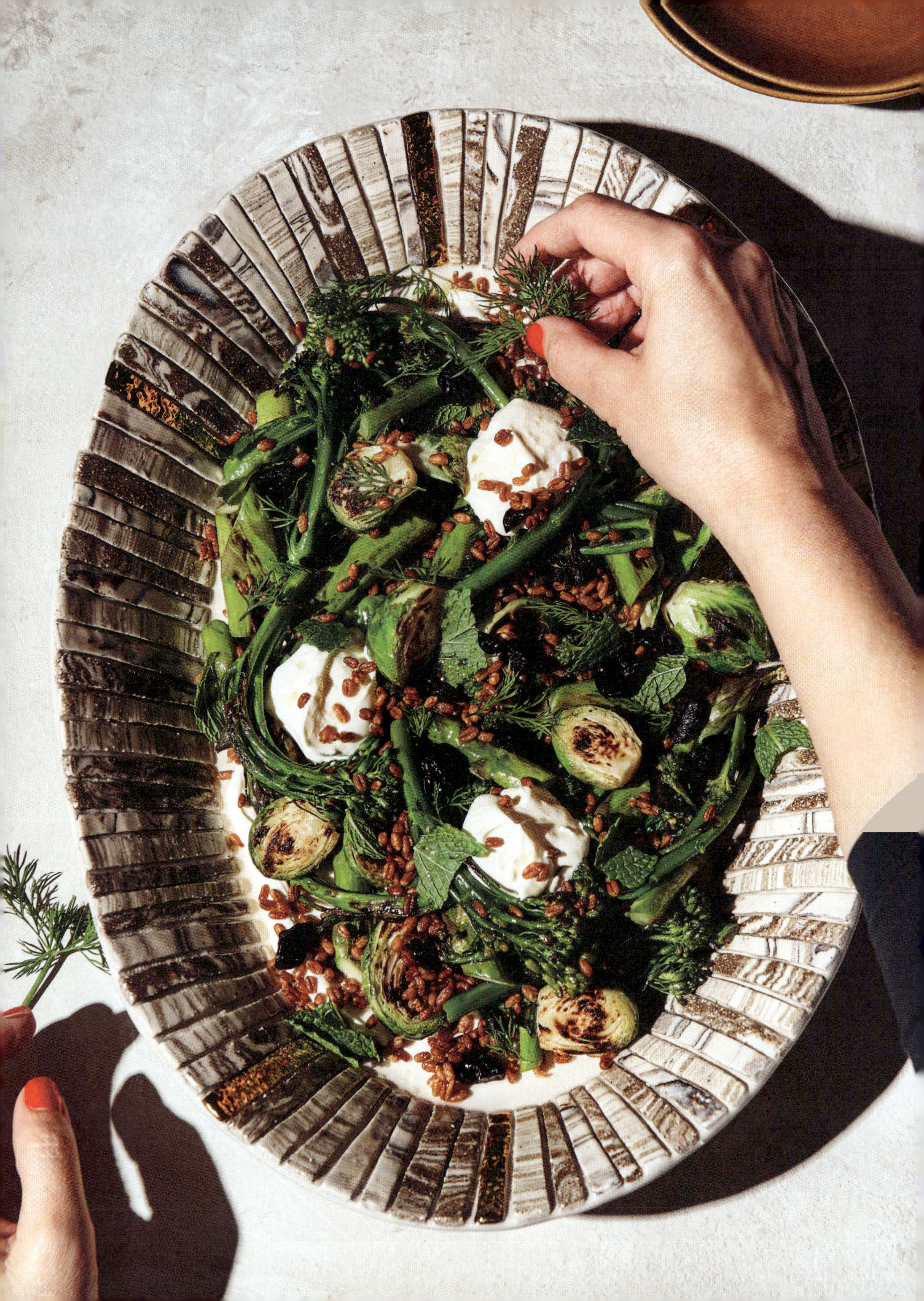

Warm greens and toasted spelt

Serves 4–6 as a side

The combination of the fresh, creamy, lemony, garlicky GOAT dressing with the smokiness of hearty greens cooked on the barbecue is a surprising and welcome combo for hot days. Adding to the surprise is the toasted spelt, which has been teased into a crispy, crunchy, nutty morsel using the magic of heat and oil.

Dressing

1 quantity The GOAT dressing (page 43)

Salad

1 handful (30 g/1 oz) spelt or farro
olive oil, for cooking
1 bunch asparagus
1 bunch broccolini
1 zucchini (courgette), cut into 4 cm (1½ in) batons
6 brussels sprouts, halved
1 quantity Whipped feta (page 198)
2 tablespoons dried cherries
small handful dill, to garnish

Cook the spelt in lots of boiling water for 15–25 minutes (the time will depend on whether you are using pearled or wholegrain – pearled will cook a little quicker, as it's had its outer germ/grain removed). Drain, rinse in cold water, then set aside to completely dry. Once dry, toast the spelt in a hot frying pan with a generous glug of olive oil until lightly golden all over. Transfer to a paper towel-lined plate and allow to cool.

Trim the woody ends from the asparagus then cut into 4 cm (1½ in) pieces, on a diagonal.

Trim the woody ends from the broccolini then cut into 4 cm (1½ in) pieces, leaving the tops intact and splitting any extra-wide pieces of stalk in half lengthways.

Toss all the veggies in a large mixing bowl with 1 tablespoon olive oil and a generous pinch of salt.

Cook on a hot barbecue in a single layer. Avoid moving the slices around too much while they cook, to ensure they develop a nice char.

To assemble, spread most of the whipped feta over the bottom of a serving dish. Pile the cooked greens and dried cherries on top, then dollop with the remaining whipped feta and top with toasted spelt and dill.

Serve immediately.

Swaps

1. Cook the vegetables in batches in a frying pan over a medium–high heat instead of on the barbecue.
2. Use any grain in place of spelt.

Roasted pumpkin with raita and tempered spices

Serves 4 as a side

This just might be the cheekiest side of all because it's definitely not a salad! What it is though is showstopping and it goes so well with anything – be it a wintery feast or a summery barbecue.

Raita

1 Lebanese (short) cucumber, grated
¾ cup (185 g/6½ oz) full-fat Greek yoghurt
1 teaspoon ground cumin
½ teaspoon sea salt

Pumpkin

¼ kent pumpkin (winter squash) (approx. 500 g/1 lb 2 oz)
olive oil, for cooking
1 tablespoon whole cumin seeds
1 tablespoon whole coriander seeds
1 teaspoon mustard seeds
2 strands of curry leaves
handful roasted cashews, roughly chopped
handful pepitas (pumpkin seeds), toasted

To make the raita, scoop up handfuls of grated cucumber and squeeze over the sink to release as much liquid as possible. Place in a mixing bowl along with the yoghurt, cumin and salt and stir to combine.

Preheat the oven to 180°C (360°F) and place an oven rack on the bottom third of the oven. Cut the pumpkin into chunky wedges. Place on a baking tray skin side down. Lightly coat in olive oil and salt, and bake for approximately 40 minutes, or until fork tender, turning the tray 180 degrees about halfway through the cooking time.

Once the pumpkin is cooked, heat 2 tablespoons of olive oil in a large frying pan over a medium–high heat. Add the spices and curry leaves, and cook, swirling constantly, until the spices are popping and fragrant.

Place the raita on the bottom of a serving dish. Top with cooked pumpkin, then spoon the spices, curry leaves and oil over the top. Garnish with cashews and pepitas, and serve.

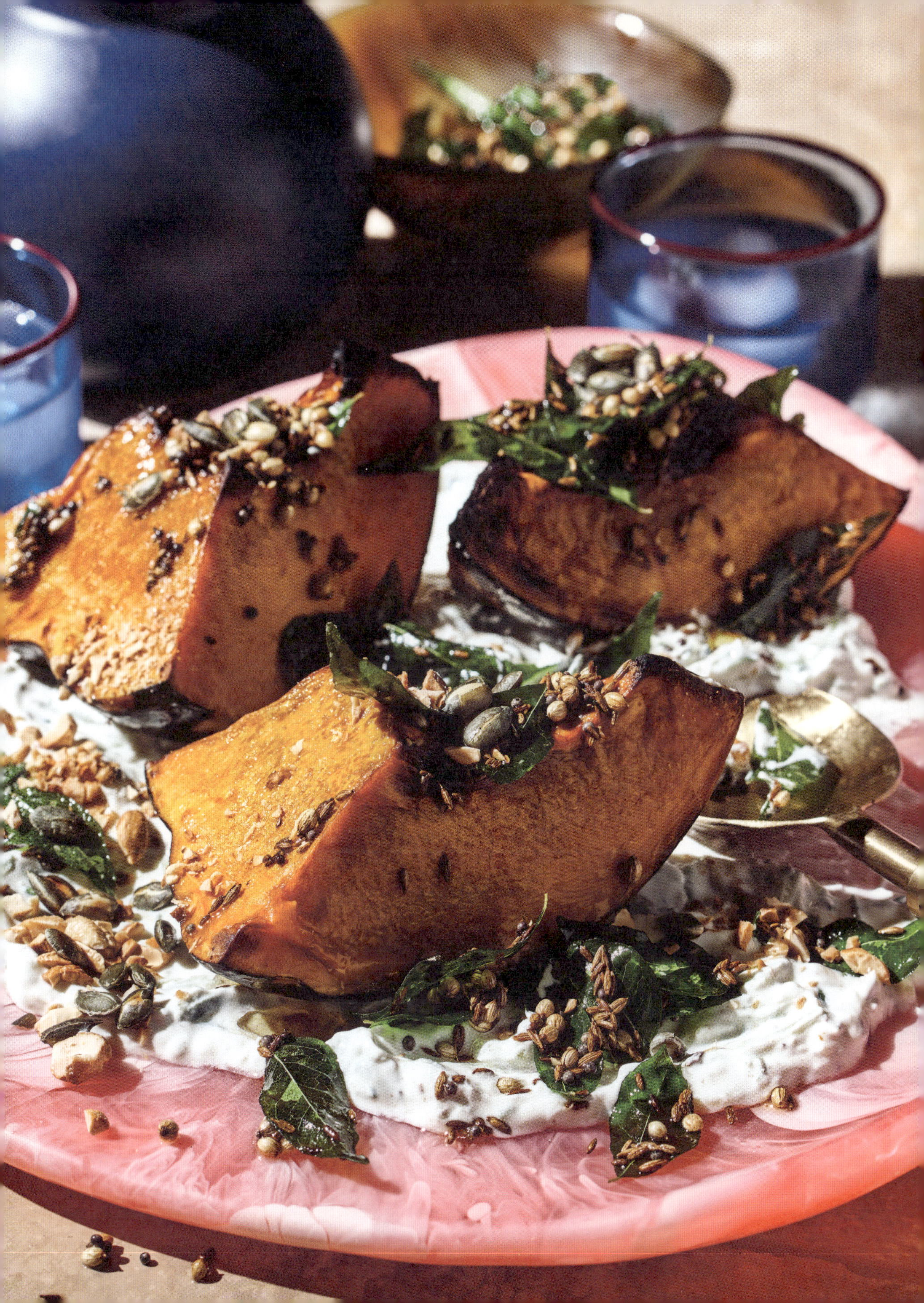

MAKE IT

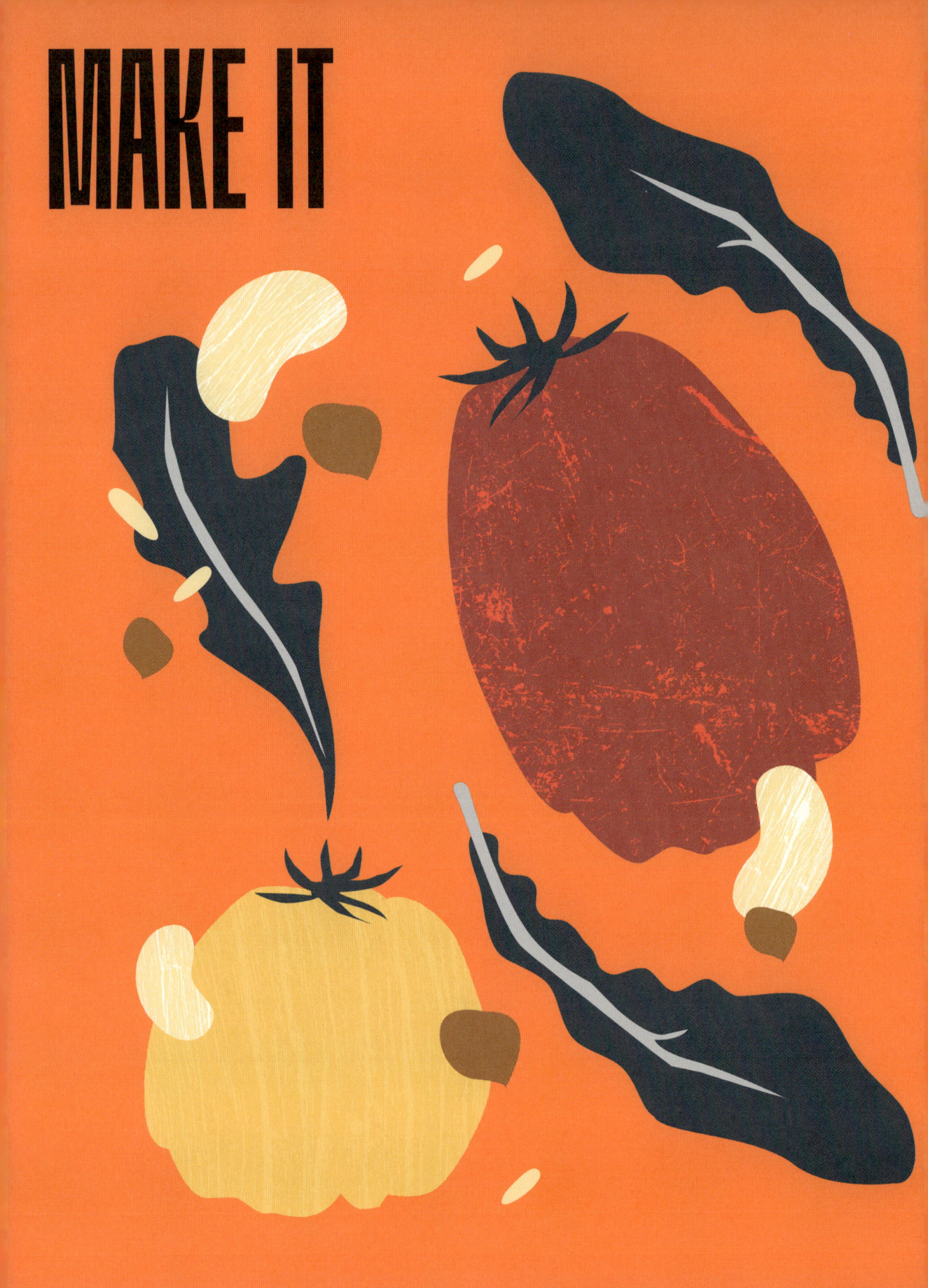

A PARTY

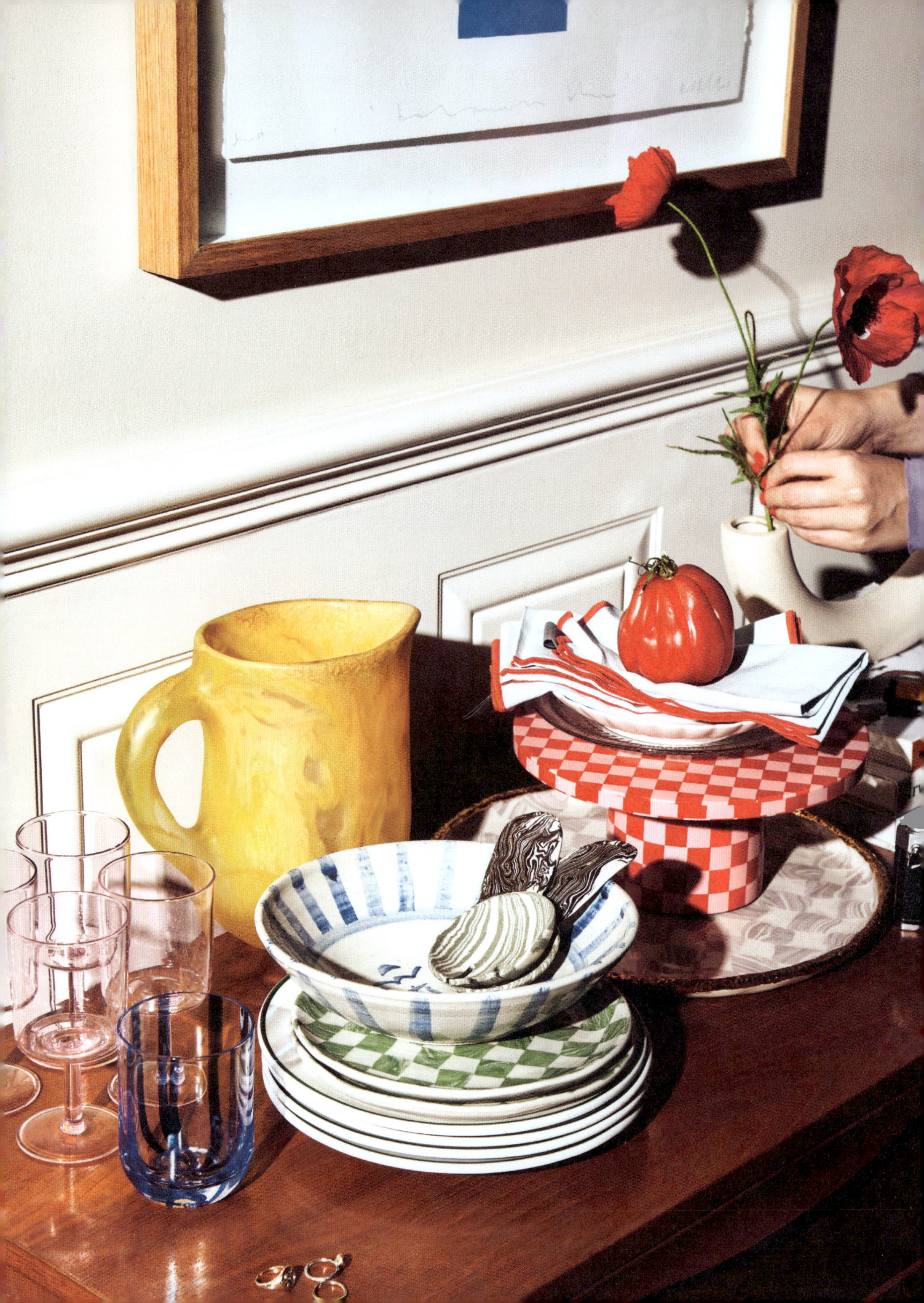

What's better than one salad? A salad party! The recipes in this chapter are things I serve when hosting salad parties – dishes that perfectly complement an array of salads and can be served before or alongside your main spread.

Here you'll find recipes for some of my signature creamy, loaded dips and well as springy focaccia and even a cake! Perfect additions to a table of salads when you want to take things up a notch.

Salad club

A genius way of sharing healthy food with your coworkers is to start a salad club. You each bring a salad to work on Monday, and share it for the following few days; that way you only have to cook lunch once but still get to enjoy a home-cooked lunch throughout the working week. This works best with three to four people, but if you have a lot more, just adapt the approach so each person cooks once a fortnight, instead of once a week.

Make it a party

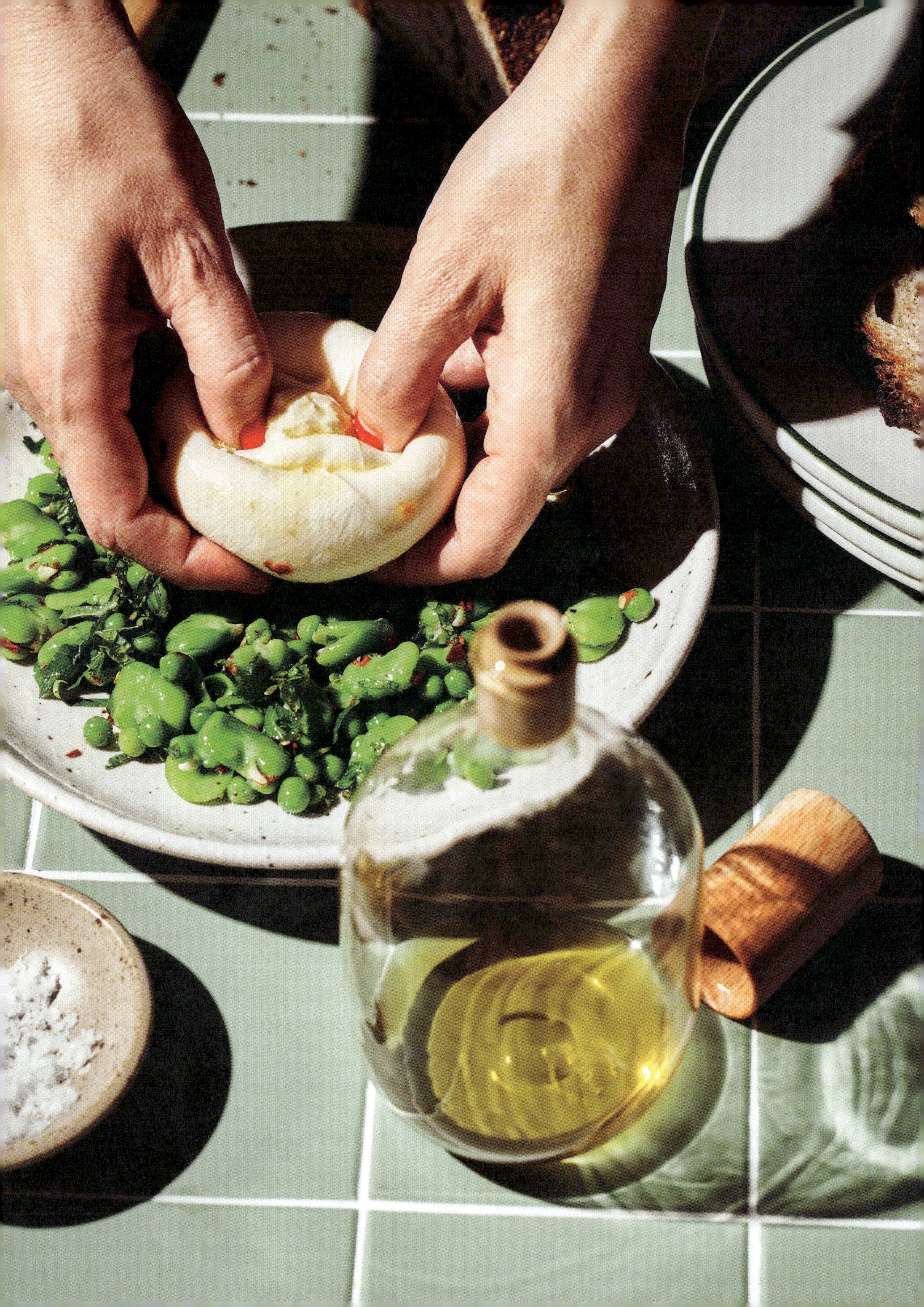

Burrata with broad beans and peas

Serves 4–6

Burrata is a soft cheese ball with a creamy centre. Breaking through the soft outer layer to reveal the creamy inner is one of the greatest parts of eating it. The vibrant green of the peas and broad beans against the white of the burrata is really quite showstopping. The simple dressing of lemon, fresh herbs and olive oil complements both the legumes and the burrata, rendering this dish the perfect thing to make for a gathering.

1 ball of burrata, room temperature
½ cup (80 g/2¾ oz) frozen broad beans
½ cup (80 g/2¾ oz) frozen peas, defrosted
zest of 1 lemon
generous glug of olive oil
¼ cup (15 g/½ oz) mint, chopped
¼ cup (7 g/¼ oz) flat-leaf parsley, chopped
chilli flakes, to taste
fresh sourdough (see page 206) or bruschetta, to serve

Take your burrata out of the fridge about 30 minutes to an hour before serving to let it come to room temperature. This will ensure you enjoy its rich, creamy texture and delicate flavour to the fullest.

Bring a saucepan of water to a boil and prepare an ice bath. Boil the broad beans for 2 minutes, then submerge in the ice bath. Pop the beans out of their skins and discard the skins, leaving just the soft, inner bean.

To prepare your peas, place in a heatproof bowl and cover with boiling water for a couple of minutes — either with the cooking water from the broad beans, or boiled water from the kettle. Drain and submerge in the ice bath to set the colour.

Combine the broad beans, peas, lemon zest, olive oil, mint, parsley and chilli flakes to taste, then season with salt and pepper to taste. Stir to combine.

Spoon the pea and bean mixture into a serving dish. Place the burrata in the centre and gently break it open to reveal the gooey insides. Enjoy with a glass of wine and a big chunk of bread.

Epic tip

Can't find burrata? Swap for stracciatella, place this on the bottom of a serving dish and spoon the peas and beans over the top.

Whipped feta with balsamic roasted grapes

Serves 6

While this whipped feta is a feature in many of the recipes throughout this book, you can turn it into an absolute showstopper of a dish by topping it with balsamic roasted grapes and serving it with soft, pillowy foccacia (see page 206).

Whipped feta

400 g (14 oz) Danish feta
½ cup (125 g/4½ oz) full-fat Greek yoghurt
½ teaspoon lemon zest
½ teaspoon minced garlic
½ teaspoon salt
1–2 tablespoons olive oil

For a vegan version

400 g (14 oz) block of firm tofu, drained and broken into bite-sized pieces
½ teaspoon lemon zest
½ teaspoon minced garlic
¾ teaspoon salt
2 tablespoons olive oil
1 tablespoon lemon juice
150 ml (5 fl oz) water

Grapes

1 small bunch red grapes
1 tablespoon olive oil
1 tablespoon balsamic vinegar
a few sprigs fresh thyme leaves, plus extra to garnish

fresh focaccia or crusty bread, to serve

To make the whipped feta or tofu, place all ingredients except the olive oil in a high-powered blender or food processor and blitz until they come together. You may have to pause a few times, scrape the sides down and give it a bot of a jiggle, to get it going. Scrape down the sides once more, then turn the blender/food processor back on and pour the olive oil in, adding it in a constant stream until you have a creamy, silky-smooth dip.

Place in an airtight container in the fridge for 30 minutes, or until ready to use.

To make the grapes, preheat the oven to 190°C (375°F).

Toss the grapes in the oil, balsamic vinegar, salt, pepper and thyme leaves, then transfer to a roasting tin. Roast in the hot oven for 15 minutes, then set aside to cool.

Smear the whipped feta into a serving dish using the back of a tablespoon. Gently place the roasted grapes on the feta, then spoon the juices from the roasting tray over the grapes. Serve with focaccia or another crusty bread.

Epic tip

Optional add-ins for the whipped feta include fresh herbs such as dill, chives, basil, parsley or coriander (cilantro). These can be stirred in once finished, or blitzed with the other ingredients to make a vibrant green whipped feta.

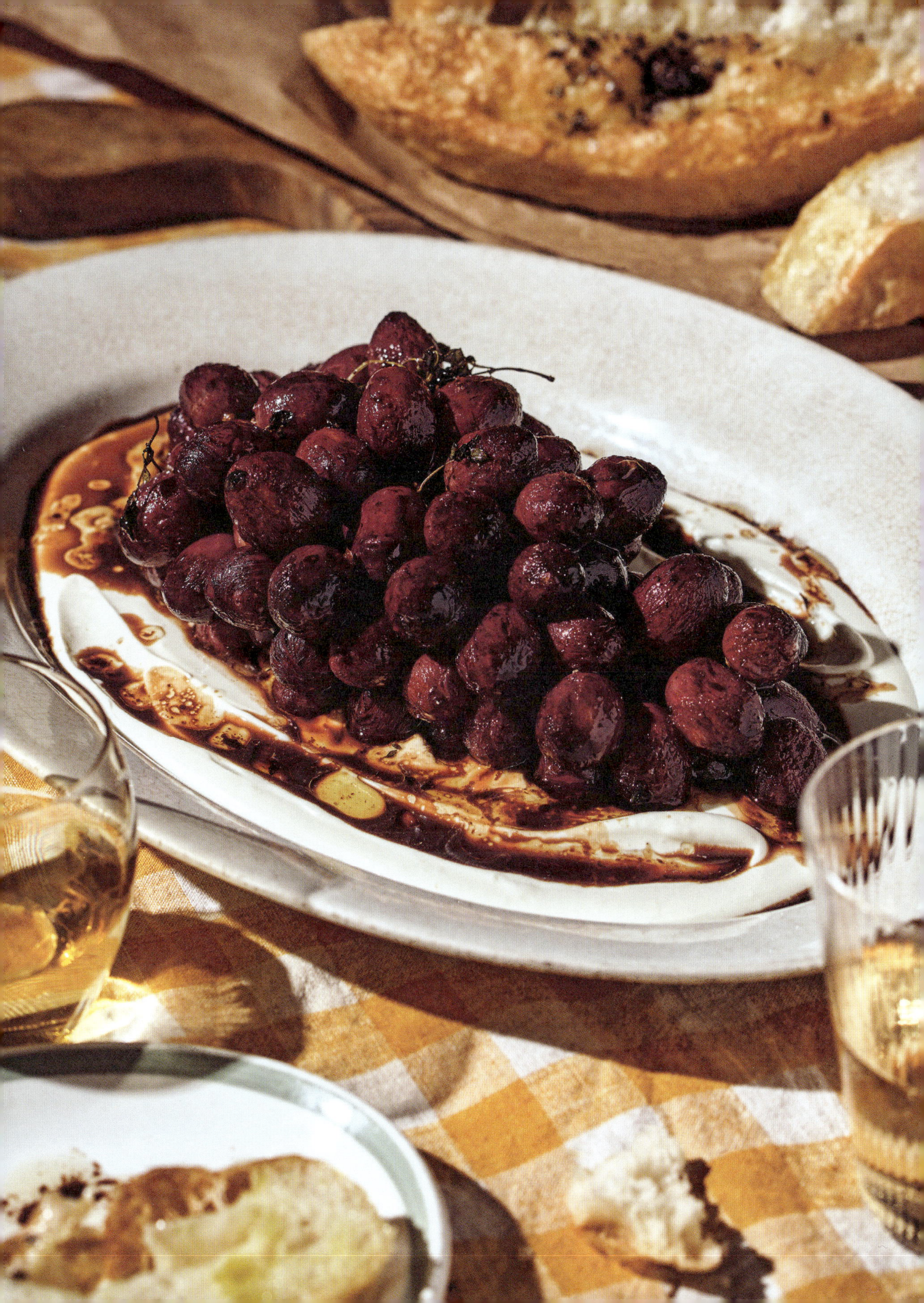

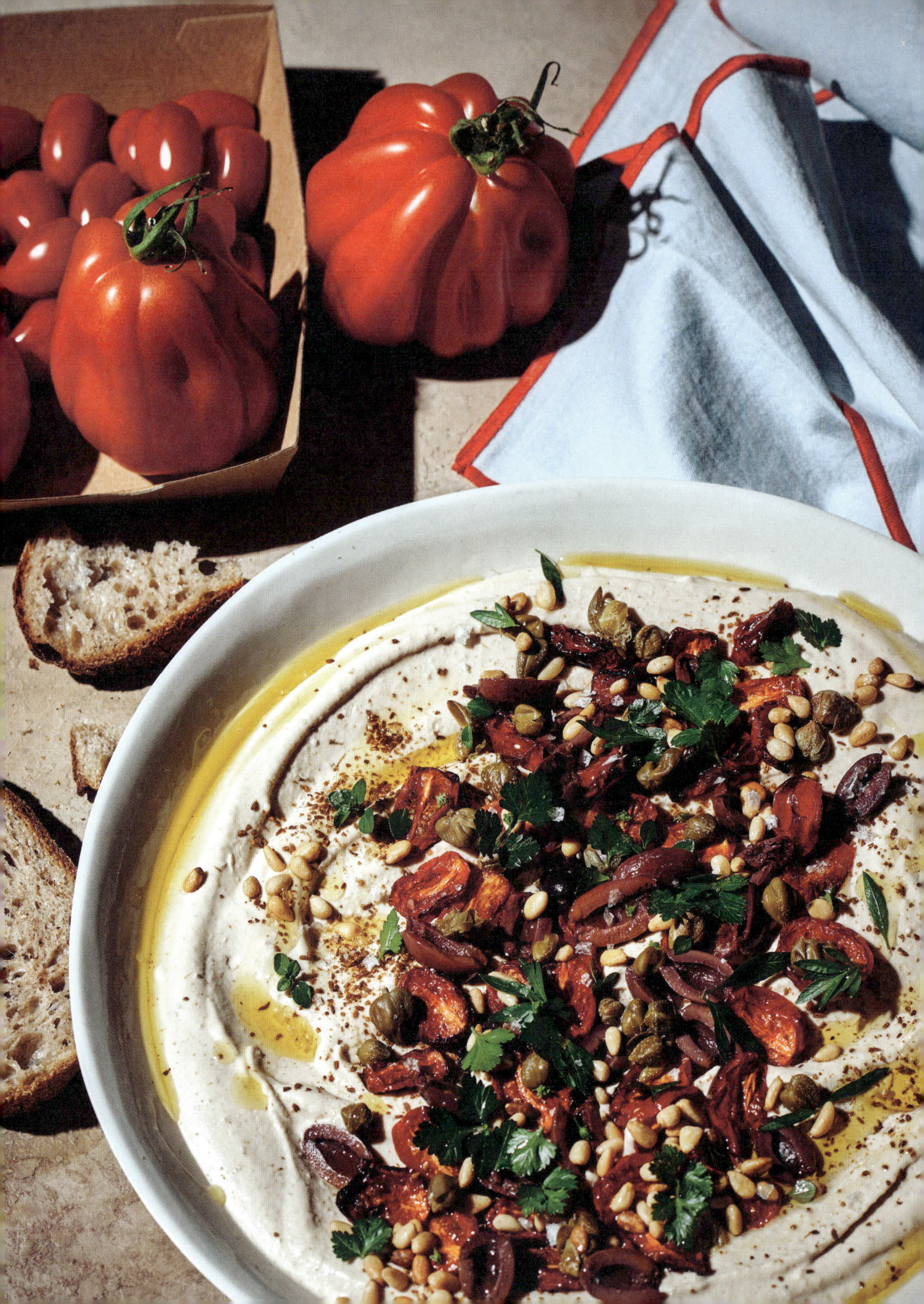

Dreamy creamy loaded bean dip

Serves 4–6

Loaded dips are my signature. They're dishes that I return to time and time again, and they're the dishes friends and family expect me to bring to gatherings, along with a loaf of freshly-baked sourdough to dip, dunk and schmear with. And this concept doesn't stop here. The dreamy, creamy loaded guac on the following page is further testament to how special the combination of a creamy base with flavoursome toppings can be.

It's not often that I call for specific kitchen equipment, but for this recipe a high-powered blender is really important. If you don't have a good blender, you won't get a smooth and creamy dip.

Bean dip
- 2 × 400 g (14 oz) tins butter (lima) beans, cannellini beans or chickpeas
- 200 g (7 oz) unhulled tahini
- juice of 1 lemon
- 75 ml (2½ fl oz) olive oil
- 1 teaspoon ground cumin
- 1 teaspoon ground coriander
- 1 teaspoon sea salt
- 2–4 garlic cloves, crushed
- approx. ½ cup (125 ml/4 fl oz) water

Toppings
- 200 g (7 oz) baby roma tomatoes
- olive oil, for drizzling
- pinch of sea salt
- pinch of caster (superfine) sugar
- 1 teaspoon cumin seeds
- large handful kalamata olives, halved
- large handful capers
- large handful toasted pine nuts
- large handful oregano or flat-leaf parsley leaves
- freshly baked sourdough, crackers, or corn chips, to serve

To make the bean dip, place all ingredients, except the water, in a high-powered blender or food processor and blend until well combined. Add the water – a little at a time – and blend until you have a smooth, creamy dip. Transfer to a large serving bowl and smooth with the back of a tablespoon. Alternatively, store in an airtight container and refrigerate until ready to use.

Preheat the oven to 160°C (320°F).

Slice the tomatoes in half lengthways and put them in a mixing bowl with a drizzle of olive oil and a pinch of salt and sugar. Toss to combine, then transfer to a baking tray, cut side up, and bake for 40 minutes, or until shrivelled and starting to blacken.

When you're ready to load up your dip, drizzle it with oil, then add cumin seeds, slow-roasted tomatoes, olives, capers, pine nuts and herbs.

Serve with sourdough, corn chips, crackers, corn fritters or any other delicious morsel you fancy.

Epic tip
If making this for a special event or gathering, you can make both the slow-roasted tomatoes and the dip up to two days ahead, and assemble before serving.

Make it a party

Dreamy creamy loaded guac

Serves 4–6

This recipe is perfect when avocados are inexpensive and in abundance. While guacamole (guac) is often served on the chunkier side, making it in a food processor gives it a smooth, creamy, whipped texture that makes the perfect base for the toppings I love to load onto this – grilled corn, jalapeños and pepitas (pumpkin seeds).

This loaded guac pairs really well with Grilled corn and edamame salsa (page 79), Roasted capsicum dip (see opposite) and a big bag of salted corn chips.

Toppings
2 ears of corn, husks removed
1 jalapeño, sliced paper-thin
handful pepitas (pumpkin seeds), toasted
chilli flakes, to garnish
coriander (cilantro) leaves, to garnish (optional)

Guac
2–3 ripe avocados, peeled and stoned
juice of 1 lime
1 tablespoon olive oil
½ teaspoon sea salt
½ teaspoon ground cumin
½ teaspoon ground coriander
½ teaspoon garlic powder
corn chips, to serve

Cook the corn, following any of the methods outlined on page 23, then remove the kernels from the husks and set aside.

To make the guac, place all ingredients in a food processor and purée until smooth. Transfer to a serving dish, scraping out as much of the guac as you possibly can with a silicone spatula. Smooth the top of the guac with the back of a tablespoon and top with sliced jalapeños, corn and pepitas. Garnish with additional olive oil, as well as chilli flakes and coriander leaves, if desired.

Serve with corn chips.

Swaps
Take things up a notch and serve with slow-roasted tomatoes, à la the Dreamy creamy loaded bean dip (page 201).

Roasted capsicum dip

Serves 4–6

It's creamy, it's tangy, it's smoky, it's moreish and it goes with everything. I take this dip everywhere. Serve this with a bowl of corn chips or a plate of raw veg. It's also excellent on tacos or nachos, in burritos or stirred into pasta, and incredible in an egg salad with corn. You can also use it in the Chipotle corn and chickpea salad (page 134). A high-powered blender is the key to making sure you can get a smooth and creamy dip.

1 cup cashews
¾ cup (185 ml/6 fl oz) water
2 teaspoons freshly squeezed lime juice
1 chipotle in adobo
1 teaspoon adobo (sauce)
1 teaspoon garlic powder
1 large roasted red capsicum (bell pepper)
½ teaspoon salt
smoked paprika or chilli flakes, to garnish
corn chips or raw veg, to serve

Place all ingredients, except the paprika and chilli flakes, in a high-powered blender and process until silky smooth.

Transfer to a serving bowl, using a silicone spatula to scrape all the goodness out of the blender, then dust with smoked paprika or chilli flakes (optional).

Serve with corn chips or raw veggies. This dip is especially good with celery.

Pictured overleaf →   Make it a party

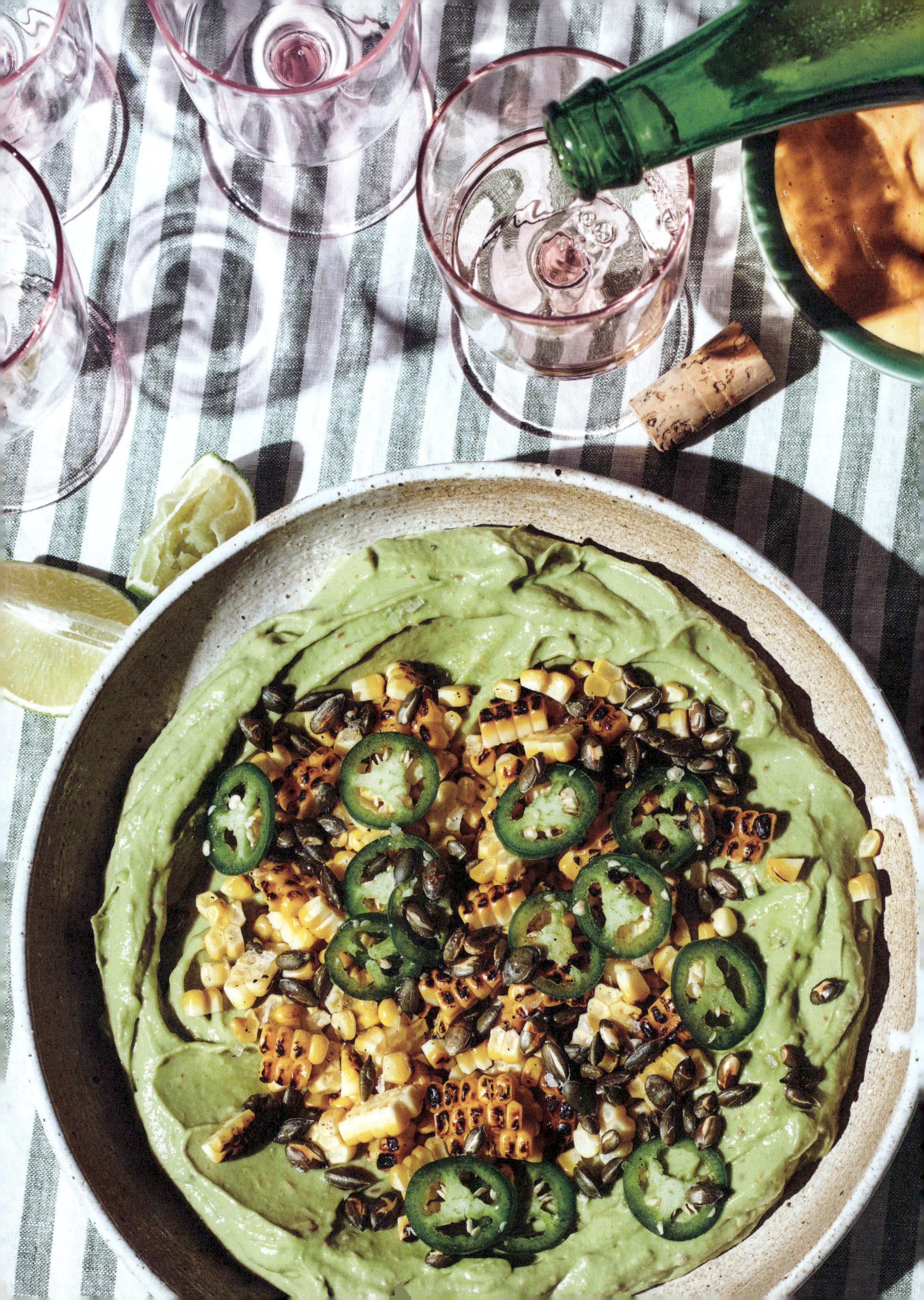

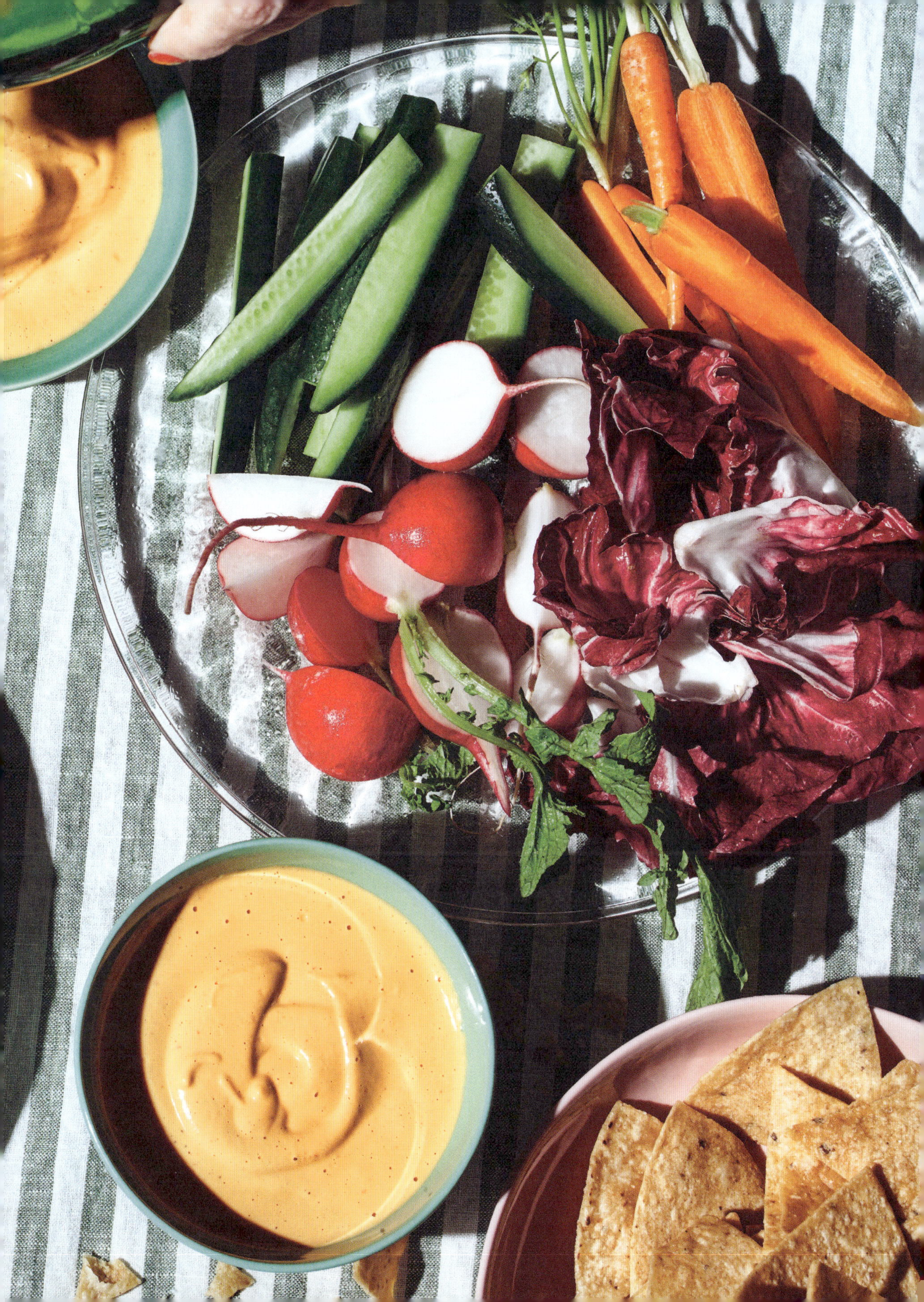

Sourdough focaccia

Serves 4–8

What's a focaccia recipe doing in a salad book, you ask? While it may seem odd at first, hear me out – there is no better way to tie a table of delicious food together than with a loaf of some kind. While sourdough is my jam, not everyone has the right tools at home to shape and bake a perfectly rotund loaf. Focaccia though – anyone can make focaccia. All you need is some simple ingredients and some time. And if time is not on your side, half a teaspoon of yeast is your best friend.

This recipe assumes a little bit of sourdough knowledge and starts with a recently fed sourdough starter.

For the focaccia

100 g (3½ oz) fresh sourdough starter
350 g (12½ oz) water
25 g (1 oz) olive oil, plus extra for drizzling
500 g (1 lb 2 oz) white bakers (strong) flour
10 g (¼ oz) salt
toppings (see suggestions below)
½ teaspoon yeast (optional)

For the toppings

My toppings vary depending on what I have at home and what I'm serving with the focaccia. Here are some ideas:
Red onion, sliced
Baby roma tomatoes, halved
Olives, pitted and halved
Capers
Rosemary
Garlic
Pesto
Feta, crumbled
Roasted red capsicum (bell pepper)
Boiled potato – thinly sliced, crumbled or cut into wedges
Cooked mushrooms.

Night before: Feed your starter – see the introduction above. Feed your starter by mixing 30 g (1 oz) starter with 25 g (1 oz) bakers flour, 25 g (1 oz) wholewheat flour and 50 g (1 3/4 oz) water. Stir, cover and set aside overnight.

9 am: Weigh 100 g (3½ oz) of the fed starter and combine with the instant yeast (if using), the water and the olive oil and whisk to combine. Add the flour and salt and scrunch/mix until well combined. Scrape any excess dough off your hands, then leave the dough to sit for 40–60 minutes.

10.00 am: First stretch and fold.

10.30 am: Second stretch and fold.

11.00 am: Third stretch and fold.

11.30 am: Fourth stretch and fold.

12.00 pm: Transfer the dough to a well-oiled focaccia tin, approximately 20 × 30 cm (8 × 12 in) in size. Cover, and allow to sit.

12.30 pm: Using oiled hands, gently coax the dough towards the edges of the pan. It will naturally spread as it proofs, so don't use so much force that you tear the dough.

3:30pm: If you haven't used the ½ teaspoon of yeast, cover the dough and place in the fridge overnight. If you have used yeast, proceed to the next step.

Make it a party

Continued →

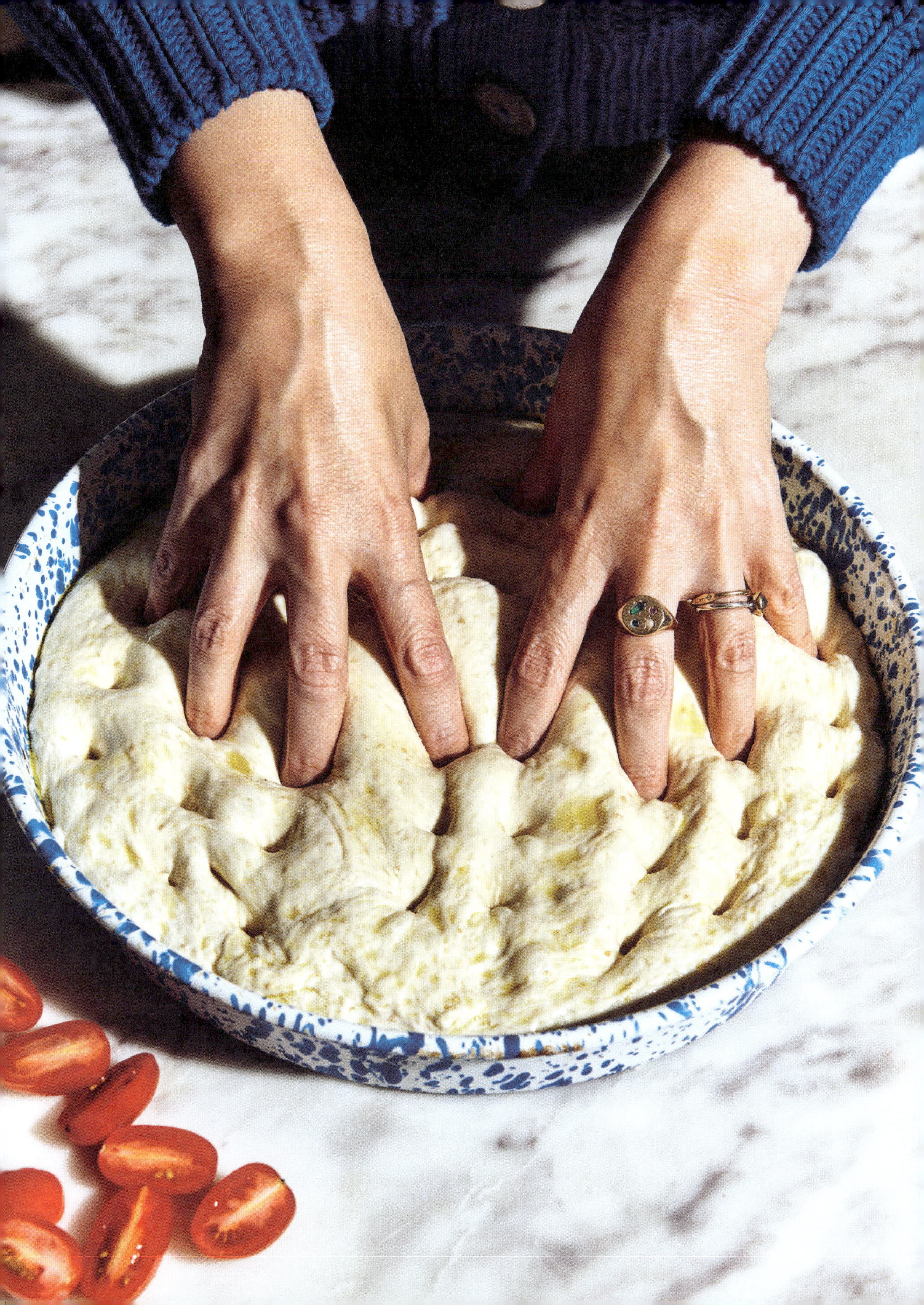

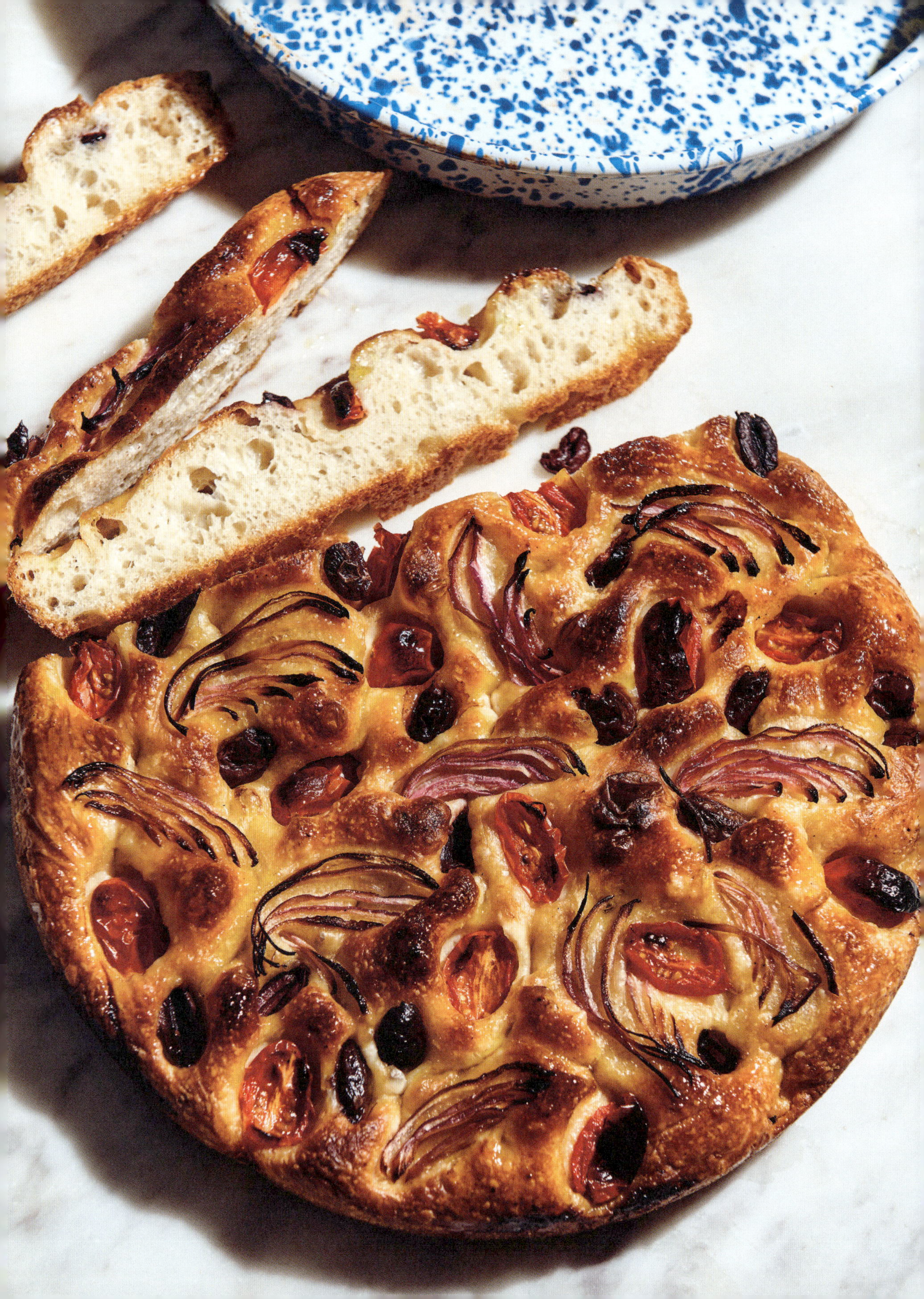

30 minutes before you're ready to bake: Turn your oven to the highest heat and move an oven rack to the bottom third.

4.00 pm: At this point, the dough should be bubbly. Using wet fingers, create dimples in the dough. Ideally, you want them evenly spaced and all the way to the bottom of the dough, but don't be too fussy – it's just focaccia, after all! Have some fun with this – it's a great way to involve the kids.

Drizzle the top of the dough with 2 tablespoons of olive oil. Lightly rub your chosen toppings in olive oil then arrange on top of the dough – I like to start with the biggest ones and finish with the smallest ones. Press them into the dough so they are nestled in the focaccia. Finish with a generous sprinkling of salt and then reduce the oven temperature to 240°C (465°F). Bake the focaccia in the hot oven for approximately 30–40 minutes, turning the pan 180 degrees about halfway through the cooking time.

Once cooked, allow to rest in the tin for 10 minutes, then tip onto a wire cooling rack and allow to cool for another 20 minutes.

Slice, and serve with any array of dips, cheese and salad.

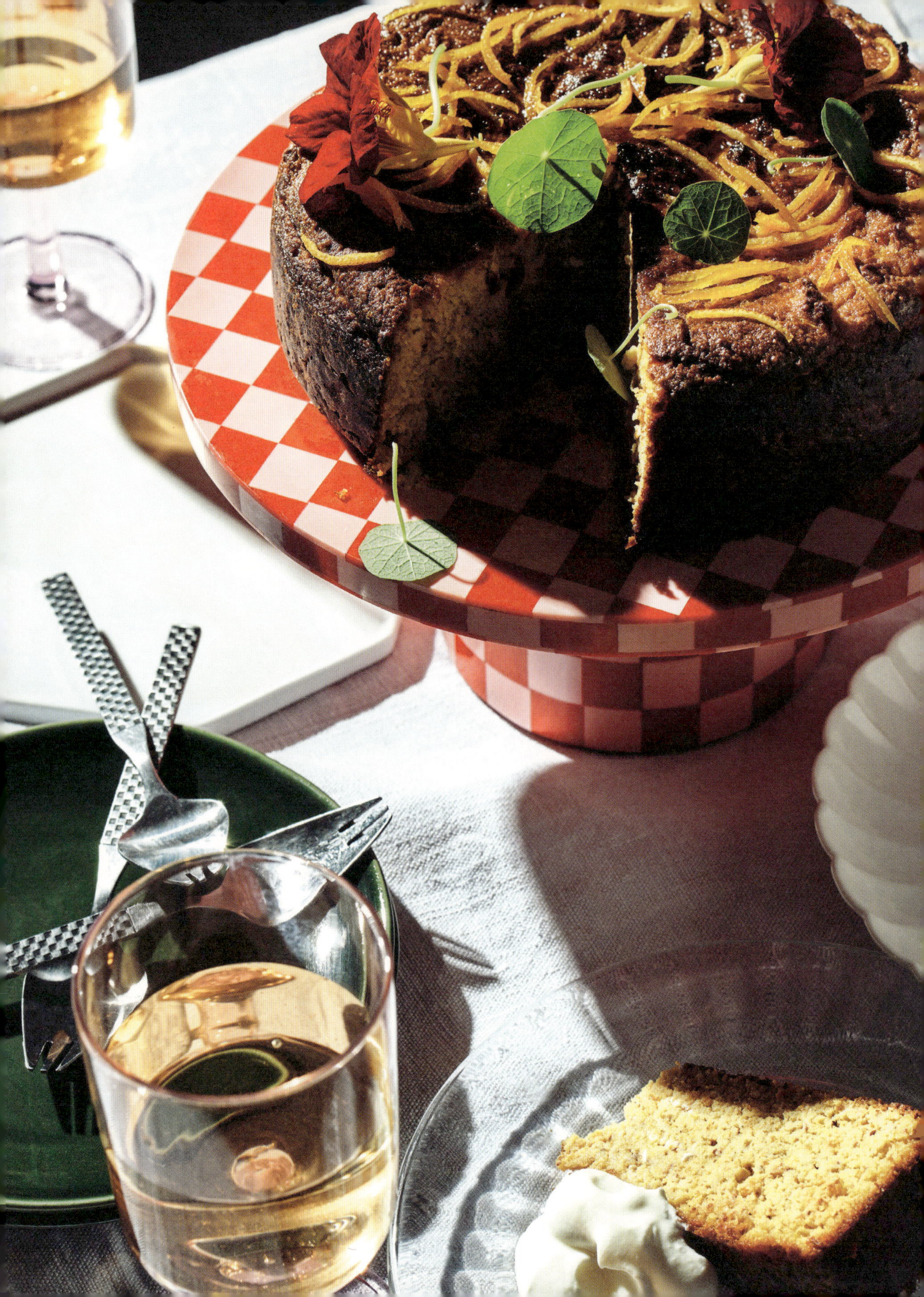

Everyone's favourite orange cake

Makes a 20 cm (8 in) cake

I first made Claudia Roden's classic version of this cake when I was working in a cafe in Berlin. It's a recipe that saw me through my vegan years and one that I come back to time and time again. I always make this for gatherings, as it's gluten free and can easily be veganised. The version with eggs will yield a fluffier cake, but both are delish.

3 oranges
4 eggs or 150 ml (5 fl oz) aquafaba
¾ cup (165 g/6 oz) raw cane sugar, plus ¼ cup (55 g/2 oz) for the syrup
3 cups (300 g/10½ oz) ground almonds
1 teaspoon baking powder
1 teaspoon pure vanilla extract
pinch of salt
your favourite yoghurt, to serve

Place two oranges in a saucepan, cover with water and bring to the boil. Cook for 30–40 minutes then drain and rinse the oranges in cold water.

Preheat the oven to 180°C (360°F) and line a 20 cm (8 in) springform cake tin with baking paper.

Roughly chop the oranges, discarding any seeds, and then purée them in a food processor until no large chunks remain.

For the non-vegan version: Add eggs, ¾ cup (165 g/6 oz) of the sugar, almonds, baking powder, vanilla and salt to the food processor and process until well combined.

For the vegan version: Place the aquafaba and ¾ cup (165 g/6 oz) of the sugar in a large mixing bowl. Using an electric whisk or stand mixer, beat for 3–5 minutes, until the mixture starts to turn white. Add the puréed oranges and beat for another 30 seconds or so, then add the ground almonds, baking powder, vanilla and salt and beat until well combined.

Pour the cake batter into the tin. Smooth the top and bake for 1 hour, or until a skewer comes out clean. Allow to cool in the pan.

To make the syrup, remove a 2 × 5 cm (¾ × 2 in) piece of peel from the remaining orange. Cut the peel into thin strips, then juice the orange. Pour the juice into a small saucepan along with the strips of peel and the remaining raw sugar. Bring to a boil over a medium–high heat, then reduce to the lowest setting and simmer for about 5 minutes, until the sugar has dissolved.

While the cake is still in the tin, prick holes in the top using a toothpick or skewer, then gently pour the syrup on top. Leave for 30 minutes or so before running a knife around the edge of the cake and gently removing it from the tin. Serve with any kind of yoghurt.

Fun fruit salad

Serves 4–6

While it's a total rule breaker when it comes to my definition of a salad, fruit salad is the embodiment of simplicity, sweetness and vibrancy. Each forkful is a celebration of sweet, tart and tangy flavours that burst on the tongue and refresh the palate. This is great as a light meal on a hot day but also makes for a showstopper of a dessert when hosting or attending a party.

While I do love this particular combination of fruits, this is more of a reminder that such delights exist than a recipe to follow to a tee.

1 cup (250 g/9 oz) vanilla yoghurt
1–2 mangoes, sliced
1–2 cups berries
2 passionfruit
handful slivered almonds, roasted handful mint leaves
edible flowers, to garnish

Spread the yoghurt over a serving dish and top with the mango and berries. Spoon passionfruit pulp over, then scatter with roasted almonds and top with mint and edible flowers.

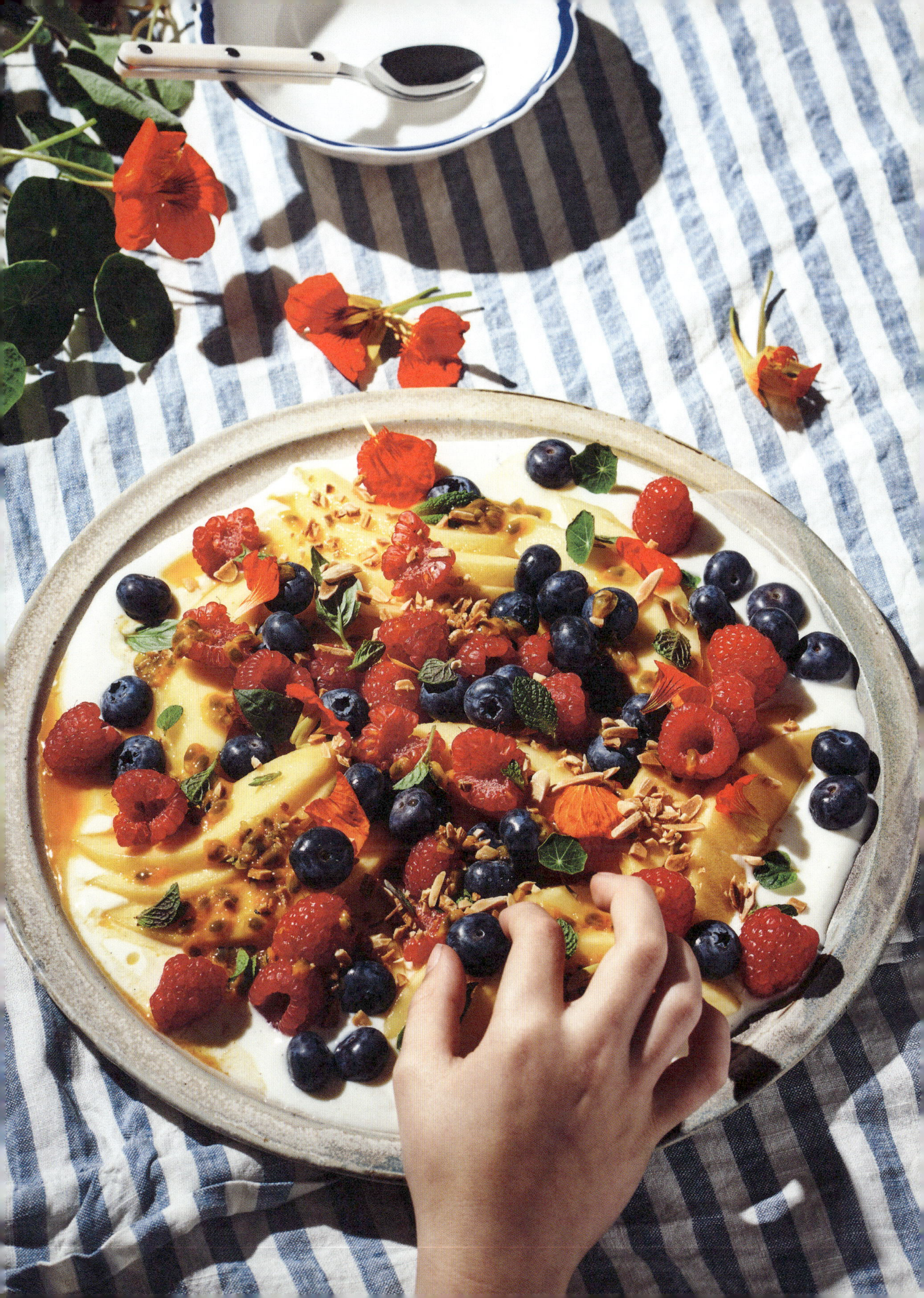

Dinner party menus

There is nothing quite like sitting down to a meal with people you love. In my twenties, hosting and attending potlucks was the norm, and through the sharing of food I forged bonds, drowned sorrows, consumed multiple glasses (okay, sometimes bottles) of wine, and felt socially connected to those in my community. I recently realised that as I've grown older, become a parent, moved countries and then suburbs, become busier with work, and figured out how to socialise in a post-Covid world, I don't host as often as I used to. No one does. Having people over feels harder than ever because we are all exhausted.

The antidote to this is to invite friends over and ask them to each bring a salad or a bottle of wine with them. It's an easy and effortless way to host a gathering when you can't spend hours in the kitchen but still want to gather your loved ones around a table of nutritious food. When I do have the time and energy, I love a full-blown cooking bender where I make multiple salads and all kinds of dips and sides, and sweet treats to accompany them, but the opportunity for such joys are few and far between these days.

No matter the approach, whenever I gather a group of loved ones around a few salads, everyone leaves full and happy. No matter how hard it feels or how much tidier I wish my house was, the moment my guests arrive I am always glad I followed through. Nothing beats that feeling you get when everyone is together. It's what matters most, after all.

Menu One

To start
Whipped feta with balsamic
   roasted grape (page 198)
Sourdough focaccia (page 206)

Salads
Haloumi chickpea salad (page 118)
Roasted cauliflower salad (page 129)

Sides
Roasted zucchini, crispy pitta and beans (page 130)
Greens with radish, parmesan
   and garlic croutons (page 171)

Dessert
Everyone's favourite orange cake (page 211)

Pictured overleaf →

Menu Two

Sides
Dreamy creamy loaded guac (page 202)
Roasted capsicum dip (page 203)

Salads
Chipotle corn and chickpea salad (page 134)
Marinated black beans with crispy
   tortilla strips (page 121)

Dessert
Fun fruit salad (page 212)

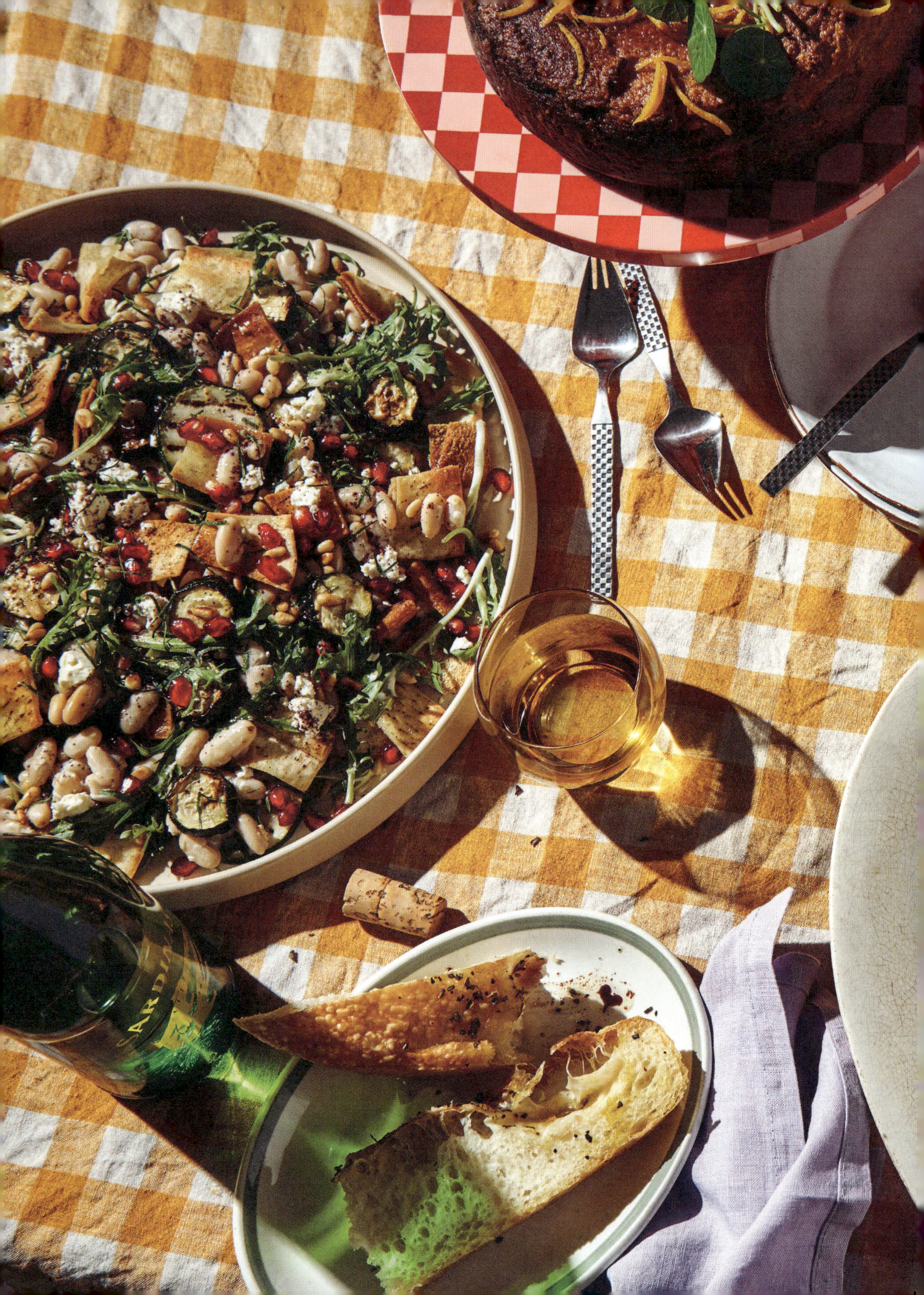

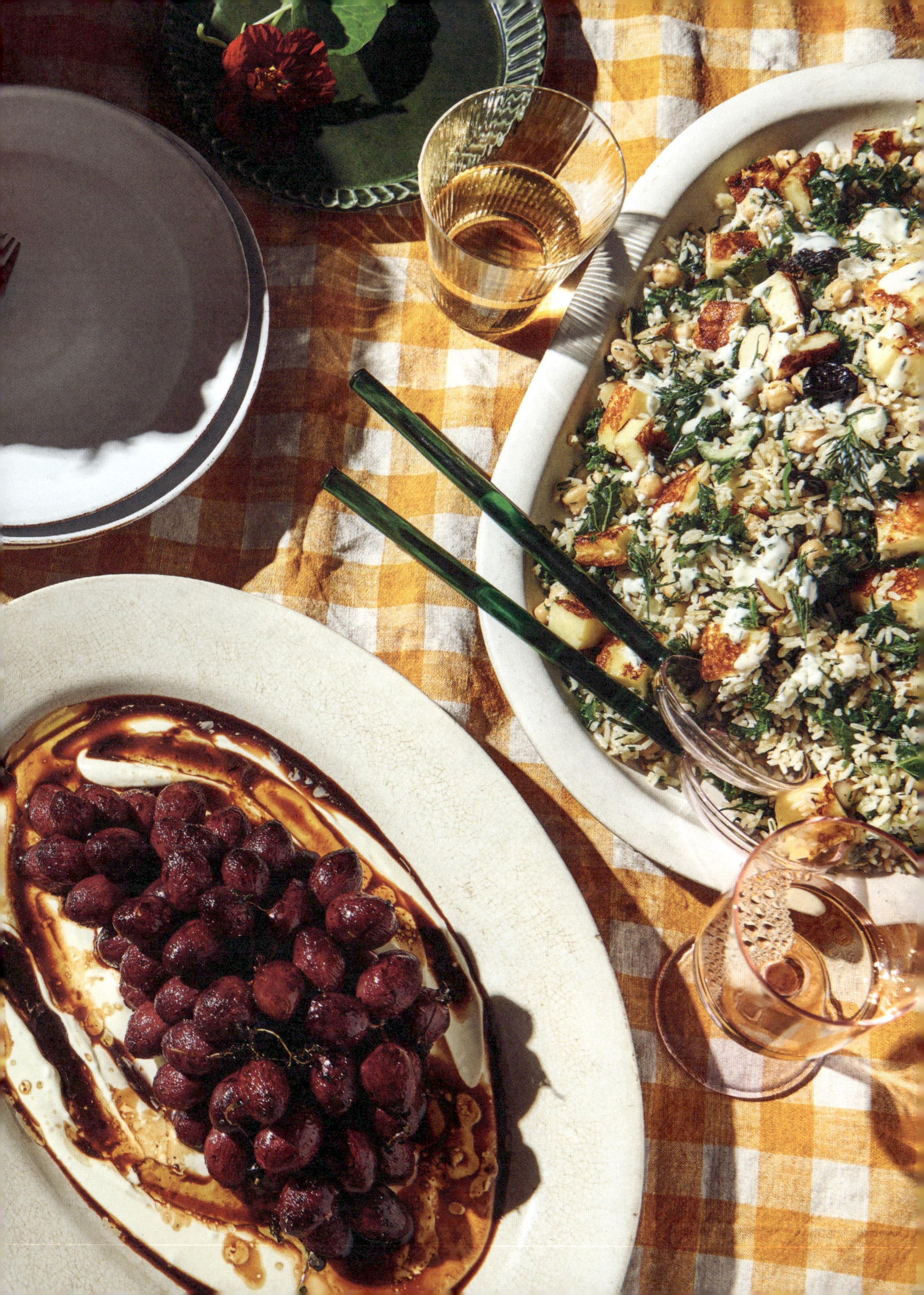

Index

A

almond
    Forever favourite chopped salad 75
    Grain salad 114
    Raw cauliflower and broccoli salad 186
    Roasted cauliflower salad 129
    Spicy peanut slaw with tofu croutons and almonds 68
Antipasti pasta salad 142
asparagus
    Warm greens and toasted spelt 189
    Warm greens noodle salad 165
avocado
    Avocado salsa 98
    Butter bean breakfast salad 105
    Chilli lime pinto bean salad 109
    Coriander pesto and roasted pumpkin pasta salad 143
    Dreamy creamy loaded guac 202
    Forever favourite chopped salad 75
    Greens with avocado, pepitas and sesame seeds 170
    Marinated black beans with crispy tortilla strips 121
    Marinated chickpea, avocado and feta salad 82
    Monday salad 106
    Soba salad with edamame and corn 161
    Super salad 97

B

Basic balsamic dressing 39
basil 21
beans (*see also* broad bean, cannellini bean, chickpea, edamame bean)
    Burrata with broad beans and peas 197
    Butter bean breakfast salad 105
    Chilli lime pinto bean salad 109
    Chipotle corn and chickpea salad 134
    Coconut-crusted pumpkin and chickpea salad 110
    cooking 27
    Dreamy creamy loaded bean dip 201
    Haloumi chickpea salad 118
    Honey mustard carrot and chickpea salad 125
    Late summer rusk salad 78
    Marinated black beans with crispy tortilla strips 121
    Roasted zucchini and feta with sorghum 122
    Roasted zucchini, crispy pitta and beans 130
    Super simple broad bean salad 93
    Three bean salad 107
beetroot
    Root-to-leaf beetroot salad 133
    Super salad 97
bread
    croutons 24, 48
    Greens with radish, parmesan and garlic croutons 171
    Kale and crouton side salad 171
    Marinated black beans with crispy tortilla strips 121
    Pangratatto 48
    Roasted feta and grape fattoush 89
    Roasted zucchini, crispy pitta and beans 130
    Sourdough focaccia 206–8
broad bean
    Burrata with broad beans and peas 197
    Super simple broad bean salad 93
broccoli
    Charred broccoli and pea pasta salad 149
    Raw cauliflower and broccoli salad 186
    Roasted cauliflower and broccoli salad 186
    Warm greens and toasted spelt 189
Butter bean breakfast salad 105
Burrata with broad beans and peas 197

C

cabbage 21
    Cabbage and pea slaw 176
    Crispy nori tofu with simple slaw 72
    Peanut tofu with green slaw 86
    Pomegranate, eggplant and cabbage 115
    Satay tofu and edamame bowl 90
    Spicy peanut slaw with tofu croutons and almonds 68
cake, Everyone's favourite orange 211
cannellini bean
    Dreamy creamy loaded bean dip 201
    Roasted zucchini and feta with sorghum 122
    Roasted zucchini, crispy pitta and beans 130
    Three bean salad 107
capsicum
    Antipasti pasta salad 142
    Forever favourite chopped salad 75
    Greek salad 71
    Grilled corn and edamame salsa 79
    Monday salad 106
    Rice noodle salad with marinated tofu 153
    Roasted capsicum dip 203
    Spicy tofu puffed rice salad 94
carrot
    Honey mustard carrot and chickpea salad 125
    Monday salad 106
    Satay tofu and edamame bowl 90
    Spicy peanut udon salad 154
    Super salad 97
cashew nut
    Coconut-crusted pumpkin and chickpea salad 110
    Coriander pesto 39
    Ever-versatile tomato and cucumber salad 180
    Five-spice tempeh and cauliflower salsa 113
    Roasted capsicum dip 203
    Roasted pumpkin with raita and tempered spices 190
cauliflower
    Five-spice tempeh and cauliflower salad 113
    Raw cauliflower and broccoli salad 186
    Roasted cauliflower salad 129
celery
    Chickpea, celery and walnut salad 64
    Monday salad 106
    Peanut tofu with green slaw 86
Charred broccoli and pea pasta salad 149
Cheese (*see also* feta, haloumi, parmesan)
    Cos, parmesan, fried pasta and basil 170
    Greek salad 71
    Greens with radish, parmesan and garlic croutons 171
    Haloumi chickpea salad 118
    Lemon ricotta pasta salad 150
    Marinated chickpea, avocado and feta salad 82
    Raw zucchini, pea and stracciatella 158
    Roasted feta and grape fattoush 89
    Roasted pumpkin, maple walnut and blue cheese 126
    Roasted zucchini and feta with sorghum 122
    The GOAT dressing 43
    Whipped feta 198
    Whipped feta with balsamic roasted grapes 198
chickpea
    Chickpea, celery and walnut salad 64
    Chipotle corn and chickpea salad 134
    Coconut-crusted pumpkin and chickpea salad 110
    Dreamy creamy loaded bean dip 201
    Forever favourite chopped salad 75
    Haloumi chickpea salad 118
    Honey mustard carrot and chickpea salad 125
    Marinated chickpea, avocado and feta salad 82
    Pomegranate, eggplant and cabbage 115
    Three bean salad 107

chilli
    Chilli lime dressing 39
    Chilli lime pinto bean salad 109
    Coriander pesto and roasted pumpkin pasta salad 143
    Ever-versatile tomato and cucumber salad 180
    Sesame, soy and crunchy chilli tofu 32
Chipotle corn and chickpea salad 134
climate considerations 11
coconut
    Coconut-crusted pumpkin and chickpea salad 110
    Coconut satay dressing 39
Coriander pesto 39
    Coriander pesto and roasted pumpkin pasta salad 143
corn
    Avocado salsa 98
    Chipotle corn and chickpea salad 134
    cooking 23–4
    Grilled corn and edamame salsa 79
    Soba salad with edamame and corn 161
couscous, Roasted eggplant and zucchini with pearled 157
cos (romaine) lettuce 21
    Cos, parmesan, fried pasta and basil 170
Crispy nori tofu with simple slaw 72
crouton 24, 48
    Greens with radish, parmesan and garlic croutons 171
    Kale and crouton side salad 171
    Roasted zucchini with crispy pitta and beans 130
    Spicy peanut slaw with tofu croutons and almonds 68
cucumber
    Ever-versatile tomato and cucumber salad 180
    Gado gado salad plate 76
    Greek salad 71
    Monday salad 106
    Quick pickled cucumber 90
    Roasted feta and grape fattoush 89
    Satay tofu and edamame bowl 90
    Three bean salad 107

D

dip
    Dreamy creamy loaded bean dip 201
    Dreamy creamy loaded guac 202
    Roasted capsicum dip 203
Dreamy creamy loaded bean dip 201
Dreamy creamy loaded guac 202
dressing 10
    Basic balsamic dressing 39
    Chilli lime dressing 39
    Coconut satay dressing 39
    Honey mustard dressing 78
    Lemon tahini yoghurt dressing 42
    Pomegranate dressing 42
    Sesame mayo dressing 42
    Spicy peanut dressing 42
    Spicy soy dressing 43
    Supergreen dressing 43
    The GOAT dressing 43
dukkah, Hazelnut 51

E

edamame 37
    Grilled corn and edamame salsa 79
    Satay tofu and edamame bowl 90
    Simple soba for one 141
    Soba salad with edamame and corn 161
    Super salad 97
egg
    Egg salad for one 64
    Gado gado salad plate 76
    omelettes 37
    Soy sauce eggs 36
    The perfect boiled egg 34
eggplant
    Pomegranate, eggplant and cabbage 115
    Roasted eggplant and zucchini with pearled couscous 157
equipment 58
Ever-versatile tomato and cucumber salad 180
Everyone's favourite orange cake 211

F

fattoush, Roasted feta and grape 89
feta
    Coriander pesto and roasted pumpkin pasta salad 143
    Grain salad 114
    Greek salad 71
    Marinated chickpea, avocado and feta salad 82
    Roasted feta and grape fattoush 89
    Roasted zucchini and feta with sorghum 122
    Roasted zucchini, crispy pitta and beans 130
    Super simple broad bean salad 93
    Whipped feta 198
    Whipped feta with balsamic roasted grapes 198
feta, Tofu 33
Five-spice tempeh and cauliflower salad 113
focaccia, Sourdough 206–8
Forever favourite chopped salad 75
fruit salad, Fun 212
Fun fruit salad 212

G

Gado gado salad plate 76
Gochujang tofu 32
grain
    cooking 24–5
    Five-spice tempeh and cauliflower salad 113
    Grain salad 114
    Roasted eggplant and zucchini with pearled couscous 157
    Roasted zucchini and feta with sorghum 122
    Super salad 93
    Warm greens and toasted spelt 189
grape
    Roasted feta and grape fattoush 89
    Whipped feta with balsamic roasted grapes 198
Greek salad 71
Greens with avocado, pepitas and sesame seeds 170
Greens with radish, parmesan and garlic croutons 171
Grilled corn and edamame salsa 79

H

haloumi 37
    Haloumi chickpea salad 118
hazelnut
    Hazelnut dukkah 51
Honey mustard carrot and chickpea salad 125
Honey mustard dressing 78

I

iceberg lettuce 21
    Gado gado salad plate 76
    Grilled iceberg lettuce with capers 179

K

kale 21
    Cabbage and pea slaw 176
    Kale and crouton side salad 171
    Marinated black beans with crispy tortilla strips 121

L

Late summer rusk salad 78
leaves 16, 18–21
    drying 20
    washing 18
    storing 20
lemon
    Lemon ricotta pasta salad 150

Lemon tahini yoghurt dressing 42
Lemongrass tofu 32
legumes 26
   cooking 26
lentils
   cooking dried 27
   Grain salad 114
   Monday salad 106
   Roasted cauliflower salad 129
   Roasted pumpkin, maple walnut and blue cheese 126
   Root-to-leaf beetroot salad 133
lime
   Chilli lime dressing 39
   Chilli lime pinto bean salad 109

M

Maple walnuts 51
Marinated black beans with crispy tortilla strips 121
Marinated chickpea, avocado and feta salad 82
meal planning 9
measurements 10
Monday salad 106
Mushroom and tofu laab 85

N

noodle (*see also* soba noodle)
   Rice noodle salad with marinated tofu 153
   Simple soba for one 141
   Soba salad with edamame and corn 161
   Spicy peanut udon salad 154
   Spicy soy noodle salad with warm tofu puffs 162
   Warm greens noodle salad 165
nut (*see also* almond, cashew nut, hazelnut, peanut, walnut)
   Chickpea, celery and walnut salad 64
   Ever-versatile tomato and cucumber salad 180
   Forever favourite chopped salad 75
   Grain salad 114
   Hazelnut dukkah 51
   Lemon ricotta pasta salad 150
   Maple walnuts 51
   Peanut tofu with green slaw 86
   Raw cauliflower and broccoli salad 186
   Roasted pumpkin, maple walnut and blue cheese 126
   Roasted pumpkin with raita and tempered spices 190
   roasting and toasting 50
   Root-to-leaf beetroot salad 133
   Spicy peanut dressing 42
   Spicy peanut slaw with tofu croutons and almonds 68
   Spicy peanut udon salad 154
   storing 50
   Tomato salad with fried capers and pine nuts 185

O

olive
   Antipasti pasta salad 142
   Forever favourite chopped salad 75
   Late summer rusk salad 78
   Raw zucchini, pea and stracciatella 158
orange cake, Everyone's favourite 211
oven temperature 10

P

Pangratatto 48
Panko tofu salad for one 67
parmesan
   Antipasti pasta salad 142
   Cabbage and pea slaw 176
   Charred broccoli and pea pasta salad 149
   Cos, parmesan, fried pasta and basil 170
   Greens with radish, parmesan and garlic croutons 171
   Grilled iceberg lettuce with capers 179
   Lemon ricotta pasta salad 150
pasta
   Antipasti pasta salad 142
   Charred broccoli and pea pasta salad 149
   Coriander pesto and roasted pumpkin pasta salad 143
   Cos, parmesan, fried pasta and basil 170
   Lemon ricotta pasta salad 150
   Raw zucchini, pea and stracciatella 158
   Roasted tomato orzo salad 146
pickled cucumber, Quick 90
pea
   Burrata with broad beans and peas 197
   Cabbage and pea slaw 176
   Charred broccoli and pea pasta salad 149
   Raw zucchini, pea and stracciatella 158
peanut
   Peanut tofu with green slaw 86
   Spicy peanut dressing 42
   Spicy peanut slaw with tofu croutons and almonds 68
   Spicy peanut udon salad 154
pepita
   Chilli lime pinto bean salad 109
   Coriander pesto and pumpkin pasta salad 143
   Forever favourite chopped salad 75
   Grain salad 114
   Greens with avocado, pepitas and sesame seeds 170
   Roasted pumpkin with raita and tempered spices 190
   Super salad 97
pesto, Coriander 39
pomegranate
   Pomegranate dressing 42
   Pomegranate, eggplant and cabbage 115
   Roasted cauliflower salad 129
preparing veggies 22
protein 17, 26
puffed grains 25
pumpkin
   Coconut-crusted pumpkin and chickpea salad 110
   Coriander pesto and roasted pumpkin pasta salad 143
   Roasted pumpkin, maple walnut and blue cheese 126
   Roasted pumpkin with raita and tempered spices 190

Q

Quick pickled cucumber 90
quinoa
   Five-spice tempeh and cauliflower salad 113

R

radicchio
   Cos, parmesan, fried pasta and basil 170
   Lemon ricotta pasta salad 150
radish
   Cabbage and pea slaw 176
   Gado gado salad plate 76
   Greens with radish, parmesan and garlic croutons 171
   Roasted feta and grape Fattoush 89
Raw cauliflower and broccoli salad 186
Raw zucchini, pea and stracciatella 158
rice
   Chilli lime pinto bean salad 109
   Coconut-crusted pumpkin and chickpea salad 110
   Haloumi chickpea salad 118
   Monday salad 106
   Satay tofu and edamame bowl 90
   Spicy tofu puffed rice salad 94
Rice noodle salad with marinated tofu 153
Roasted capsicum dip 203
Roasted cauliflower salad 129
Roasted eggplant and zucchini with pearled couscous 157
Roasted feta and grape fattoush 89
Roasted pumpkin, maple walnut and blue cheese 126
Roasted pumpkin with raita and tempered spices 190
Roasted tomato orzo salad 146
Roasted zucchini and feta with sorghum 122
Roasted zucchini, crispy pitta

and beans 130
Root-to-leaf beetroot salad 133

S

salsa
    Avocado salsa 98
    Grilled corn and edamame salsa 79
satay
    Coconut satay dressing 39
    Satay tofu and edamame bowl 90
seed (see also pepita, sesame) 50
    Coriander pesto and roasted pumpkin pasta salad 143
    Dreamy creamy loaded guac 202
    Grain salad 114
    Greens with avocado, pepitas and sesame seeds 170
    Roasted pumpkin with raita and tempered spices 190
    roasting and toasting 50
    Sesame mayo dressing 42
    Sesame, soy and crunchy chilli tofu 32
    Sesame, soy and peanut 32
    Soba salad with edamame and corn 161
    Super salad 97
sesame
    Greens with avocado, pepitas and sesame seeds 170
    Sesame mayo dressing 42
    Sesame, soy and crunchy chilli tofu 32
    Sesame, soy and peanut 32
    Soba salad with edamame and corn 161
    Simple soba for one 141
Simple soba for one 141
slaw
    Cabbage and pea slaw 176
    Crispy nori tofu with simple slaw 72
    Peanut tofu with green slaw 86
    Spicy peanut slaw with tofu croutons and almonds 68
soba noodle
    Simple soba for one 141
    Soba salad with edamame and corn 161
Sourdough focaccia 206–8
soy
    Sesame, soy and crunchy chilli tofu 32
    Sesame, soy and peanut 32
    Soy sauce eggs 36
    Spicy soy dressing 43
    Spicy soy noodle salad with warm tofu puffs 162
Spicy peanut dressing 42
Spicy peanut slaw with tofu croutons and almonds 68
Spicy peanut udon salad 154
Spicy soy dressing 43
Spicy soy noodle salad with warm tofu puffs 162
Spicy tofu puffed rice salad 94
Super salad 97
Supergreen dressing 43
Super salad 97
Super simple broad bean salad 93

T

tahini yoghurt dressing, Lemon 42
tempeh 37
    Five-spice tempeh and cauliflower salad 113
    Gado gado salad plate 76
The GOAT dressing 43
Three bean salad 107
tofu 28–31
    Crispy nori tofu with simple slaw 72
    fresh vs packaged 28
    Gochujang tofu 32
    Lemongrass tofu 32
    Mushroom and tofu laab 85
    noodles 37
    Panko tofu salad for one 67
    Peanut tofu with green slaw 86
    puffs 37
    Rice noodle salad with marinated tofu 153
    Satay tofu and edamame bowl 90
    Sesame, soy and crunchy chilli tofu 32
    Sesame, soy and peanut 32
    Spicy peanut slaw with tofu croutons and almonds 68
    Spicy soy noodle salad with warm tofu puffs 162
    Spicy tofu puffed rice salad 94
    Tofu feta 33
    Whipped tofu 37, 198
tomato
    Avocado salsa 98
    Butter bean breakfast salad 105
    Ever-versatile tomato and cucumber salad 180
    Greek salad 71
    Late summer rusk salad 78
    Roasted tomato orzo salad 146
    Spicy tofu puffed rice salad 94
    Tomato salad with fried capers and pine nuts 185
crispy tortilla strips, Marinated black beans with 121
Two-minute tofu – four ways 32

V

vegetables
    Cooking 23
    Preparing 22
vinegar
    Basic balsamic dressing 39

W

walnut
    Chickpea, celery and walnut salad 64
    Lemon ricotta pasta salad 150
    Maple walnuts 51
    Roasted pumpkin, maple walnut and blue cheese 126
    Root-to-leaf beetroot salad 133
Warm greens and toasted spelt 189
Warm greens noodle salad 165
Whipped feta with balsamic roasted grapes 198
Whipped feta 198
Whipped tofu 37 198

Y

yoghurt
    Lemon tahini yoghurt dressing 42
    Roasted pumpkin with raita and tempered spices 190
    The GOAT dressing 43

Z

zucchini
    Raw zucchini, pea and stracciatella 158
    Roasted eggplant and zucchini with pearled couscous 157
    Roasted zucchini and feta with sorghum 122
    Roasted zucchini, crispy pitta and beans 130
    Super simple broad bean salad 93
    Warm greens and toasted spelt 189
    Warm greens noodle salad 165

Acknowledgements

Andy, Louie and Jude, for your patience and support while this cookbook stole your wife and mama away for extended periods of time. I promise it's the last one.

My family and friends for listening to me talk about food non-stop, testing my recipes and taking leftovers off my hands and heaving fridge, and cheering me on when the book-writing fatigue hit.

Elise, my MVP. Your encouragement, support and cheese through the final stretches of writing this book has made it better than I could have ever imagined.

Lee and Rochelle — my Kiwi Dream Team! Your commitment to my vision, and ability to execute it, has blown me right out of the water.

Alice, Tahlia, Kristin, Elena and the rest of the team at Hardie Grant for trusting me with this book idea, helping me bring it to life, and guiding me past any questionable ideas I floated, haha.

Vanessa and Andrea for your editing and proofreading prowess.

Evi-O.Studio — it has been a dream to work with you since I first started writing cookbooks over a decade ago, and you did not disappoint! Thank you for bringing my book to life with your bold colours and clever design.

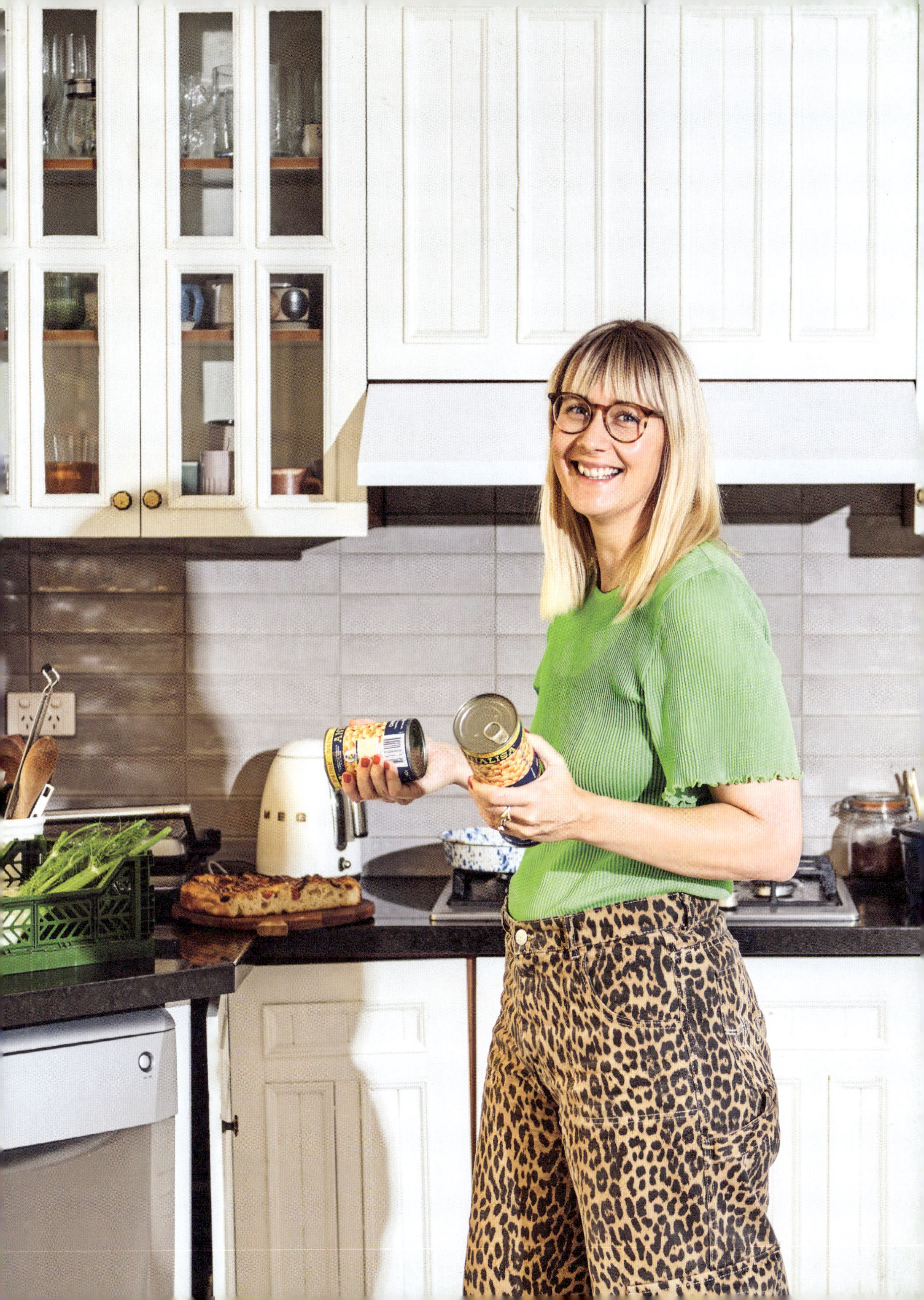
SMEG

Published in 2024 by Hardie Grant Books, an imprint of Hardie Grant Publishing

Hardie Grant Books (Melbourne)
Wurundjeri Country
Building 1, 658 Church Street
Richmond, Victoria 3121

Hardie Grant North America
2912 Telegraph Ave
Berkeley, California 94705

hardiegrant.com/books

Hardie Grant acknowledges the Traditional Owners of the Country on which we work, the Wurundjeri People of the Kulin Nation and the Gadigal People of the Eora Nation, and recognises their continuing connection to the land, waters and culture. We pay our respects to their Elders past and present.

All rights reserved. No part of this publication may be reproduced, stored in a retrieval system or transmitted in any form by any means, electronic, mechanical, photocopying, recording or otherwise, without the prior written permission of the publishers and copyright holders.

The moral rights of the author have been asserted.

Copyright text © Jessica Prescott 2024
Copyright photography © Rochelle Eagle 2024
Copyright illustrations © Evi-O.Studio 2024
Copyright design © Hardie Grant Publishing 2024

A catalogue record for this book is available from the National Library of Australia

Epic Salads
ISBN 978 1 74379 975 8
ISBN 978 1 761 44175 2 (ebook)

10 9 8 7 6 5 4 3

Publisher: Alice Hardie-Grant, Tahlia Anderson
Head of Editorial: Jasmin Chua
Project Editor: Elena Callcott
Editor: Vanessa Lanaway
Design Manager: Kristin Thomas
Designer: Evi-O.Studio | Emi Chiba
Typesetter: Evi-O.Studio | Doreen Zheng
Photographer: Rochelle Eagle
Stylist: Lee Blaylock
Home Economist: Elise Pulbrook
Head of Production: Todd Rechner
Production Controller: Jessica Harvie

Colour reproduction by Splitting Image Colour Studio
Printed in China by Leo Paper Products LTD.

MIX
Paper | Supporting responsible forestry
FSC® C020056

The paper this book is printed on is from FSC®-certified forests and other sources. FSC® promotes environmentally responsible, socially beneficial and economically viable management of the world's forests.